PERSIAN *LIONS,*
PERSIAN LAMBS

OTHER BOOKS BY CURTIS HARNACK

PERSIAN *L*IONS,

PERSIAN LAMBS

An American's Odyssey in Iran

BY CURTIS HARNACK

IOWA STATE UNIVERSITY PRESS, AMES

FOR

ELIZABETH C. HARNACK

AND

JOHN F. HARNACK

Printed by The Iowa State University Press, Ames, Iowa 50010

This paperback edition is an unabridged republication of the work originally published by Holt, Rinehart and Winston in 1965, to which has been added a Preface prepared especially for this reprint edition by the author.

Map by Linda M. Emmerson

Library of Congress Cataloging in Publication Data

Harnack, Curtis, 1927–
    Persian lions, Persian lambs.

    1. Iran—Description and travel. 2. Education—Iran. 3. Harnack, Curtis, 1927–
DS259.H37   1981   955′.053   81-8323
ISBN 0–8138–1336–0   **AACR2**

CONTENTS

PREFACE

In 1979, twenty years after my time in Tabriz, Iran, as a Fulbright professor of American literature, a number of us who had been there gathered in Washington, D.C., for a reunion. Together with a few Tabriz natives who happened to be in town (one a faculty member of Teheran University, now closed by the government; another married to an American), we feasted on *koresh*, a spicy meat casserole; *borek*, filo leaves baked with cheese and spinach; long-grained Mazandaran rice cooked with cherries; and *baklava* for dessert. Sipping tea out of glasses Persian style, we spent eight hours together catching up, looking at photographs, listening to Iranian songs, and reflecting on what we had done in Iran—in the light of present circumstances, with the Shah's power being challenged by rioting crowds and his royal downfall imminent.

When we had lived in Tabriz, during the Dulles-Eisenhower Cold War years, the fact that we were Americans abroad created a bond among us which in retrospect seems enviable—similar to the all-together spirit that buoyed the World War II effort. Whether we happened to be in Iran as teachers, missionaries, foreign service officers, technical assistance advisors, or U.S. Army personnel training Iranians in the use of American weapons, we were fellow countrymen all, and we highly approved of ourselves and our nation. Iran was a remote "underdeveloped country" and only a check in the atlas, for most people, could reveal its precise location—a nation with a name Americans mispronounced "Eye-ran."

Now, as Iranian hatred of America poured from television screens each day, those of us gathered at the reunion could not help but wonder over the meaning of our involvement in the life of that country. Who were we and why had we done this to them?

An agricultural technical assistance man travelled to our get-together from his native state of Idaho. He and his wife had spent several hard years in extremely primitive regions of Iran, working on irrigation projects, herd improvement through breeding, bank credit systems for farmers, the uses of hybrid seeds, and setting up craft industries for rural women. His Iranian "counterpart," whom he trained, carried out many of these programs after the Idahoans had left, and they exchanged frequent letters.

A public health man from Maryland had worked on controlling communicable diseases, water pollution, and immunization of school children. His wife, a nurse, had headed a hospital in Japan after the war, service for which the Japanese government had recently honored her. The medical aid this pair gave poor Iranians came at a crucial time. In addition,

American Presbyterian missionaries ran a hospital and drug dispensary, practicing Christianity in service to the needy.

The former American consul in Tabriz and his wife organized this reunion. They were superior foreign service people in every respect, had learned Farsi and Turki languages, and within the boundaries of traditional diplomacy accomplished their job with style, decorum, and an admirable feeling for the local citizenry. The U.S. Information officer on the consulate staff, whom I call Paulus in this book, was of Greek parentage, and twenty years later he and his Turkish wife still seemed the sort one would like to have representing our country in far places—or enjoy as friends. We all spoke of absent colleagues: one had died, another was now ambassador to a Persian gulf state; a third had retired—the one I found to be involved in what Kipling called "the game," with his powerful binoculars and tiny Minox camera. His role hadn't been ours, but he, too, was part of the picture, for Iran in the late 1950's was full of intelligence-gatherers from various countries, and we were living within a few miles of the U.S.S.R. border.

I was warned immediately upon arrival not to ask one of the Tabriz girls present about her family (her sister had been my student, I also remembered her parents) for she might break down in tears. Her brother had been accused of radical activity, thrown in jail, and although family influence got him out the first time, after a subsequent arrest he was never heard from again and presumed killed.

We looked at slides in the afternoon, revisiting Tabriz streets crowded with dark-suited men, women in *chedurs,* burros, droshkies, and turbaned Kurds. I glimpsed a corner of my old garden and the sunny porch where I used to sit. Then, a shot of some of us around the Christmas dinner table: how young I looked, and with a decidedly Persian moustache!

Were those days with their sense of accomplishment, doing useful services for people in need—who had asked for them—just down the drain of time? Would the awful consequences of the political uses the United States made of Iran obliterate all of these good works?

It is easy to be sweepingly cynical about America's international adventurism, unfashionable and even suspect to think that any of us who were involved in Iran were motivated by an idealism to be cherished. However, I remember putting Thoreau's "Civil Disobedience" on my students' reading list, and it interested them mightily. The revolutionary message of that essay also represents our country and may have had its effect.

The worst thing about having world-shaking historical events catch up with one's private history is the strong temptation to claim prescience, or at least remarkable powers of astuteness. However, a great many foreigners living in Iran in the late 1950s knew as well as I that the tyrannical Shah Reza Pahlevi could not last in power indefinitely. I thought the end would come much sooner than it did. I under-estimated the amount of money Iran would generate through its oil and how those billions of dollars purchasing U.S. armaments would bolster the Shah's regime. From a few thousand Americans in Iran during my time there, our presence grew to over 40,000. The moral implications of this huge involvement cannot be overlooked. The fury of the mob-masses shown to the world on television screens—orchestrated though it doubtless was—had its roots in rage over what the United States had done to their lives and their society. I remember the severe disapproval of the chief mullah of Tabriz regarding my presence at the university, since I was purveying western ideas and attitudes. His holy anger foreshadowed the coming to power of the Ayatolla Khomeini. Our C.I.A. agents did indeed train and work with the Iranian secret service, the *Savak,* whose deadly activities touched the lives of so many Iranian families. As a nation we have much to answer for, though the hostage issue clouded over these questions and caused many Americans to feel self-righteous, indignant, and put upon. The very point the militant terrorists hoped to make—that we must understand what we had done to them—was lost in the dramatic event itself and its long, painful unwinding.

The psychological makeup of Iranians, their various cultures and customs, I still feel, remains a mystery to most of my countrymen. More than anything, I hope this book helps to reveal some aspects of the complicated Iranian social and religious heritage—and especially why many of us who came to know Iranians and their country grew so fond of them. In spite of all that has happened, a future reconciliation is desirable, and probably more necessary for us as a people than for them.

March, 1981

PERSIAN *Lions,*
PERSIAN LAMBS

1 ARRIVAL IN TABRIZ

THE plane from Teheran to Iran's northernmost province followed the jagged inner rim of the Elburz mountains, which cut off a view of the Caspian Sea. A dusty brown haze hung over the great desert plateau. "There isn't much to see," I said to my seat companion, a black-haired, pretty nurse-trainee, on her way home for a vacation. *"Vaqti-ké Engelisi harf mizanam mifahmid?"* "Do you understand when I speak English?" I asked. It was the only complete Pharsi sentence I knew; I had been in the country a little over a week.

"Na." She blushed and snapped open a sunflower seed with the skill of a chickadee.

"How do you do that?" I asked, pantomiming.

We did not have a language in common, but we had a fine time. My students were later to show me how to peel an orange, pointing out that it was much easier to start at the blossom end instead of the stem. I willingly instructed them in English grammar; they showed me how to smoke a narghila pipe. In these exchanges, each side gave and received more than was readily apparent. The facts of travel chart an inward course, a maze of the spirit, but awareness of this comes later, not when one is involved in timetables, maps and the first impact of a new country.

From the air Tabriz, the capital city of Azerbaijan, looked like a large oasis with orchards, vineyards, groves and flower gardens —all neatly contained in small rectangular dried-mud walls. Round, blue, winking pools were set in front of modest adobe homes. The ruins of the Ark, or Citadel, a fortress built by Ali

3

Shah in the fourteenth century, and the only unmistakable land-mark of Tabriz was a solid block of ochre bricks resembling from a distance a cluster of grain elevators. Within the shadow of the Ark, in a street named after it, I was to live for nearly a year.

As we disembarked, the local U.S. Information Agency officer, whom I shall call Jim Paulus, took charge of my gear, and we drove in a Jeep to his home, where I would stay until final ar-rangements about my flat were worked out. He was rather alarm-ingly cheerful about Tabriz, the people, and the work I would be doing at the university. If he felt such a selling job were neces-sary, I surmised that perhaps I had committed myself to some extraordinary difficulties—and that he was trying to keep the truth from me as long as possible. I began to see, however, that his smiling Jaycee manner was a genuine expression of his love for the Middle East, enthusiasm for his job and delight that I had come.

He was relieved to hear me say I already knew that the curricu-lum in Iranian universities allowed for no course in American literature, though this was the subject I was supposed to teach, under the terms of the Fulbright grant. On the way to the airport in Teheran, a harried U.S.I.A. official had reluctantly told me that courses were dictated by Teheran University for the national university system, and provincial institutions (Tabriz had been elevated to university status at the time of the Russian occupation during World War II) were obliged to follow the program—otherwise the students could not be certified for their degrees. The head of the English department at Teheran University re-garded American authors as part of the canon of English letters and would not countenance an influx of Fulbright professors who were supposedly specialists in "American literature." There-fore it was impossible to have a course with this title in a stu-dent's program. But I had decided that the content of any course could be determined by the teacher, and there would be no need to quibble over the title.

We entered the outskirts of the city and crossed an ancient bridge, arched like an eyebrow. The mountains rimming the val-ley were in slag-heap colorings: coppery green landslides, carnelian cliffs, purple outcroppings—very painterly mountains some-what resembling the buttes of Utah. The air had that light mountain buoyancy which makes the sky seem the blue of outer space, incredibly deep and pure in its blueness. I felt exhilarated but also a little queasy in the stomach. Every lurch of the jeep over potholes made me think I was about to vomit. Paulus, when apprized of my condition, said he had a bottle of Kaopectate at home which would fix me up, but that I would do as the natives and eat plenty of the local yogurt, called *mast* and made from the milk of the water buffalo.

The dusty road soon became pocked and pitted asphalt. Be-tween the edge and the sidewalk was an irrigation canal called the *jube*, still used as a water supply by many of the 300,000 in-habitants, though a British engineer was supervising the installa-tion of a new, sanitary water system. There was a story, probably apocryphal, that when the Teheran water system had been in-stalled, debates in the Majlis had broken out, some statesmen ar-guing that this was obviously a case of foreign graft and mis-management. Why, for instance, were the engineers putting in two whole sets of plumbing when there were sewage pipes al-ready throughout the city? It seemed simple to arrange matters so that sewage flowed through the pipes at night and water dur-ing the day.

Paulus waved toward a two-story yellow brick building. "See those racks of dyed yarn on the roof? A carpet factory—not one of the good ones, though." Skeins of brilliant red, blue, and green wool were looped on wooden frames, their colors "fixing" in the sunlight.

Most women on the streets were veiled to the eyes in black silk or flowered cotton print *chedurs*. A group of them washing clothes in the *jube* and leaning far down toward the water, still managed to conceal most of themselves as they squatted on the edge like waterfowl. The trees growing along the *jube* were a variety of poplar called *Tabrizi*. All the streets were mud-walled, and everything seemed hidden behind doors. Our progress was impeded by herds of goats, brown, grey and black sheep, and long pack-trains of burros loaded down with burdens of straw laced into packets like enormous hand grenades. Russian droshkies plied the streets looking for customers; the carriages were drawn by two thin horses, often splotched with henna dye and wearing brilliant blue beads or hammered metal necklaces. The droshky driver charged one *toman* (about fifteen cents) for a trip anywhere in Tabriz. Russian-built automobiles also served as taxis, and there were a number of garishly painted buses wheezing down the avenues.

In the center of town we came to the area of shops, set in two-story brick buildings, and on a corner passed a man in a red fez playing a silver flute, with many listeners gathered around. Street venders were hawking baked turnips and beets, fresh sheep feet and brains (a breakfast delicacy), sturgeon from the Caspian, charcoal-broiled kidneys and hearts, while children with trays of caramel candy on their heads ran through the crowds of dark-suited, shabby men, shouting like newsboys.

Paulus unlocked the heavy street door of his walled compound, flung it wide, and there below us was a neat garden with a fish-pond, water spraying in the air. Pear and quince trees were heavy with fruit. We walked down steps into the sunken garden and then up a short flight to the front door of the house. The spacious rooms had high ceilings, and French windows along the back gave out upon a balcony that afforded a splendid view of the strange, purple-red mountain called Analzanal, with its Moslem shrine on top. The carpets were warm-colored and deep, giving a hushed seclusion to the place in striking contrast to the dusty chaos of the street—as if we had crept into our tent and had closed the flap.

I stayed inside that walled domain for several days, except for brief forays into the downtown shopping area and explorations in the ancient bazaar. I had laughed at the clichés about "cultural shock" so much tossed about among overseas personnel, for I thought that I was adaptable to unexpected situations, had no preconceived notions as to what Persia would be like (although of course I did), and therefore could not be "shocked." I slept a great deal but assumed that my body was becoming used to the change in altitude—Tabriz being about as high as Denver. Still, I was feeling strange. A desire to withdraw, to contemplate the new surroundings from some safe perch, lasted for several days, and I basked in the sunshine under that bowl-blue sky, leisurely letting Persia come to me, rather than going out to seek it.

My only real contact was with my host, Jim Paulus. Paulus was of Greek extraction, a native of Amherst, Massachusetts, and he had first visited Tabriz in 1950 while doing graduate work for his doctorate in history. For a number of years he taught at Robert College, Istanbul; he married a Turkish woman, educated at Edinburgh and Yale, who taught English at Ankara University. The atmosphere of their home was a blend of the Turkish and American: white goatskin blankets on a box-spring bed; Ronson table lighter on a hammered copper tray which served as an end table; stuffed eggplant on the same menu with apple pie; she was a Moslem, he reminded me of a deacon in a good New England church. The harmony they achieved in their personal lives was a model of what we were all striving to bring about in international life. I had come to Tabriz believing the world to be one—not that east was east and west was west. I expected my experiences to confirm the idealism I felt concerning the possibility of accord between peoples. I came to teach but ended being taught. I spent a long time trying to figure out just what the lesson was. At the beginning, I simply did not know.

Even in my highly circumscribed existence, those first few days, I encountered strangeness. A tall, thin, grey-haired man, his face beatified through suffering, appeared to live in a series of rooms along one wall of the Paulus compound. He would nod and smile whenever he saw me sitting by the pool in the sun, an unread book in my hand, then slip back into the shadows of his rooms, drawing the drapes shut after him. Jim Paulus explained that he was the landlord, a recluse because of ill health, straitened circumstances, and the death of his wife. We were introduced, and thereafter we would speak briefly, though I could never detain him for very long. Years ago he had studied in the United States, at Wabash College, and the English language came back to him in luminous bursts that seemed to surprise him, like a half-forgotten patois of childhood.

Later, from Mrs. Paulus, I learned that he was an aristocrat of the Qujar line deposed by the present Shah's father in 1925, and he had once held much property and a prominent position in Tabriz. Now he lived in two rooms of the servant quarter and was forced to lease his home. He had lost his money at about the time his wife died of tuberculosis. His love was so intense that he devoted his days to keeping fresh his grief, making constant pilgrimages to her grave, fondling her personal ornaments, and meditating on their past life together. Friends found that his necrophilic absorption pre-empted his time; they no longer saw him, and he was eventually half-forgotten, though the touching tribute of his love remained a legend to hearten one's faith in the durability of the affections.

When the Pauluses had come to Tabriz two years before, they were the first tenants of this house; his removal to the servant quarter was another stage in his self-flagellation. At first he referred to the Pauluses as his guests and would accept no rent payments unless they were forced upon him. Mrs. Paulus told me that when they moved in, all the portraits of the owner's ancestors were still hanging on the wall of the bedroom. He explained, when she asked about it, that he simply did not know how to solve a very delicate problem: in his two rooms he did not have the space to honor his ancestors by hanging them in the proper positions of esteem. He could not place his father at the foot of the bed! Rather than dishonor his kin, he would leave them hanging in the big house.

I do not know how Mrs. Paulus solved the problem, but when I visited the bedroom of the elderly man one day as he lay weak from incessant nosebleeds, I saw the gallery of family portraits surrounding him. Perhaps Mrs. Paulus had pointed out that now, since she and her husband were occupying the house, they had their own ancestors to think about—their own family portraits to be placed in honored positions on the wall.

There were numerous callers every day. The doorbell on the street (placed high up, out of the children's reach) would buzz noisily, and in the kitchen the *bodgee* (maid) would utter a cry, urging one of her underlings to run out and open the door; but if no one were free at the moment, she would grudgingly fling a *chedur* over her head and clatter out to the door in shower-clog shoes. Usually the guests were women friends of Mrs. Paulus, socially prominent ladies of Tabriz who attended the English classes given by Mrs. Paulus during the winter. Her husband also conducted weekly discussion sessions in English, for the leading professional and businessmen of the city. Current events was the topic; the tensions between Russia and Iran and Russia and the U.S. were so ominous that many Iranians believed whatever radio or newspaper report presented the situation in its direst aspects. The forum in the Paulus home served to provide them with accurate information on world events.

One visitor to the household was an expatriate American whom Paulus called "Uncle" Moore. He had been born and raised in a little town in southwest Iowa, but he had lived most of his life in the Middle East (and still hated the smell of garlic on anyone's breath). Upon retirement from the faculty of Robert College, where he had been Paulus' friend, he discovered that America did not really interest him as a place to spend the rest of his years. He returned to Turkey, and now, riding the rough, crowded, dirty provincial buses, he had traveled through the mountains of ancient Armenia and had arrived in Tabriz. Having taken his chances on uncertain food and infested beds in roadside inns, his journey had just begun: his immediate destination was Isfahan, and he was timing it so that he would arrive at full moon. He explained to me that he had never been in Isfahan when the moon was right; before he died he wanted to sit in the gardens of the Ala Kapi palace on the Imperial Square at Isfahan, under a full moon, and listen to the nightingales singing. After that he was bound for Kabul, Afghanistan. We never heard from him again, but I thought of "Uncle" Moore the following June when I finally got to Isfahan and in the moonlight walked the flowered paths along the silvery Zayandeh Rud River, with its magnificent bridges, and viewed the glittering domes and minarets of Shah Abbas' fantastic city. I thought of him because there were no nightingales singing.

Another visitor, a physician and his wife who lived nearby, presented an invitation to a dinner party a few days hence. The doctor, probably not yet forty, was short, clean-shaven, and had crew-cut, brown hair. He was an eye-ear-nose specialist, and though he had been practicing only a few years, he was already a very rich man; he had recently taken his second wife, who was living in a separate establishment. It angered Mrs. Paulus that this intelligent, enlightened, Europeanized physician resorted to the polygamous code of the Koran, obviously for his sexual convenience. An ardent feminist, she vowed that the Middle East would someday not be so totally a man's world—though probably not in her lifetime. The doctor's first wife was lushly beautiful, opulently fleshed, the way the Persians like their women: black hair, olive skin and enormous dark brown eyes. Her smile was shy, her voice and manner intimate, gentle and very feminine. She had come from a higher-placed family than the doctor's, and part of his instantaneous success in his profession and in society had come about through his having married above him and having received a handsome dowry.

With a party in the offing at which I would meet most of the elite of Tabriz, I decided to get a haircut, not having had one since I left New York more than a month before. Paulus dropped me off at his barbershop near the main intersection of Shahnaz (named after the king's daughter) and Firdousi (the classic Persian poet); he introduced me to the barber and explained in Turki, the local dialect, what I wanted. Then he drove his Jeep on out Shahnaz avenue to the consulate, which was located near the edge of the city.

A white-coated assistant barber with a slightly fawning smile helped me remove my jacket; he disappeared in back with it. I noticed the hushed, strange peacefulness of the place. Across the wide window on the street, yellow plastic cafe curtains shut out most of the view; we were in pleasant seclusion. The owner of the establishment kept smiling at me and nodding his head. He was performing with a pair of shears on a customer who was deeply preoccupied, staring at himself in the mirror. Several men waited in chairs along the wall and I sat down among them, eyes lowered, allowing them to look me over; I picked up an Iranian magazine filled with cheesecake pictures of Italian movie stars. The other customers wore dark, badly cut suits of good English wool; their shoes were in terrible shape, and only much later did I understand why this was frequently the case. Most Persian men regard footgear as serviceable equipment for use outdoors; in the house shoes should be removed, slippers worn. Therefore, they are not part of one's costume, to be kept looking neat and attractive.

The three men receiving haircuts sat on walnut barber thrones obviously put together by a local carpenter: the headrest was a jutting crescent of wood padded on top, which could be moved up and down and fixed into place by a peg. The light fixture was a ring of neon tubing, the latest fad in Tabriz, and, I suspected, only rather recently imported from Germany. Now and then the head barber lifted his hand in some sort of signal and two boys of eight or nine, his apprentices, rushed to the rear for basins, water, another type of shears or brushes.

Finally it was my turn. A completely clean cloth was unfurled and wads of cotton were gently packed around my neck so that the harsh noose of cloth would not be abrasive—and also to prevent snippets of hair from falling inside my shirt. Up close I was struck by the barber's face—not its physical aspects, for he was an ordinary sort of Azerbaijani, rather tall, with dark greying hair, a thickly featured, strongly handsome face, and great sensitive eyes; it was somehow satisfactorily lined, the smiles playing across it like ripples on a pool. I sensed immediately his spiritual well-being, an inner radiance that was comforting to be around.

He brought out a small alcohol burner with a violet wick and struck a match. It burned directly in front of me, since my legs were tucked under the sideboard as if I were sitting at a desk, a great mirror facing me. From a drawer he pulled out three hand clippers, two scissors, and a razor, and one by one swept them across the flame, the burning hairs crackling. I wondered if this rite of cleanliness were especially on my behalf—the American from that land of the clean and gilded spoon. But I saw by glancing at the other customers that this was not an unusual process. No one was paying attention to the barber. Each was watching himself in the mirror with complete absorption. The man on my right, handsome in a mustachioed regimental style, was gazing raptly into his own eyes. On my left the assistant barber was clipping away on a patron who was considering the lean, strong angle of his chin. He tilted his head slightly and turned partially away—yes, that was better. He frowned—ah, very fierce indeed!

Then he smiled at himself in charming approval. The men occupying the chairs along the wall were looking at themselves, too. In this male beauty shop there seemed nothing extraordinary about such narcissistic concerns.

When the instruments had been sterilized the two boys rushed up and took away the burner. The barber surveyed my hair intently, then began to comb and brush it, massaging the scalp with his hands and smiling at me in the mirror. A boy returned with a tin bowl of hot water, and the barber placed a glass jar of cotton on the shelf in front of me, detached a blob, and after dipping it in hot water, began to swab me behind the ears, at the bottoms of my sideburns, and across my neck. Then he picked up the razor and I squirmed; he had failed to apply shaving soap! But he scraped away and miraculously I felt no pain. Upon finishing he squirted me with an atomizer of powerful rosewater until I was enveloped in a mist; then he administered talcum powder with a small feather duster. I could only conclude from all of these finishing touches that *he* thought I didn't need a haircut, but he intended to give me my money's worth in fringe benefits.

He reached for the cotton again and began plugging up my ears. He picked up the scissors and fell to work. It was a long process. He would stop frequently and experiment with my hair, as youngsters do, by parting it at odd angles or swirling it about in unnatural, faun-like shapes. After careful arrangement so that all my hair flowed in one direction, he would snip the two or three miniscule strands that were too long. Then he would suddenly reverse the field, running everything backward, and just as it is uncomfortable for a dog to have its coat stroked the wrong way, so I was made vaguely uncomfortable and a little angry. It seemed to amuse him to comb my hair up until it stood on end for a moment, five inches in the air; then, as it rapidly slipped through his comb, falling back to my head, he swooped down with the scissors and caught the tips. My hair was a cascade in front of my eyes when he suddenly stopped, opened a drawer and drew out a sheet of white paper, which he slipped under my forelock. I thought it might be some Persian scheme for seeing every filament more clearly. His scissors began cutting decisively, right across my eyes, although having the illusion of safety behind the paper, I had no inclination to flinch for fear of having an eye poked out. The barbers out here, I realized, had considered all the nuances of the trade.

At last I sensed that the job was over. The boys raced toward the back for a large mirror, which they thrust in the air over their heads so that I could see the back of my neck. The barber, highly pleased with himself, was obviously waiting for my reaction. Not just a nod and the usual *merci* was in order, but a look of wonder, astonishment, and delight must cross my face, as I perceived my transformed appearance. I did my best. The barber unhitched the shawl from my shoulders, removed the cotton from around my neck, and began feather-dusting my cheeks, chin, ears and forehead. As he leaned close with his four-day growth of beard, gold-toothed smile, and compliments about my *mū* (hair), I realized that I had come close to a kiss on both cheeks. I climbed out of the chair, smiling, to show him that he had truly renewed my vigor and pleasure in myself. He began to use a black roller brush, something like a small carpet sweeper, on my shirt and trousers.

When I brought out my wallet and gave him thirty rials (about forty cents), I noticed his slight hesitance. Had I blundered? Perhaps only an assistant barber soiled his hands with money—I might have offended him. He took the smudged bills, however, quickly tucking them away, and then reached for my coat, which the boys had brought out from the rear. Surely a tip to someone was in order—I gave coins to the boys—they were delighted. Their heads were clipped close to the skull, like novitiates in a monastery, and that old priest of a barber nodded, smiling his approval.

As we exchanged hearty *khoda hafez*'s in farewell, I noticed that the assistant barber who had greeted Paulus and me upon entering was now busily at work sweeping up my fallen hair. He seemed to be trying to communicate something to me, for he kept glancing over his shoulder, nodding, and hurrying with his task. He gathered all my hair in a piece of folded newspaper and somewhat reverently moved with it to the rear, still smiling proudly at me. I realized I was witnessing the final touch to the process: this part of me which I had left behind on the floor

13

would be disposed of properly, with due respect, just as one must take care in destroying the national flag or church vestments. No foreign foot would trample upon these hairs, shards of my own existence. I had not been in the hands of some functionary who was a mere barber—nor had I been simply a man in need of a haircut. I had undergone a ritual, and when there is soul-sharing involved, one cannot be casual about it.

2 A LOOK AT SOCIETY

THE evening of the party at the physician's, we had a hearty high tea before leaving the house at 8:30, since Mrs. Paulus said we would not dine until close to midnight. She wore a conservative, brown American dress with a square cut neckline and a heavy Turkish necklace of silver charms (miniature beggar's bowl and tiny flat hands to ward off the evil eye). Small, auburn-haired, with large brown eyes, she was too thin, but so high-strung she could not gain weight. She wore glasses, as did her husband. Having spent years studying and teaching the English language, there was only a slight liquidity of vowels, an occasional blurring of consonants, which marked her as a foreigner. Tonight I admired her for wearing the peasant jewelry of her native land, for I suspected that the Tabriz ladies we'd meet would be adorned with diamonds, rubies and emeralds from Teheran's smartest jewelry stores. Mrs. Paulus, unlike most of them, was comfortably at ease about her heritage.

A servant opened the courtyard door before we had a chance to ring the bell. Several automobiles, among them a Buick, Mercedes and Cadillac, were parked along the *jube,* with chauffeurs standing guard to prevent hub caps, tires, radio antennas and other items from disappearing in the night. We walked through a garden of red geraniums, blue and white petunias and other flowers growing in paisley patterns. The trees were burdened with fruit. A butler in a white jacket showed us into the main drawing room where about forty people were assembled, men on chairs along the left wall, women seated on the right. They rose, we bowed and smiled, and everyone exchanged loud *salaams.* Paulus turned to the line of women, introducing each of them to me; he knew the proper, personal remark for each of them. Mrs. Paulus took her seat at the end of the line, and the row of women sat down.

We crossed an expanse of carpet to the men's side. Most of the leading doctors were here, since the occasion was to honor a physician who was soon leaving for Chapel Hill, North Carolina, on a U.S. study grant. I met them all, and while Paulus continued conversing with individuals here and there, I found a place next to a fat colonel in a dark blue civilian suit with a cream-colored satin tie. Yes, the affable colonel said, he knew English. His brilliant blue eyes gave his jowly face a cherubic touch; he was, I learned later, Security Chief, one of the local strongmen.

Tea was served in glasses set in filigreed silver. Each of us had a little end table placed beside or in front of his chair. The three incredibly beautiful, matching carpets continually drew my eyes; the Tabriz carpets for some odd reason have never been especially popular in the U.S. These had probably taken six or seven years to weave and were works of art. The floral design was in muted beige, pale blue, yellow, light green and scarlet; it was a closely cropped, velvety Primavera. Like a stray piece from a German middle class home, in the center of the room was a small oval table draped in a long lace cloth and laden with bowls of nuts, mounds of fruit, candy and assorted pastries. A servant passed before us with plates of delicious pistachio macaroons. I took something of everything, as did the others; it was not expected that everything must be eaten in a "waste not, want not" fashion. Someone "out there" beyond the luxury of this room would eat what was scraped from our plates; it was *senevesh,* fate. The elements that shape a man's destiny were so much beyond his comprehension, so far removed from his personal responsibility, that only a stoical acceptance of fate was possible. Consequently, there was no compassionate notion of I-am-my-brother's-keeper. Fate had decreed that one man was rich and fortunate, whereas another was furtively picking over the garbage for his supper.

I continued to look closely at the room. Some of the chairs were locally made, rather crudely fashioned wooden pieces, but most of the room was furnished in garish, teal-blue overstuffed

16

chairs, Montgomery Ward style of the 1930's. It was round, heavy, and ugly—pressed plush in swirling shell patterns. The lighting in the room was sharp and hard on the eyes, perhaps because electricity was a fairly recent arrival in Tabriz. The brighter the room, the more it was an achievement of civilization. The ceiling lightshades were tulip-shaped, and the wall sconces were electrified torches. I had time to observe all of this because the colonel's knowledge of English turned out to be extremely limited, and once he had uttered his five phrases, and I in my ignorance had babbled away in full response, there could be no further communication between us. The colonel felt no embarrassment about this. He fell into a smug silence, apparently because he believed he'd made as much of an effort as this social situation, and a foreigner like me, called for. After all, I was as much at fault for not knowing Turki. He smiled at me now and then, unconcerned about our muteness.

A few empty seats inspired the host to attempt musical chairs, but some of his guests were too deep in conversation to pay attention to him. At last he came over to me and sat down. By this time the nut course had been served three times; with each new serving, the waiters would dump nutshells and uneaten nuts into gleaming brass bowls, then present each guest with a new plate and pour out almonds and pistachios. Potato chips were also served; they had a strange, sour Crisco taste because they'd been fried in ghee, the aged butter used in India and the Middle East for deep fat cooking. Then came bottles of locally brewed beer, Pepsi-Cola, and orange soda pop, followed by several courses of sweet, chewy candy somewhat resembling Turkish Halvah. My host was pleased to see me eating heartily. Like the compulsive hand-to-mouth movements of other guests in the room, it was mostly a nervous reaction. One or two of the men had their strings of beads out, toying with them, to keep their hands busy at something—but it was a low-class thing to do, and the more sophisticated among the men smoked cigarettes. The ladies had no such devices to drain off their agitation, but then, women were considered to be the solid, practical, unemotional, down-to-earth sex, whereas men were afflicted with delicate sensibilities, unstable emotions and excessive nervousness.

17

Dr. Bazarghan and his wife entered and we all rose and bowed; he was chancellor of the university. My host asked if I'd met them, and I said no; as soon as possible he brought Mrs. Bazarghan to my side. She spoke fluent English and had a blunt, self-confident manner that was refreshing. "You like it here?" she asked, a sly smile on her lips, as if she were waiting for me to lie. I told her truthfully that I did, but she hastily went on to say that *she* was from Teheran, and it was extremely difficult to adjust to a place like this. It had taken months to find a suitable house and more months to get it furnished in a halfway civilized fashion. She described in some detail her domestic situation, the piano lessons for the children, and her brave attempt to get used to the provinciality of Tabriz.

She was inquisitive about the apartment I had contracted to take. It was the old Turkish consulate, now a private home, and one of the few furnished apartments available in town—spoken for, very providently, by the wife of the American Consul, weeks before I arrived in Tabriz. Mrs. Bazarghan was frankly inquisitive about how much I would pay for it. "Too much, I'm sure," she added. I decided not to tell her, though she was persistent and direct. If I admitted that rent and servants would cost approximately $90 a month, she would have been horrified; some local citizens rented large houses and whole servant staffs for that price. I didn't wish her to gossip about my finances, which would only further enlarge the notion that rich Americans in Tabriz could be easily taken in by landlords and would spend a fortune for what could be had for next to nothing.

Dr. Bazarghan himself joined us—a warm, generous man, whom I liked at once; because of his exalted position in Tabriz, I was never to know him well. He was Iran's most distinguished nuclear physicist and had just returned from an Atoms for Peace conference in Geneva. He was modest, somewhat shy, and greatly honored in his country. This was partly due to the fact that Iranians were eager to fix their interest upon someone who was so fully abreast of today's world, who symbolized the persistent desire for modernity which underlay so much of the recent ferment in the country. Iranians were impelled to be as modern as possible, but were drawn back because of custom and tradition to the ancient ways and values. Few Iranians I met were not caught in this struggle. They were cast in the mold of their heritage but felt they must slough it off and become Westernized in order to participate in the mid-twentieth century. "They are the most schizophrenic people imaginable," said one glib European to me in Teheran. "You can't say you'd wish they'd be themselves. They don't know who they are."

A burst of laughter came from the women. I learned later that they were amused over a language error. One woman had thanked Mrs. Paulus for suggesting where she could get an oven in which to bake cakes. The conversation was in Turki, and the word for baking cakes is the same as the one for making love. After a happy time, relishing the joke, the ladies all rose and filed into the dining room for the buffet supper. Their dresses were modeled after Paris magazine illustrations, copied by local dressmakers. The style involved low necklines showing some cleavage, tight fitting bodices, bell-shaped puffy skirts and bouffant hair-dos. Most of them were much younger than their husbands; some were striking, dark-haired beauties; all were plump.

Surfeited by sweets and nuts and beer, I was not really hungry but hoped that solid food might settle the bilious state of my stomach. The men, now standing, were smiling and murmuring "befarmeid" to one another, bowing, extending their arms in an after-you-Gaston manner. But no one of the twenty-five men would agree to step forward and leave the room ahead of anyone else. The British Council director would definitely not be the first, and he was sternly definite with his "No!" Dr. Bazarghan was urged by many to be the first man out of the room, but he would not go, out of genuine humility, I think. Then the vice-chancellor of the university was prevailed upon, but he of course would not hear of it. The guest of honor, the physician soon to depart for America, seemed a likely choice, but he bowed and smiled enigmatically and hid behind the huge colonel. No, no, the colonel would not go—he blushed at the very suggestion. Then they began urging Jim Paulus—he must go, but he too demurred. I was next, but they did not beseech me for very long, since perhaps I would not understand the intricacies of protocol and would actually accept their suggestion, which would have been a disastrous error, embarrassing for me, Paulus, and the United States government. Eventually I realized that every man in the room recognized Dr. Bazarghan to be the most distinguished person present. Even he knew it, and although the Director of Labor for Azerbaijan was also honored and two other generals of the Iranian army were asked, they all refused and at last Dr. Bazarghan reluctantly moved toward the door.

But then, who was the next most distinguished? The *befarmeids* started in a chorus once more, until suddenly, either tiring of the game or feeling it a discourtesy to leave Bazarghan alone with the women, while his friends quibbled over their relative importance, the group moved in unison toward the door and out into the foyer.

The ladies were already deeply absorbed in eating. Platters of shish kebab, tender lamb in tomato sauce, saffron-flavored long grain white rice with pine nuts, dismembered chicken in sweet gravy, salad, sliced onions, pickles and preserved fruits were located in the center of the table. In boarding house style the buffet offering was being assaulted from all sides; any holding back out of politeness would mean no supper. There was very little talking, since the business of eating was undertaken with some mechanical difficulty—everyone stood about, plate in hand, or tried to establish a place on the table. I finally found a niche on a sideboard to rest my plate; the food seemed marvelous. My hostess came by and I told her how delicious everything was. She smiled wistfully, perhaps with some amusement, for I discovered later that the menu for all society parties in Tabriz was invariably the same. They hired the same catering service, which never varied the dishes. Most Persian food, I was to discover, was delicious but amazingly monotonous, just a few favorite items, repeated again and again. I thought the chicken fricassee a little too chickeny—the fowl's barnyard diet of manure had strongly flavored the meat—or perhaps it hadn't been butchered properly, the guts left in too long. Everyone was drinking Pepsi-Cola. It seemed an abominable thing to do, but I was thirsty. Jim Paulus had become so accustomed to the habit, and to the need to drink Pepsi-Cola when the safety of the water was in doubt, that he claimed he actually liked it with a meal. We shared a bottle, then had another. I belched and felt initiated.

Just as supper was about over, two doctors arrived; one of them was determined to contribute some gaiety to the party. He declaimed a poem he had composed in tribute to his departing colleague, the guest of honor. Everyone was greatly pleased—truly now the party was a success and happy faces were everywhere.

The meal over, we assembled in the drawing room again, ladies on the right, gentlemen on the left. The host adjusted the phonograph and put a fox-trot on the spindle. He began going around the room, traversing those extraordinarily beautiful carpets, urging his guests to dance. Finally he found a pretty dancing companion, wife of the Director of Labor for Azerbaijan. Their efforts to get the party moving, however, did not work, and only one other couple felt bold enough to dance about, Western style, in front of a large circle of people who were watching with interest and amusement. Meanwhile, servants passed among the guests with baskets of fruit—peaches, apples, pears, grapes and cucumbers—in containers the size of laundry hampers. The next course consisted of candies, cookies and endless glasses of tea.

I saw a chair next to the British Council man, whom I shall call Fanshawe, and went over to talk, beginning by asking about the library in "the British consulate."

Indignantly he replied, "I am not a consul and there is no British Consulate in Tabriz. The consul is under the Foreign Office. I am a schoolmaster, and I direct the British Council. Council. C-o-u-n-c-i-l. Now do you understand the difference?"

"Yes," I said; the slip had been accidental, but to him it indicated the full measure of my American ignorance. I recognized him as the chaffing type of Englishman who can only be dealt with by giving back what-for. We had it out. I inquired who paid his salary—was it not the Foreign Office? He admitted it was. The United States, I affirmed, was considerably more honest in its propaganda efforts. A man like Paulus, who was the Information Agency's representative in Tabriz, was not technically under the Secretary of State, but he was officially a vice-consul; he was publicly acknowledged to be part of the United States' efforts abroad. I could see, however, that there might be some gain in the effectiveness of Fanshawe's program here if English study and the dissemination of information about Great Britain were divorced from governmental activity—and the fiction of complete independence from consul-type activities were maintained—but in truth, there seemed something slightly deceitful about it.

He smiled. From that point on, Fanshawe and I were friends.

He could not resist needling me over the absurdity of my presence in this primitive part of the world, ostensibly to teach American literature. The University of Tabriz, he assured me, was actually in need of good teachers of English, but as for proceeding to a study of "literature," that was perfectly ridiculous! Most of my students scarcely had a vocabulary of four hundred words. "Wait until you begin lecturing to them on *Moby Dick*," he chuckled. "You'll see."

I wouldn't admit it to him, but I knew very well that part of the reason for my presence in Iran was quite other than simply to lecture on Melville, Whitman and Emerson. I was also to be a good spokesman, win friends and influence people. This of course I would feel foolish saying to Fanshawe. I was a little unclear at that point about my feelings on this score. Even the advance material from the State Department before I'd left the United States was somewhat ambivalent about my role in the foreign country to which I had been assigned. On the one hand I was a free and uncommitted citizen, with my own political opinions and beliefs, but I should never forget that I would be judged as a representative American, that my appearance in Iran was tantamount to being an ambassador from the American people. I was being paid by the U.S. treasury, given privileges such as use of the commissary in Teheran, the army post office, and I even received mail at the U.S. consulate, where a vice-consul was my advisor and guide, if not actually my boss. And yet I was not considered a government employee in the usual sense at all.

I shall not soon forget my surprise when, one day, I wandered into the private office of a clerk at the consulate in Tabriz, and how he hastily, and with some embarrassment, asked me to leave and pointed to the sign on the door: No Admittance: Authorized Personnel Only. I had not been "cleared," I was not really "authorized" at all, and whereas every other American employee at the consulate could legally carry the diplomatic pouch to Teheran, it was of course nothing I was asked to do nor would have been allowed to do.

This strange role I was placed in, of being official and yet not official, was somewhat confusing to me, but especially puzzling to nationals of other countries, trying to figure out my exact place. Certainly the Iranians never believed I was anything but a bona fide American careerist in the diplomatic corps, despite my protestations that I was "just a teacher," that I had been a university professor in America and would go back to teaching. It seemed too improbable. And so in some ways I understood Fanshawe's adamant insistence on the independence of the British Council system, which was supposed to have the image of being a benevolent, philanthropic, even self-paying institution, through which the English language and British culture were better understood throughout the world; if any political benefits accrued, it was purely incidental.

Although my students could not believe the independence of my role in Iran, I kept wishing that they would: nothing seemed a better example of a free, democratic society than that it would dare to send a man who had not been "cleared," who was not official in any way, to one of the world's most politically sensitive spots, without even a briefing in Washington before going and without a call to Washington to "report" when he got back home. That any country would trust its ordinary citizens to such lengths could only be to its glory, and I wished somehow that my students would believe in the true innocence of my sojourn among them.

3 CIRCLING LAKE REZAIYEH

I BEGAN to feel restive; classes at the Faculty of Letters had not begun, and I was being denied my purposes in having come to Azerbaijan: I had not charmed a single Iranian into liking my country, nor had I taught anybody about American literature. Paulus, sensing my impatience, invited me along on a trip around the great salt lake, Rezaiyeh, formerly called Lake Urmia; he would arrange to have me speak in the schools of the city of Rezaiyeh.

With an Iranian at the wheel of the Jeep, we chose the northern route, going counterclockwise around the lake, following the ancient caravan trail between India and Istanbul. The condition of the road had probably changed little over the centuries, but we drove at a speed of sixty, flying over the ruts and pits. Peasants with black oxen were tilling the irrigated, yellow-clay soil with crude wooden plowshares. Now and then we had to pause, horn blaring (our driver, Sumat, enjoyed this) to scatter shepherds with their flocks of black and white turkeys, sheep and goats. I asked Paulus about tenant farming, and he said that shares of profit were divided five ways: to the landowner, to the holder of water rights, to the provider of the seed, to the owner of the plows and oxen (all four were usually the same man), and lastly to the peasant laborers. "Not much left for the peasants, I'm afraid."

"Where do they live?" I asked, for on the vast plain there was not an adobe cottage in sight.

"Look back against those mountains—look hard."

Then I saw the mud-walled village, blending into the foothills the way an animal might hide its lair; except for the rectangular black doorways and tiny dark squares of windows, it was scarcely visible at all. Each day the peasants walked miles from their homes to work the tiny plots of land assigned them. Their clothes were very different from the dark Western suits of men in the cities; the hand-loomed costume consisted of a coarse, dun-colored jacket and floppy burlap-type trousers, usually gaily patched with chintzes and other prints imported from Russia and found in all the bazaars. Hand-knitted woollen socks reaching up their shanks were often bright orange or fuchsia or flaming red. They were shod in a simple leather sole laced to the sock with thongs and whimsically turned up on the end. Their faces were gypsy-colored, walnut-stained by the ever present sunshine, and deeply creased. The men's black hair was closely cropped and many of them wore small crocheted skullcaps of an intricate, snowflake design.

We passed a man bathing in a small, shallow stream. Modest, shy Iranian men were extremely skillful in manipulating their garments so that although they relieved themselves in public along a roadside or bathed in open streams with women nearby washing clothes, their own sense of privacy was maintained, and always on their faces was an expression of calm dignity, as if God alone were witness.

We kept rising, and as the valley became narrower and higher it also became greener, except that, since it was autumn, the grass was now yellowing. I saw a group of peasants winnowing wheat in front of a granary; they tossed the grain into the air, caught it in large sieve-bottomed pans; the chaff blew away in the wind. Soon we arrived in the small city of Morand, situated on a mountain slope. We stopped to buy fruit and vegetables, for which Morand was renowned, and also to collect a few native-dyed baskets of crudely woven straw, which resembled Mexican craft. Our driver Sumat, who worked as a handyman and general assistant at the consulate, purchased a handsome basket and put in grapes, pears, cucumbers and apples as a present for his mother. We told him he was a good boy and would surely be rewarded in heaven.

By local standards Sumat had advanced far in the world, especially considering that he was only twenty-two years old. The U.S. consul prior to the present one had hired Sumat as a houseboy when he was about fifteen. Before long Sumat had learned to cook and to speak English, although he was hard to understand, since he did not articulate by using his lips or tongue; rather, the sound would emerge from his thick, parted mouth as if he were speaking from behind a mask. He had coarse, curly brown hair, blue eyes, fair skin and a shy, dignified manner. Very early Sumat revealed an aptitude for mechanical things—he could repair almost anything; he was reliable on errands, faithful and responsible. The consul hoped to send him to the United States for a college education, but as it developed, this was rushing matters too much. Sumat dropped out of the local university and expressed no interest in a career abroad. He was supporting his father and mother, who, on the strength of his job with the Americans, had purchased a house. His "rise" had already been considerable, and he was content to enjoy his hard-won privileges.

Hurrying on, we made Khoi by lunchtime, and on the way crossed the high mountain pass called Yom, a summer resort and a ski area in winter; the small buildings looked forlorn and unfestive on the bare mountain slope. Beyond the pass we descended into a desolate valley of great length and flatness where herds of camels were grazing, distinctly etched against the distant mountains. The yellow-brown clay foothills were bleak and uninteresting; the same color of dung seemed everywhere, on field, mountain and sky.

A friendly policeman in Khoi, who nevertheless checked our credentials as if we were spies, babbled to Paulus in English—a nonsense string of phrasebook sentences. He had studied the language all by himself, and although he could say some recognizable English words, he was at a loss as to how to apply them, except to fling them in the face of the first English-speaking man encountered, then grin with pleasure over his accomplishment. Paulus had come prepared, for he'd met this policeman before, and presented him with two books on English self-taught—the kind of thoughtfulness that made Paulus loved throughout Azerbaijan. Even those who did not know his name referred to him as "the friendly American who always smiles."

We ate lunch in a restaurant where Paulus had eaten on his first swing through Iran in 1950. We walked through the "kitchen," just as one does in Greece; strips of mutton were sizzling on glowing charcoal beds. The place smelled, typically, of fresh meat and frying blood, the sheep having been slaughtered only that morning. In the dim dining area, where light filtered down through a dirty skylight, tables were arranged around a gurgling fountain and pool. Above us was a balcony dining area, where some customers sat, looking down. Only dark-suited, black-mustached men wearing hats were present, for women were seldom permitted in public places. Some restaurants in Tabriz allowed them, but special booths were assigned, which could be completely closed off from the men by sliding drapes. At one end of the marble pool, orange soda pop and Pepsi-Cola were cooling; at the other, a bloody pile of raw mutton was kept chilled, close to the water. Around the spurting fountain in the center, several large pink fish swam, looking up at the customers with yellow wall-eyes.

We started on our way, down the western shore of Lake Rezaiyeh, and again we entered a fertile agricultural region. Flocks of sheep and goats dotted the hills and tiny plumes of smoke were seen in the mountains—shepherds having their noon meal. After passing the earthquake-destroyed village of Shahpur, an ancient and historic spot (a new village exists nearby), I began searching the hill crests overlooking the lake for Zoroasterian cairns, reportedly still in evidence. The birthplace of Zoroaster, a native of western Media, about 500 B.C., was said by some to be Shahpur; others claimed Rezaiyeh. In any case, Zoroasterianism, based on the principle of the eternal struggle between good and evil and the worship of fire, was still of some influence in these parts—and gaining adherents in Teheran, in cultist fashion. I saw several stone piles on promontories, but they did not look promising enough to stop and explore. We sped on.

Villages along the way, though only glimpsed from the Jeep, were mired in mud; heavy rains had recently descended and human life was on an animal level. The mud homes had a few holes cut in the walls for windows, doors and an aperture in the ceiling for smoke to escape. Chickens, sheep, children and goats wallowed in the filth together, while the men sat on plaited straw mats on the verandas of the teahouses and smoked their waterpipes. Because of the shortage of wood for fuel, here as elsewhere in the Middle East, dung piles were gathered soon after they dropped from the animals and were plastered against the walls to dry in the sun, then stacked in round piles with broom-like plumes at the top. Sometimes these discs were arranged artistically, not flat like a plate of cookies but on edge like miniature wheels. Perhaps it was easier to pull them apart when needed, and they were better preserved from the rains this way.

Although the afternoon was waning, we stopped near an outcropping of giant pink rocks, not far from the shores of the lake. Carved on the side was a six- or seven-foot high Sassanian period bas-relief. Though somewhat eroded by storms, it was an impressive piece of art. Here an ancient army had supposedly camped after a victory, to rest, and an artist (or several of them) had chipped away at this commemorative design. Two horsemen were clearly distinguishable, emerging from the rock with a ghostly, monolithic presence. They were graceful, curvilineal creatures, their trappings done with some detail. The horsemen's headpieces resembled the gear of the present-day Kurds. The leader here was clearly accepting a gift from a conquered subject—an old theme in Persian art. The triumphant horseman's beard was carved with ringlets and part of his cape flowed out regally behind him. With all the military implications of this tableau, the message had an Ozymandian touch, for this windswept rock looked out upon nothing, on a land that seemed coveted by no one, on an emptiness especially telling because of the deadness of the salt lake itself.

Entering the outskirts of Rezaiyeh at dusk, I found a duplicate of Tabriz: the same walled orchards, the *jubes* lining the streets, the towering poplar trees, and the two-story ochre brick buildings of the shopping area. But somehow, with its location near the lake, tilted toward it, there was an atmosphere of a coastal town, a watering place. And one was struck by the women without *chedurs,* walking freely about the streets in Western dresses; the population here was largely Christian Assyrian.

Sumat drove us to a pension kept especially for American workers in the area, where it cost about $3.50 to stay, not counting meals. This was the so-called "Point Four Guest House," where Djavid presided as cook, and Anna his wife as housekeeper. Wizened little Djavid in his white chef's hat knew about American life; he'd lived in Chicago himself, had been a cook at the Palmer House. Incredible!

Yes, really, he insisted. And as proof he began rattling off names of things in Chicago. "Michigan Boulevard," "Clark Street," "Wabash Avenue," "Lake Michigan," "The Loop," "Illinois Central Railroad," "the stockyards—Chicago stockyards."

Finally convinced, the visitor could only ask: but how come you're here?

Oh, he loved America. He wished he were there now, but he had made one mistake—one little mistake, or rather, a very big error in the eyes of the United States government. And now he could never go back.

Trouble with the police?

Never! Never! He had returned home to Iran to see his sick parents. He did not understand the rule that applicants for U.S. citizenship could not do this. Now it was too late, and never again would he see Chicago, Lake Michigan, or the Illinois Central Railroad. He had broken America's rule. He knew how to fix pancakes, though, make apple pie and home-fried potatoes. We must eat while staying with him just as we would if we were back in the U.S.A.

His wife Anna (round Slavic face with high cheekbones, sunken eyes, a babushka tied under her chin) had her own sad story, but nobody could get it out of her. She was Russian but denied it for fear that her working in the Point Four Guest House would seem suspiciously inappropriate. She took a great deal of teasing from all her guests. Sometimes Paulus would ask Anna a question in Russian, to try to trick her into replying. "No! No!" she would cry, blushing. English was the language she wished he would use, only English. She understood none of that Russian.

The speaking engagements Paulus arranged for me next day were to take place at two high schools originally built by American missionaries, well situated in compounds that had enormous *Tabrizi* trees and spacious playing fields. It was a blue and gold October day, and glancing down the streets of Rezaiyeh I saw the purple-red mountains across the lake. The air was crisp and pure, the sun brilliant; I'd had an uneasy night, however.

At about 2:00 a.m. I awoke because of a strange, muffled noise in the street, and going to the window, had looked down on a long string of solemn camels walking along the road. They were velvet brown, packed high with cargo—it was a caravan coming in from the south, festive and strange as the arrival of a circus. But the silence of the march, the strange, melodic tinkling of the camel bells (an insistent rhythm, a steady beat, as if all those club-footed animals were waltzing along) seemed an eery manifestation of a land that was not merely odd to me now, but would remain forever foreign, inexplicable. It was a recognition, I suppose, an eager tourist must always come at last to accept. I had my first intimation that life in Azerbaijan for me would not be what I had anticipated—and, more important, that I had no control over what experiences might be forthcoming or what they would do to me. The land was asserting itself; and I was beginning to feel it.

In the bright, salubrious mountain air of morning, I recovered my well-being and felt ready to venture forth again. I prowled about the bazaar, which glittered as if it were the plunder discovered by Ali Baba in the robbers' cave. The bazaars of the cities of Persia seemed to join one another, continuing shop after shop, winding along deep in the earth, coming out into the open air for the space of a block, then burrowing under again, as if in one long connected splendid tunnel. Older than the buildings of the towns, more established than the lineage of the people, these bazaars became in one's mind the eternal womb of the Middle East.

When the time for my talks neared, Sumat drove Paulus and me to the boys' school, and we met Mr. Mehibe, director of education for Rezaiyeh. He informed me that I was the first American speaker to appear at the school, perhaps since the days of the missionaries. Glasses of tea were served while faculty members came in to meet me. After a few minutes and a brief, ceremonious sip of tea, we marched upstairs to the auditorium, where about five hundred boys were awaiting my lecture. What in God's name would I say? I had somehow neglected to think much about it, but when I was introduced in Pharsi, with many compliments, and I mounted the stage, I suddenly decided that perhaps they'd be interested to hear about schooling for a typical American boy. Crafty propagandist that I was, I meant to imply that all schoolboys had much in common—they would all be friends, if they just knew one another.

I spoke for thirty minutes in a slow, repetitious, overly enunciatory way that I'd been told to adopt for my classes, and I was surprised to see that they were more or less able to follow. They laughed in the right places. Dressed in dark suits, white shirts, ties, some with mustaches, they were like impish, diminutive men; the contained energy of their attention seemed to charge the room. Later, during the question period, one student asked about Edgar Allan Poe, America's most famous writer; another wanted me to describe universities and hotels in America. Some of their questions I was later to find verbatim in such standard texts on the local market as *Brighter English*.

I left the crowded auditorium at the insistence of my aides; like a man running for office, I could only spend a certain amount of valuable time in one place. Sumat was waiting to rush me over to the girls' school, where I was due at 3:00 p.m., in the Jeep. They were playing games at recess when I arrived; a charming scene— hundreds of little girls in grey dresses with white collars, all of them with dark hair and enormous eyes. The missionaries had laid out the compound on a grand scale, and now the towering *Tabrizi* trees, fully grown in their regimented places, formed long alleys.

The headmistress of the school greeted me in French and tea was served in her office. After a few minutes Mr. Mehibe arrived with Paulus, and I was introduced around the room. Unlike many Iranian officials with a pocketful of power, Mr. Mehibe showed no contempt for his underlings, no desire to make them grovel before him. The teachers were all women, but they were clearly not afraid of him, and not only respected his position, but actually liked him.

My speech was a variation of the one just delivered, except that stress was put on the education of women in America. With part of my mind, as I talked, I wondered what the effect of my words might be. In the question period following, one girl asked if home economics were an important subject in American high schools. I was surprised to hear such a pertinent query, certainly not out of *Brighter English,* and I tried to give an honest answer, especially in terms of what "important" meant. I said it depended on what the girl and her parents expected from her education. Some prepared for college, others developed business skills; still others cultivated domestic arts. An English teacher pressed me to clarify my remarks. She rephrased the question: were credits in homemaking as important as credits in other subjects? Finally I said yes, grades were given for homemaking courses and were averaged in with grades from academic courses in most public high schools.

Not until the assembly broke up, when I was given a tour of the premises, did I fully understand the reason for the home-economics questions. Proudly, the headmistress showed me a large, beautiful stainless steel, American-built, American-donated kitchen, with sewing areas as well. Obviously, home economics was the chief subject here—it was why girls went to school, as well as to learn to read and write. But as far as a woman's career was concerned, there was little change in this mode of education from the old-fashioned way of learning everything at home from the mother. Was this modern kitchen a sign of progress in women's education? I think the bold young lady who asked the question had other ideas. Iranian women were struggling to be released from purdah, from their inferior position in society. She had probably hoped I would dismiss home economics as unimportant and stress training for professions, business, and other careers—an education for an independent, self-sufficient life of equality, of the sort led by women in the United States. Many of these girls had perhaps hoped to hear from me not merely what was pleasant to say—or what would make them kindly disposed toward America—but what I felt to be the truth. But I had been equivocal, and I was sorry.

Early next morning as we drove out of Rezaiyeh, heading south, continuing our circling of the lake, the first rays of the sun hit the mountains across the great water table. The roseate mountains near Tabriz glowed incandescently with simple splendor.

We passed geometric orchards; vineyards corded the slopes; I gazed down crossroads through long columns of golden *Tabrizi* trees and at small streams brilliantly reflecting the azure sky. The sun was rising with more than its usual drama, and we were all speechless. Ahead on the side of the road an old man, white-bearded and bare-headed, got down on his knees to praise Allah, while his donkey, as if quite accustomed to his master's ritual, slowly ambled on ahead. In the east the sun was breaking over the edge of a particularly jagged, black mountain, and the rays were refracted, bent down and up in striations. Then the sun burned through the mountain and burst fully upon us, ordinary as daylight.

At times the road ran close along the lakeshore, where an overwhelming stench arose from greenish, red-and-blue slime at the water's edge, a mud famous throughout Persia for its power to cure arthritis. It smelled bad enough to cure anything. "Shall we stop and scoop up a sample?" asked Paulus.

"Not unless you have some enemies you want to get rid of."

When would we come to Hasanlu, I wondered, and would there be time to stop and look over the archeological site. A crew from the University of Pennsylvania had discovered a golden bowl and other treasures in a palace 2800 years old. "If we don't miss the turn off," said Paulus looking at his watch, "I think there'll be time for Hasanlu. But I've never been sure of the cross-road to it; we'll have to hope Sumat sees it."

"What time are you supposed to see the Army general in Mahabad?" I asked.

"He doesn't know I'm coming. I just hope to catch him during the noon hour, sometime."

"How far are we now from Mahabad, Sumat?"

He'd been daydreaming and hadn't heard; I asked again. Looking at his speedometer, he mumbled a reply, but it was inaudible—and what difference did it make? We were going so fast I had little hope that the intersection would be noticed. Sumat didn't slow down—ever. We crossed a small, ancient stone bridge with a crest in the middle, like a drawbridge starting to open. We literally flew through the air and landed with a jolt on the other side. Some boys tending camels in a nearby pasture lifted their

33

staffs in the air and shouted in alarm. I had hit my head on the ceiling and had come down equally hard.

But suddenly Sumat slowed, smiling; we had arrived at the road east to Hasanlu. Beyond a small ridge of hills we descended into a waterless lake basin that presumably had once been part of Lake Rezaiyeh. Here and there salt marshes obtruded, with the mud showing frosty, saline crusts; vegetation was sparse. The road followed along the putative shore, the basin itself was about ten miles across. Ahead, the blue mountains of Iraq looked alien and sinister. Soon the road turned into an overused automobile track; the ruts by now were too deep even for a Jeep's axle, and Sumat had to drive it along the rim of the wheel tracks. It was the sort of challenge he loved, and sweat stood out on his brow; a faint smile edged his lips. Our whole enterprise out here suddenly seemed to depend on his skill. He sensed our anxiety and knew, surely, that we trusted him to get us through.

At last we spotted a large mound in the distance, a kind of leviathan grave. As we drew closer, the pockmarks where the archeologists had been digging became clearly visible. A tiny mud village was located at the foot of the mound, and, following no road at all now—just rolling across the desert—we were hailed by an Iranian dressed in cast-off U.S. Army clothes, who came loping toward us, signaling us to stop. He was the caretaker, instructed to protect the place, since the archeologists had returned to Philadelphia. He was a very friendly caretaker, more like a man who had the concession for one of the Seven Wonders of the World. He led us along the exposed palace walls, and we walked on top, looking down into the rooms. Shards of bowls were everywhere, including the bottoms of several man-sized burial urns. We located the chamber where the golden bowl had been discovered. Supposedly a thief had been in the act of stealing the bowl in the midst of a fire in the palace, when he had been suddenly trapped and buried alive by falling beams. A number of dead puppies lay on the dirt floor of the room now, dashed down by a local resident eager to get rid of an unwanted litter. The compartment seemed destined as a place of death.

After gathering some of the wild rue which grew everywhere abundantly, we climbed into the Jeep and were about to start.

The watchman was very disappointed—not that he expected a gratuity, but didn't we suppose that there were some little extra things, bowls and trinkets and keepsakes, still here in the village? Wouldn't we be interested in seeing them—perhaps buying them? Paulus scolded him good-humoredly, saying he sounded more like a thief than a caretaker. Just where did he get these artifacts and how did they happen to be in his possession? No, we certainly weren't interested in his wares.

As we drove away, I expressed my disappointment; I'd like to have seen the treasures he and his friends made off with during the night, when the archeologists weren't looking. "You might've been tempted to buy them," said Paulus. "And anyhow, they're very likely clever imitations, or worthless pieces from other villages, brought here, now that Hasanlu is famous." He shrugged off the matter, but I felt that his New England sense of morality had risen strongly.

Once again on the main road to Mahabad, we entered Kurdistan, in recent years one of the most politically turbulent regions in the Middle East. The Soviets during their occupation of Persian Azerbaijan during World War II had encouraged the nationalistic feelings of the Kurds and had helped set up a regime that declared itself independent of Iran, strongly Russian in sympathy. The Kurdistan Republic had been crushed by Shah Reza Pahlavi's army with very little difficulty, once the Russians had withdrawn from Iran, but latent feelings of nationalism remained in the Kurds and the Soviets fanned these hopes. The general land area of the Kurds, to complicate matters, lay in Iran, Iraq and Turkey.

Now as we approached Mahabad, former capital of Kurdistan, I began to see a few natives. Astride beautiful, well-groomed Arabian horses, the Kurdish men wore swathes of blue or white or pink silk around their heads; decorated with tassels in contrasting color, the swirls of cloth fell to their shoulders and flew out behind, as they rode their swift horses. Their Western coats were of dark, imported wool, tailored with a military cut; they hung open, revealing scarlet or white linings and a wide cummerbund of the same material as the headgear, with a dagger tucked in the folds. The outfit was completed by baggy, full

35

trousers, which ballooned out like harem pajamas. On their wrists they wore white bands of cloth, like bandages. The combinations of materials and hues varied widely in splendor, but their eye for color was invariably sure, and the peacock spectrum in which they presented themselves was breath-taking. In addition, Kurdish men are husky six-footers, exceedingly handsome, with complexions much fairer than either Turks or Persians and eyes that are frequently the blue of a Siamese cat or a startling green; their faces are quite broad, with high cheekbones and straight, well-molded noses and firm chins. Their women are beautiful but muffled modestly, not in somber grey or black *chedurs,* but in petticoats of gay prints, headbands of white cloth, and many layers of contrasting colors.

Since the main road to Mahabah was being repaired, the only way we could enter the town was to drive up the river bed in water a foot deep; Sumat watched carefully to avoid deep holes. With a great burst of energy the Jeep careened up the banks and we arrived as if by attack in the capital city of the Kurds. It was another mud-walled, dun-colored town, with trees planted along the *jube* for comfort after the desert wastes. While Paulus talked to his general, I walked through the uncovered bazaar and watched a group of metal workers pounding out a design in copper and brass bowls. I emerged into the street just as a great commotion started up.

"Hi! Hup! Hup! Hup!" screamed a half-wit in burlap rags, his face scrofulous, pock-marked, his beard lice-ridden, and his eyes staring wildly, out of focus. As he cavorted through the street, a crowd of onlookers taunted and cheered him. He pulled the tails of burros, scared little boys so that they screamed and ran, turned cartwheels, squatted in the street, and all the while uttered strange, comic sounds. Like a medieval jester, he would do anything to amuse—try anything—and obviously his audience loved it. The fool's trousers were split completely open in the rear, and every now and then he would let out a piercing shriek to get attention, then expose his bare buttocks; the crowd roared with laughter. They gave him coins freely; and later, in the deep recesses of the bazaar, when I was buying a velvet, spangled hat, traditional Kurdish woman's headgear (which they wear concealed under

36

their head-scarves), the fool came screaming along and held out his hand to me, saying *"Baksheesh! Baksheesh!"* His eyes had a dazed look of insanity, as if he'd just been clouted over the head. I handed over one toman, and he reached out to embrace me, but Sumat intervened, struggling to fend him off and laughing as he shoved aside the madman. As other men and boys came up to give chase, the fool streaked off, cackling, running between the legs of a pack train of burros loaded with carpets—his tormentors in gay pursuit.

Sumat, seeing that I was fascinated, said: "He is a happy fellow."

I glanced at him, saw that the remark was meant in all seriousness, and nodded.

Paulus' business was soon finished and we drove out of Mahabad by way of the river and started toward Tabriz, though dark would descend long before we reached it. Some of the peasant villages through which we passed had pigeon towers in the corners of the walls, like crude battlements. Pigeon dung was utilized for fertilizer, since animal manure was burned for fuel; and squab made good eating. In Miyanduab we stopped in a *chaikhane* for glasses of tea, and ate the last of the picnic lunch Mrs. Paulus had prepared for our journey. The village was extremely poverty stricken, the people in rags, many of them diseased and dying, and it seemed that every other native had white trachoma spots in his eyes or was blind entirely. A huge bird's nest atop one of the buildings seemed symbolically portentous, as if some evil carrion creature had cast its blight upon the town.

In the dim tea house swarming with flies, while we sat and drank from our glasses (the slightly galvanized flavor caused by the samovar seemed to enhance rather than spoil the tea—or perhaps I fancied this, since the medicinal taste was somewhat reassuring), a rather healthy looking young man, ruddy, bright-eyed, and dressed in a used but reasonably clean dark suit, came in and went from table to table begging. Paulus said something admonishing to him, in Turki, and for a moment the young man sheepishly hung his head. Then Paulus handed him two and a half rials. At once the beggar sat down at a nearby table, ordered tea and kebab and set to with relish. It pleased us to have this happen so ingenuously, and later, when the young man had his turn at the narghila and began sucking on the nozzle of the colored hose, Paulus called over to him: are you enjoying yourself? A look of rapture crossed his face. He dropped the pipe, stood up, and went through an elaborate curtsy; he bowed with a concluding skip—a sort of lilt—and then sat down. We all laughed.

"There are so many jokers in this part of the country," I said to Sumat. "Why is that?"

"It is good to laugh and joke," he said with a slow, sad smile. "There is nothing else that can be done."

Again on our way, Paulus waved his arm out the window, saying: "See those black tents in the distance? They're nomads and always camp far from the road. They won't have a thing to do with anybody. They graze their animals on other people's land."

I was struck by the exceedingly graceful pagoda shape of the tent. With the sides rolled up, the sloping tent roof seemed to float in the air against the distant mountains. A small herd of sheep and goats were mere dots in the landscape. These people were gypsies and not to be confused with the nomadic tribes of the south who traveled from winter grazing grounds to the high green mountain lands in summer. Staying clear of all tribes and villages, these outlaw gypsies had customs and mores of their own. The black tent, like a pirate flag, was their symbol.

In Azershahr we stopped to inspect a drapery factory because Paulus thought I should witness all the land had to offer, though we were still far from Tabriz. As we walked into a courtyard, a huge dog barked fiercely from a loft in the factory; a boy in an opposite window tried to hush him. The manager greeted us and was delighted to give us a tour. The only light came from occasional unenclosed skylights, but the impression was of a vast dim room filled with looms set close together. Sudden shafts of sunlight in the gloom were startling in contrast to the darkness. The crude looms were constructed of wood and operated by foot and hand power. The operator rested on the edge of a board which looked like an oar; his buttocks served as his only point of gravity. At the loom his whole body was in constant movement, except for his left leg and foot—this single limb seemed the only thing that bespoke his dignity as a human being, for when operating the loom he became a kind of cataleptic creature. He wore pajamas, and he beat with his bare right foot upon a board, as one might pump bellows for a foot-trundle organ. The shuttle was sent across by a downward pull of the left hand, and the woof was made by a downward jerk of the right hand. The operator threw himself into the rhythm slowly, but once in the wild dance of the loom, he seemed beyond powers of self-recovery, controlled entirely by the demands of the machine.

The pattern for the cloth was determined by a sheet of cardboard on a roller drum—a cardboard cut-out very much like a player-piano scroll. In this instance, strings passed through the holes, and these in turn controlled the spacing of the threads. Examined closely it was an ingenious machine of wood, string, pins and hope, held together by Persian magic, and it produced splendid drapes, as intricately designed as a carpet, as floral and geometric as a Persian garden. The room where the threads of gold, red, blue, white, green, pink, orange, grey, black and variations thereof were wound on spools together or combined in various ways was now filled with sunlight. Great webs of colored thread swirled out, met, joined and were rolled together on giant spools. It was a fantastic room of moving linear color, fretwork of gossamer, rectangles and bars and pyramids of changing hues, vast shifting webs.

Upon our leave-taking I asked how much money an operator of the loom made. Three rials a meter, I was told. The average worker could do about twenty meters a day. I quickly figured: the daily salary was about eighty cents, U.S. money. This was skilled labor, the manager told us, and that was why salaries were so much better than the average Iranian worker received.

The sun set very shortly after our departure from Azershahr, and I began to understand the difficulty of night driving in Iran. Drivers of on-coming vehicles seldom dimmed their lights and usually came straight down the center of the road. For the sake of safety, one had to pull over close to the edge of the gravel road and stop entirely. Clouds of dust enveloped us, further obscuring our visibility. Paulus was at the wheel now. I couldn't drive because I didn't have diplomatic immunity, and should I have an accident would be at the mercy of harsh Iranian laws. Quite recently an Englishman in Shiraz, a waterworks engineer, who had been living in Iran a number of years, ran down and killed an old woman. He knew he was in serious trouble and quickly paid-off the family very handsomely, using up six years of savings. But the law pressed and he was sentenced to prison for three months, from January to March. The two-hundred-year-old prison in Shiraz used to be one of the Shah's palaces, but there was little of the palatial about it these days. It was unheated and thoroughly primitive, but his wife brought him food and medicines now and then; he was allowed an icy bath in the courtyard once a week. He survived the ordeal, as Englishmen in foreign parts so often do, but his experiences, bruited about Iran, made me unwilling to take a chance behind the wheel of our Jeep.

While I was dwelling on these matters, Paulus slowed down, muttering "What's this?"

Sumat in back made sucking, apprehensive noises. An Iranian in our lightbeam was flagging us down. There was a parked automobile at the roadside and another vehicle that appeared to be on its side in the ditch. We stopped. There had been an accident, the Iranian said, throwing the flashlight beam deeper into the gloom at the side of the road. Then I saw a covered-up man, his head showing above the sheet, his face an odd bluish-grey color. "I think that man is dead—we must not stop," said Sumat.

Paulus, paying no attention, braked the Jeep to a total halt. "Is he dead?" he asked the stranger, in Turki.

The whiskered man clicked his teeth, half-smiled, and nodded his head. After lingering with the flashlight ray so that we could have a good look at the corpse, he informed us that the driver who had caused the accident had been taken away to jail by the police. Now he, the stranded traveler, was waiting for someone to remove the body.

We had no room for the corpse in our Jeep, nor did the stranger suggest we take it, but Sumat rather excitedly told Paulus not to pause any longer. "Please sir, do not stop. Do not stop for this man. Go on, go on!"

Paulus put the motor in gear and we started up. I asked Sumat if he had been afraid we would offer to put the dead man in the back seat with him.

But he did not smile. "It is best, on this road, never to stop, especially at night. The bandits have many tricks, and this, I think, was one of them."

"But obviously, there had been an accident," I said. "Wasn't that man in the ditch dead?"

"How did he die? And why did the man lie, saying the police had been there? Police out here? No, I think if we had stayed much longer, men with guns would be all around us. Then there might be more dead men in the ditch."

Paulus said nothing in comment. I savored the notion that we had brushed close to violence; the trip had been given its necessary fillip. Back in Rezaiyeh I had accomplished my desire to do good and win friends for my country, and now in accordance with notions of what a stay in Persia would involve, I'd had an adventure. At about midnight we reached Tabriz safely, and for perhaps the last time, I believed that events transpiring confirmed my expectations: I was still discovering what I had imagined I would find; I was still sequestered in my innocence.

4 THE UNIVERSITY
OF TABRIZ

I HAD been warned to expect the worst, but I could not hold back a rising sense of dismay when I took up my duties at the Faculty of Letters. The building itself was a crude brick structure set between shops. Heavy wooden double doors with great hoops of iron for handles made the entrance seem suitable for four-in-hand coaches. The dark, dirty, raw-brick interior, unheated and opening upon an inner court, reminded me mostly of a stable. Classrooms contained small petrol burners for heat, but these were not lit until the depths of winter, and they were continually going out. Pupils and teachers wore heavy coats; the animal warmth of many bodies packed together in a closed room raised the temperature. Dim, weak-watted lightbulbs dangled down into the rooms like coils of flypaper, and in order to read the text in my hand, I regularly brought along a flashlight, since most of my classes were in late afternoon or evening.

At first I attributed the bewildering quality of disorganization to the absence of the dean, who, at the start of school in October, had not yet returned from abroad. Classrooms kept getting mixed up; I could not find my students; they could not (or rather, did not) find me until half the hour had elapsed. School would be recessed unexpectedly; holidays were frequently declared, at the slightest pretense, and I would arrive to find the door of the building locked, the students wandering the streets. Advised by Paulus to present a ruthless countenance before my class, I terrorized them at first, or perhaps the strangeness of my presence hushed them. However, they soon became accustomed to me and

42

lapsed into their usual abominable classroom behavior: whispered, made mischief while fellow students recited, and wriggled in their seats like unruly sixth graders. The general buzz was usually so loud I had to shout to be heard.

Only theatrical displays of anger—expelling the worst offenders, or stalking out of the room in the middle of the hour—made any impression. I later learned that they were used to being cuffed on the ears when they misbehaved, and in the spring, during the final examination, the proctor knocked an obstreperous student to the floor and trounced him. The only rule they respected was the decree that attendance be taken; if marked absent too often, they would not be admitted to the examinations in spring, upon which grades were based. Roll call was handled at first by student monitors who read off the names in Pharsi— but I discovered that absent friends were not accounted for; some names were simply skipped. I appointed a student to transliterate the Pharsi into English, and I read off the names myself, concentrating on the faces that smiled and answered *Huzzahr*.

Deviousness, lying, cheating and mischief were the daily lot, all transpiring in an atmosphere of hectic gaiety and excitement; they loved me, they found college amusing and interesting, they were having a marvelous time. But I was not. As each horrendous feature of my job became revealed, I kept telling myself that somehow the difficulties would be surmounted. I would make-do, I would manage to survive. I could not risk feeling sorry for myself, not when I had nine months to go. I fixed my attention upon a few loyal and industrious students who were obviously working hard to benefit from my instruction. They were also helpful in explaining the endless regulations of the school; they reported promptly when our classroom was switched or when the university was on holiday.

The library was surprisingly well stocked with hundreds of books in American and English literature, but the old, half-senile librarian firmly announced in a mixture of German and French that no books were to be borrowed by students because they stole them. Nor could I set up a reserve shelf: pages would be ripped out, surreptitiously, even though students sat under the watchful eyes of the librarian and his assistants. But *I* was welcome to visit

43

the stacks and take out any book I wished, for this collection existed to benefit the professors—it was for them, not the students, and he was honored to have the privilege of serving me. (At this point he bowed from the waist.)

Two Faculty of Letters clerks earned their livelihoods mimeographing texts assigned in the courses and selling the sheets to students for a few rials a page. Although the State Department shipped me fifty books I had ordered, they did not arrive until half the year was over. A dozen high-school American literature texts were discovered at the consulate, but these were not enough to go around, since I had upwards of fifty and sixty students in each course. I used the mimeographed-sheet system of the school. An assistant librarian would type up a stencil from the passage I selected; the office would run it off and sell the sheets to students, and during the twice-weekly class sessions, we would go slowly, word by word, over the sentences, usually covering about a paragraph in an hour. I would attempt to define the words within the limits of their very narrow vocabularies. Students would practice reading, and I would call upon them to give definitions.

The conscientious students would memorize the entire assignment, but most of them postponed this arduous work until spring, at which time they committed to memory the entire year's reading—feverishly goading themselves to the task, pacing the walks in the parks, or wandering in the fields near Tabriz, a dazed look on their faces. Of course, I tried to tell them I did not wish them to memorize these sections from Steinbeck's "The Red Pony," Whitman's *Leaves of Grass,* or Wolfe's *Look Homeward, Angel,* but to them, studying meant memorizing. They had no experience with conceptual learning—only the rote method. They understood little of what they could frequently rattle off by heart; but they refused to believe this.

Abiding by the framework prescribed by the school, I conducted three courses entitled "Literary Texts"—first year, second year and third year. Most students were male, but a few girls from upper-class families sat with lowered eyes in the front row, and always banded together in the halls. Social sanctions were so strong that for the most part the boys did not dare converse with them; and the girls were feeling strangely exposed, without their

44

chedurs. The Armenian girls were distinctly more confident of themselves and were usually excellent students; the Armenian boys frequently tried to ally themselves with me, exercising their rights as fellow Christians, much to the annoyance of their Moslem classmates.

A senior member of the literature faculty told me that I must progress chronologically: the freshmen should read early English literature, perhaps *Beowulf,* or *The Faerie Queen;* the second-year students might suitably read seventeenth or eighteenth century works; the seniors would have the Romantic period and some twentieth century literature. He urged me also to give a course in the history of the language, but I sensed that the notion was preposterous. Following the survey scheme of literature, I would not be able to teach many American authors, but I subscribed to his dictum to the extent of beginning my freshmen on *King Lear;* the other classes read Melville, Mark Twain, Sherwood Anderson, and Hemingway. When I discovered that the first-year students had vocabularies of scarcely five hundred words, I dropped Shakespeare. We spent the year on a story by Jack London, which seemed more their speed. My mentor, I later discovered, taught no literature at all in his classes. He had the students memorize endless passages from a nineteenth century history of English literature—they never actually read the stuff itself.

After a few weeks, observing that little work was being done, I assigned a short paper, due the following week. The class was dumbfounded; then they tittered; and finally they paid no attention, while I carefully explained what I expected. At the close of the hour a student came up to tell me that no such papers during the school year would be agreed to. "What do you mean?" I asked, astonished.

"In our school the seniors *only* have one long paper to write. And there is one test, in spring, in all classes. The students know that the grade they have on the final examination is the only one that matters."

"Not now!" I replied defiantly. "Not this year—in my course! We shall proceed as we do in American universities."

"Alas, sir, you cannot."

45

"We'll see!"

And I did. The day I announced a "drop quiz" half the class rose from their seats and fled the room. As for the term papers, most of the students copied a few paragraphs from encyclopedias or books of criticism; others turned in no paper at all. Ignoring me, they were confident that the registrar of the school would only record the final mark. Now and then they were a little concerned lest my strange methods somehow penetrate the prescribed channels of the way things were done at the Faculty of Letters; in the final reckoning, when I graded their examinations, a lower mark might be given them than their test score warranted. But even in this respect, they felt reasonably secure, since the examination papers became the permanent property of the university, locked in a safe. There *had* to be a proportionate number of high grades, middle grades, low grades and failures, so that no matter how I marked the papers, the school officials could "adjust" the marks, going over the papers if necessary to determine how the members of the class should rank. If one student had a grievance—if he felt I had been unjust—once I had left Tabriz an inquiry could be initiated and his mark redressed. I also learned that functionaries of the school lived partially on bribes, and students whose families were rich and powerful made their wishes felt.

The life of learning was no special bailiwick wherein high ideals had value; it was merely an aspect of Iranian life in general, and the corruption of the universities was only an expected part of the way things were everywhere else. Many of my students could not understand my indignation. Did I not realize that favorable marks and a high rank in the class could mean benefits, privileges and positions which would be of extreme value? All students were eager to advance in some career, and, just as in business each advantage is grasped in order to attain the next, so it was in school. Cheating was not in itself dishonorable unless one were caught at it—then it was embarrassing, rather than damaging to one's reputation. Cynics that they were, they pointed out that cheating and stealing went on everywhere, all the time, and even the most exalted were guilty of it; hence, I should not be surprised to discover it in my classes.

I could scarcely deceive myself into thinking that the school year would be profitably spent, given these circumstances, nor did I wish to battle their immorality, with the hope of teaching them the difference between fair standards and corrupt practices, for I knew that no friendship for me or America would be engendered if I maintained a holier-than-thou attitude. Their characters at this point could not be made to fit my mold; the Middle East had different ways of looking at morality, and I was enough of a relativist to understand that I had no business judging them too harshly because they did not conform to my notions.

My colleagues were a mixed lot and for the most part remained aloof, partly because their salaries were dependent upon the number of pupils, and I was responsible for draining off some of their income. They were all officially courteous, but it was not worth their time to bother too much about me, since my presence was understood to be of limited duration and presumably involved some American propaganda scheme. Language barriers hindered the development of acquaintanceships, too, because at first I knew no Pharsi and my French or their English was rather inadequate. Furthermore, being professors at the school did not bind us into a community of absorbing interests, since none of them could live on the paltry salaries and each had two, three, or more jobs into which they channeled their chief energies. The most lucrative second job was private tutoring.

One of the men, whom I shall call Mr. Shirazi, was a typical educator at the Faculty of Letters. He had a master's degree from a European university and had been to America on a study grant from the State Department. He was a kindly, weak, middle-aged bachelor, ineffective as a leader and not respected by the students. His mind was nimble but dully frivolous; he was absent-minded and disheveled in appearance; simpered instead of laughed; and was obsequious before his superiors. During the time I knew him he was busily promoting a brick factory, in which he had purchased a large number of shares. He liked to mull over aspects of conditions in Iran, uttering optimistic remarks, speculating on all the things that might be done if one just had the initiative and funds. Whenever he saw from the train window the vast miles of uncultivated, unused land that lay between Tabriz and Teheran, he reportedly felt sad about the waste. I happened to mention Shirazi's observation on unused lands to my student friends one day and asked if the undeveloped countryside inspired similar thoughts in them. They snorted at the notion. "Why doesn't *he* do something about it, if it makes him feel so sad?"

"He is a teacher, not a farmer," I replied. "A teacher plants ideas."

They thought this a very wise comment and wrote my words down in their notebooks to remember—and I felt rather ashamed. Shirazi's dreamy notions, his wistful, commonplace observations were easy to make fun of. The system of education and the low regard in which teachers were held, in the society, drew weak men into academic life.

But not all of them were of Shirazi's sort; one young Iranian teacher of French was an admirable, dynamic fellow, a martinet with the students. Educated in Paris and married to a Frenchwoman, he had at first returned to Iran with long hair, horn-rimmed glasses, and a *Deux Magots* manner; then he had studied in America, and when I knew him he wore a brush haircut, Ivy League clothes, and kept saying "Okay." He found provincial life difficult, but he carried through on his tasks in a manly, energetic way, though I could sense despair hovering like shadows on the fringes of his life. He clung to a long-shot hope that friends in America would bring about a lectureship in Persian literature for him, so that he could move to the United States, permanently. He knew he would molder at Tabriz University; he had had a taste of vigorous, enlightened, intellectual life and he wanted more. For his second job, I was instrumental in getting him appointed assistant to an in-coming American municipal government specialist. But that was all I did for him. I began to see that my feelings about him were in conflict with the official position I might have been expected to take, as a visiting Fulbright lecturer. One aim of the exchange program in countries such as Iran was to have professors lend support to any uplifting of standards. Properly, I should have made an effort to bolster the young French teacher's morale, since with more good men like him around, Iranian education would be strengthened and a group of enlightened leaders might be produced. In fact, I could only feel that he would be well off if he got out—otherwise, the situation in which he found himself would drown him.

A rising sense of conflict in the purposes of my stay in Tabriz sharpened as the facts of educational life at the Faculty of Letters became clear; I knew that the rewards of my time in Azerbaijan—and my efforts—would be of a different sort from what I had expected. One pleasant fact was that I was not overworked. Class preparation was practically nil, and the total time at the university, including the "conversation" period and a later evening session, came to about eight or nine hours a week. But I could not be content merely to sit out the year, dutifully but halfheartedly going through the motions of having a job at the school and spending the rest of my time writing, reading, or exploring the country. I still wished to serve, in some way—but I waited to see in what way my role would be revealed.

When the dean of the Faculty of Letters returned from his visit to England and America, a celebration was in order. On December 11 classes were suspended and the student body gathered in the second-floor assembly room, which was large enough to accommodate three hundred people or more. As a faculty member I was asked to sit in the first two rows, but I was not to occupy any of the chairs on the aisle, which were reserved for distinguished visitors. The program would be conducted entirely in Pharsi, the only appropriate language for public affairs, though Azerbaijani Turki was the natural tongue for most of the students. With my French teacher friend on one side and a good student of English on the other (as my translator), I was kept abreast of events in the ceremony.

Before the program began, the entrance of a local poet, Shahriar, reportedly the most famous living Persian poet, resulted in a standing ovation of great intensity. I couldn't make myself heard as I asked just who this Shahriar was. Eagerly, my student interpreter supplied me with the facts. For many years the poet had held a nominal position at Bank Melli, the national bank, but he was never expected to go to work to earn his salary, for his divine purpose was to write poetry. "They are proud at the bank to have such a famous man associated with them, and that is enough for

49

them." Since his youth, Shahriar had been a successful poet and had written many honored volumes. Then for a stretch of time he had succumbed to opium and had produced little verse; only fairly recently had he kicked the habit. "You understand," said the student, "Shahriar is very, very sensitive. He feels everything so deeply. He took opium because it was the only way of shutting off the world." Once when Shah Reza Pahlavi visited Tabriz, Shahriar was to recite a poem he had composed especially for the occasion. In the act of declaiming the poem, he fainted, and the Shah himself knelt by the poet's side and helped revive him. "And the Shah gave him money, too, and praised him."

Shahriar was ushered to the number one chair on the right; he and the dean, who was on the platform, bowed to one another; then everyone was seated. The flowers on the table in front were so tightly jammed into vases they looked like nosegays in a crowded, floral carpet. On the wall behind the dais were two luridly colored portraits of the classical poets Saadi and Firdousi.

The celebration consisted largely of a marathon of versification. Some students had composed poems in honor of the dean's return; others recited appropriate welcome-home-traveler stanzas from Hafiz or Saadi. With a bad case of stage fright, one of the performers forgot his source entirely, but he was not in trouble for long; the poem was familiar to many in the audience and they shouted the sought-for line. Shahriar remained the key figure throughout the ceremony, and his "Well done!" was usually the only accolade the students on the platform needed, the only comment that really mattered. Several times, at a moment of particular poetic felicity—right in the middle of a recitation— Shahriar called *Kaili Khōb*, as if he were a balletomane shouting bravo from the second balcony. Often Shahriar's words of commendation were really tender reassurances—as in the case of the poor fellow whose poem was so bad and who recited it so abominably that the students began to snicker. He had scribbled his verse on a sheet of paper, but in his nervousness had folded it so many times that it was in tatters and illegible. Sweat dripped from his brow and his eyes had a wild expression, as if at any moment he might leap from the stage and flee the room.

An army major, a third-year student, was highly successful with a poem having the Persian word for "yet" as a refrain—each line rhyming with considerable invention and variation. The gist of the verse: sad indeed were the students, for their beloved dean had not come back to Tabriz *hanooz* (yet). Weeks passed and at last he returned—how overjoyed they were! The *hanooz* sound echoed in and out of the lines, and the poem was declaimed by the author, a husky professional military man, with his eyes closed, his rich voice thick with feeling. Shahriar was amused and thrilled by the major's performance; he clapped his hands above his head, so that the audience could see his accolade; the students shouted and applauded. Poetry for most of them was a fancy footwork in words, not unlike, in its demands, the skill employed in tumbling, ballet, or bull-fighting. Verbal pyrotechnics provided them with the kind of thrill they sought in art. They reveled in the *mot juste* and regarded Oscar Wilde as the best English author. They were quite content to repeat platitudes by dressing them up anew; cleverness in expression was the mark of merit, not originality in the thought itself. Their general disposition was toward classicism and a belief that everything worth thinking had already come to light; succeeding generations might think merely of new ways of expressing old truths. Some Western literary critics have lamented that nothing new has happened in Persian poetry since the days of Saadi, Firdousi and Hafiz. But since these poets are regarded as perfection itself, they are the models that every age must follow.

At intermission we all remained in our seats while tea and cakes were served; festive occasions always called for refreshments. Difficult as it was to pass glasses of tea down the line and circulate trays of pastries, the feat was accomplished. There were strudel-type rolls filled with custard made from water buffalo milk, and macaroons decorated with slivers of pistachio nuts. A half dozen pretty women students acted as hostesses. I never was clear who paid for all of it, perhaps the dean himself. Entertainment during the lull in the program was provided by two students playing a violin and a *santor* (a xylophone instrument played with picks resembling wire clothes hangers), but everyone talked and no one listened. Music was regarded as something pleasant-sounding in the background. Most Iranians I met did not know how to listen to "serious" music, theirs or Western. They responded beautifully to the intricate rhythms of dance music—by dancing—but they were not accustomed to thinking of music as something to engage one's full attention.

The second half of the program began with a dramatic performance. One of my second-year students who aspired to become an actor (there was little professional theater in Iran, only road companies traveling about giving old folk plays, and several movie companies) rendered a dramatic monologue he had made up. The story concerned the life of an actor who had a very sick child. It so happened that the actor was playing a part in which he was to depict a parent grieving over a child. Of course, the audience didn't realize that his moving portrayal stemmed from the fact that in real life his own child was dying. The theater-crowd's heartfelt reaction to the brilliant performance caused the actor to faint with grief. (At this point the boy keeled over.) The French teacher turned to me, an embarrassed smile on his lips, for he knew, too, that the whole thing was awfully sentimental and corny. But the students were hushed and obviously moved—then thunderous in their approval. The boy roused himself from the floor and staggered to his seat; the emotion expended had shaken him a good deal, and he was pale, his face wet with tears.

On my walk home that evening, a band of six students surrounded me and began asking questions about my reactions to life in Tabriz. At first I replied with guarded politeness, saying the usual courteous things, but I saw by their disappointed faces that my words were taken as a refusal to step out from my official shell and encounter them as individuals. I knew immediately that they had been as relieved as I to leave the bureaucratic tangle of the university behind us, that in a sense now we were, all of us, "out of school"; there was a possibility of a new relationship forming. My true role in Tabriz, I felt, would be discovered by exploring their company. "Come on home now, with me," I said. "I'll make a pot of tea—and we'll talk."

5 A PERSIAN BULL-SESSION

AND SO it was I came to know them. From my journal: "I invited six students home to have tea—which they considered a great honor, in their exaggerated words: 'the greatest evening of our lives.' We had some fruitcake and I brewed a pot of tea. We talked about their main problem: the antiquated social-life rules under which they suffer. All of them have pen-pal female friends in foreign countries, from Germany to Japan, but this is as close as any of them comes to girls, and naturally it bothers them a good deal. They were curious to learn what really happens between young men and women in America, for they had heard all sorts of rumors and had seen so many Hollywood movies. Given the Persian inclination to pessimism, they view their starved emotional lives as hopeless and indulge their sorrows by wasting time wandering the streets, day-dreaming, futilely speculating on romance, listening to sad popular songs of unrequited love, and biding their time. They are really rather bored, too, which is one reason why I am such a diversion and curiosity for them."

I felt the pressure of their desire to become intimate with me in a way that no American in his normal friendships (perhaps only in love affairs) usually experiences it, and my immediate reaction was to keep them at some distance. They were as direct as children, as frankly impertinent, but when I turned matters to inquire about *them,* a guardedness set in. This was the Persian game: come to know the truths about someone else, but be careful not to extend any valuable portion of yourself; in this way you remain in control of your relationships. I was intrigued by this subtle game of nuances and intimations, of deceptions and revelations, for I felt that in this area lay much of their interest in life; compared to their highly cultivated sensitivity to personal relationships, many Americans seemed underdeveloped, thickly literal, and missing much of the spice of life. They felt that we as a people were ingenuous, kind-hearted, but wide-eyed innocents; they could not understand just what game it was we played with life. It was clearly not theirs.

Darius was perhaps the most forthright of this group. He was dashingly handsome in the classic Persian style, and with his carefully clipped mustache shaped like matching cedillas, full lips, enormous brown eyes, arching brows, and dark wavy hair he resembled the noblemen pictured in fifteenth century Persian miniatures. He explained that unless one's parents were rich and could help provide house, furnishings and an automobile, no young man of the middle class could think of marrying for years—not until he was in a position to offer these things to his prospective bride. She in turn was expected to enter matrimony with a substantial dowry. The way it usually worked, family matches were arranged by the adults along suitable economic and social lines. "But it is love we care about, and love does not survive in the world." A man could normally not expect to marry until he was in his forties, and then he chose some young girl in her prime who could bear him children. "But so many years are wasted. It is discouraging to think about. It is best not to think of love at all."

His friends agreed. "We must joke and think of ways to be happy," said Abbas.

They were all looking very downcast. "All right," I said to Abbas, "tell us a joke to cheer us up."

"You may not think it funny."

"Go ahead, anyhow. Tell us a story."

"The others have heard it."

"But I haven't."

He thought a moment, forming the sentences in English in his mind. "Shall I?"

"Yes—please."

"A man is bringing a gift of a cooked turkey to the king. He gets hungry along the way and eats one of the legs. When he gets

54

to the palace and he presents the turkey to the king, the king sees that it has only one leg. He asks about this. The man replies: 'In my part of the country the turkeys have only one leg.' Later, when the king visits that region, he observes a gathering of turkeys—and, indeed, they are all standing on one leg. You know, that is how turkeys sleep. But while the king is looking, it comes time to chase the turkeys into the shelter for the night. The caretaker picks up a stick and shouts at the turkeys. They begin to run. 'Look,' says the king, 'they have two legs, after all.' The man thinks quickly and replies: 'You see, they were so frightened by the herder—who shouted and chased them—that they grew another leg in a hurry, so that they could run away.' "

We all laughed—or rather, they laughed after they saw that I was amused. "I can see, you are the one who tells jokes, Abbas."

He blushed and shook his head, embarrassed by the attention. "No, that is not so."

I was later to realize, Abbas was perhaps the saddest of this band of students. He was rosy-cheeked and youthful-looking for his age, which was twenty-one, whereas most of his friends appeared older than they were. Tall, slim and delicately built, he worked-out frequently in the weight-lifting room of the Faculty of Letters, hefting enormous bars to develop his muscles. His brown mustache was sparse and straggly, drooping down at the corners of his mouth with a Chinese effect. He was quiet, shy and liked to be included in adventures but did not wish to initiate them or be responsible.

Less self-possessed than many of the students, he struck me as someone who had already accepted a colorless fate and who would not stir himself to try to change his lot. Abbas' family was lower middle class. They had no spare money for him; he was on his own. Like many of his friends, he had gotten money to attend the university by signing a pledge with the government, agreeing to a minimum of five years of teaching upon receipt of his diploma. Too late, these students realized that they had made a poor bargain, had sold themselves. Teachers never received enough to live on; they were not respected in the social system, and the work was long, tedious and without gratifications. To be a teacher meant being despised or patronized by family and

55

friends, largely because it was the lowest paying job for an educated man. Whereas a professor had some status and was usually called "Doctor," a grade-school or high-school teacher had none, and the ranks were filled with incompetent men who wanted safe spots for life, who would take any amount of insult and oppression, who lived with no hope for the future.

When Abbas had signed his pledge and taken his money, he had not fully understood this about the profession; furthermore, what else might he have done? He could have elected to work part-time and go to only one or two university classes, instead of spending full time as a student. Or he might have gone directly into business, whatever line it was his family followed. If, however, there were no spot for him, he would have had a difficult time finding a place in an organization elsewhere, for there was very little business activity and each position open was fiercely fought over. Although it was true, as an Iranian writer put it, that life is like a taxi ride—you can always stop and get out—Abbas was not suicidal. He would keep on with his life and find small satisfactions where he could. He was sensitive, intelligent, and well-intentioned, but his life, in terms of productive work and satisfactory achievement, would come to nothing. However, I realized, even as I thought this about Abbas, that I was being very American in my evaluation of what was crucial for him. Abbas accepted the bleak facts: one went on to make of things what one could. The pleasures of an evening of tea and conversation at my house became one of these good things, and he was thankful for that. Whenever his face fell in deep sadness, whenever the blight of his predictable and unrewarding destiny put him in a funk, I would say: "Abbas, why are you silent? Tell us a funny story."

"You may not think it very amusing," he would always answer.

"Try it anyhow."

"You laugh very easily. I think it is out of politeness."

"No—no, really, I want to hear every humorous story you know. Can't you think of any?"

"Someone else could tell these tales better than I."

"You do nicely at it and it's good practice for your English. Come on."

"Very well. Once there was a man who stole a cock. He hid it under his coat and tried to get away. But the owner came along and said, what are you doing with my cock? The thief said, I have not seen your cock. But to this the owner said, you lie—it is there under your coat. The man answered, no, it is not. But you see, sir, the cock's tail was sticking out from the coat, and so the owner replied: shall I believe your word or the cock's tail?"

"Ah, that's a *very* Persian tale."

"Is it?" Abbas asked. "Why do you think so?"

"Because it's about cleverness and deception. Don't Iranians enjoy this?"

"I think Americans do, too."

"Perhaps."

"There is even an American proverb," he replied, with a mischievous gleam in his eye, "which I heard at the cinema."

"What's that?"

" 'If you're so clever, why aren't you rich?' "

They were all much amused by the sally; Abbas had apparently surprised me by using the wit of my own country.

"Is not everyone in America rich?" asked Karim. He was usually the serene on-looker at my tea parties, partly because he came from a well-to-do bazaar merchant family and felt secure about himself and his future. He had a handsome, well-molded face, large expressive eyes with very long lashes, and a voice that was resonant and langorous. He entered the circle of my special student friends with considerable independence of mind and confidence in his convictions; he was not groping for values or haunted by a sense of frustration and failure. "I think everyone in America is rich," he said again slowly, not with envy or an attempt to bait me, but merely as a statement of wonderful fact.

Karim had hoped to become a doctor, an ambition shared by a large number of his fellow students. He, like many of the others, had failed to succeed in the entrance tests for medical school; consequently, he enrolled at the Faculty of Letters in order to earn a university degree—his eventual career would be in his family's business. When I asked about his medical ambitions, Karim shrugged off his failure by saying that he had a poor memory. This seemed a respectable enough excuse, an understandable fact of his nature which in no way involved a loss of face. One could

57

not admit that one wasn't good enough or smart enough—the humiliation would be too great. For Karim now his goal in life was quite simply to become as rich and powerful as possible.

"And what will you do with your riches and your power?" I asked.

He smiled, enjoying this dreaming-aloud. "I shall have everything I want."

"But isn't that a rather selfish aim?"

"What do you mean? It is what everyone wishes."

"Do you think I desire to be rich and powerful—would I be *here* if I did?"

"We do not know why you are here, but we are glad," he said.

"Do you think I'm a teacher to make money?"

"Perhaps not. No doubt other men make greater amounts."

"Of course they do."

"But you are not a teacher, sir. You are a professor."

"There isn't much difference, in my country."

"Who *does* make the most money in America?" Karim persisted.

"Business people, I suppose—also some professional men, such as doctors. But physicians don't earn the fees yours do in comparison to the rest of the economy."

"Oh, but everyone in America is wealthy—compared to us here in Iran," said Ruben.

"Yes, if we're to compare. But some of our rich men—after they've made money—spend their lives helping others and giving financial aid to social causes. That's why I asked Karim what he intended to do with all the money he plans to earn."

"Oh, yes," said Ruben, "it is necessary to help others. Every decent man must give alms for charity."

"I wasn't thinking of alms," I said, for I knew that the Koran taught that a man was obliged to pay attention to the less fortunate—though not from a sense of pity as much as to insure the state of one's soul. Tossing coins to beggars did not come about through compassion; rather, it was the price of one's own good luck. The old Middle Eastern notion of fate held them, and Karim in his ambition to become rich would feel no obligation to aid those less fortunate, except as it was traditionally done. After all, would anyone help *him,* if he had fallen low? It was all a matter of destiny; one looked out for one's own welfare and was grateful for good luck.

I began to try to explain how a sense of social responsibility must arise in any civilized society; it must become a matter of prestige for enlightened men to serve the government and not expect personal monetary gains from it. I talked of Rockefeller and the Roosevelts—how wealthy men in my country served society, just as poor men such as myself did. Why were there so few civil servants in Iran? Or perhaps there were some good leaders coming along; I had heard of a Dr. Amini.

They knew nothing about Dr. Amini but assumed he must be like the other senators and members of the Majlis: rich men who had gotten themselves elected to high posts in order to increase their riches or give jobs to members of their families. Worldly, cynical observers of the scene, they accepted the fact that there was limitless corruption in high places and low—and always would be. Karim merely hoped that someday he would be rich and powerful enough to get his fingers on some of the spoils, and he was quite frank in his desires. "If you are rich, you must also be powerful. In Iran a bribe can do anything. You may own a beautiful home, furnished with carpets and expensive things. But one night comes a knock on the door. It is the police, and they have in their hands papers showing that your house is no longer yours, that nothing you thought you owned is yours—and what are you to do? Your position in this country is never sure. You must be so powerful that others cannot take your money away from you or take what you have."

"If true, that is a terrible state of affairs."

"It is more or less true," said Ruben.

"And you people are not interested in doing anything about it? You like it this way?"

Karim smiled and shrugged. He rather did—and looked forward to his chances of success. The others said they did not like it, but what was a man to do? The Shah was honest and very smart, but he was outwitted by his advisors and used by corrupt members of his family. The American government poured money into his coffers, and none of it ever got to the common

59

people. Mossadegh was the last honest man in Iranian politics; he was a saint, like Gandhi. Someday, perhaps, the National Front would come back and take over the government and kick out all the foreigners.

"Foreigners like me?"

"Oh no, sir, you are always welcome."

Politics, they averred, was a dangerous business, and they were unwilling to involve themselves in it. "The police are everywhere. Even at the school."

"What do you mean?"

"Didn't you know? The police spies are in every classroom, listening to all that is said."

"Who are they?"

They tossed their heads in the local gesture that meant "no" and merely said that everyone was aware who these students were. Some boys had spending money, fine clothes, and their tuition was automatically paid, though their families were very poor. "Where does this money come from?"

"The Savak—the secret police."

"I hope some of you will eventually want to do something about improving your country."

"We do not know what to do. It is dangerous to do anything," said Ruben. "People will think we're communists, but we hate the communists. The American system is best. We do not believe in giving away what we have, in sharing the wealth; we want to keep what we have and make money—we are capitalists."

"Yes, I can see that Karim is, at least."

"Trade is the mother of money," Karim said. "That is a true saying, and British in origin, I believe."

"And when you've gotten all your money, your conscience will not be bothered if you do nothing but spend it on yourself and your family?"

He smiled. "Of course not. There are many things I want. A beautiful home, a foreign car, and perhaps several wives. One Iranian, one Chinese, one American, one French—or maybe German. If we are dreaming of the future, that would be my dream."

"Oh, you would be a real Moslem and take advantage of the marriage laws—even though, as you've told me, you are an atheist?"

"Why not?"

"Just what does the Koran say about wives?" I asked.

Ruben informed me that if a man were in a financial position to take more wives, he must first consider his physical abilities, for he should be capable of visiting each wife at least twice a week. According to my calculations, that made an eight-day week, unless he lay with one of them twice or two of his wives on a single day. Yes, that would have to be the way, and a nervous titter passed among them as they considered this pleasant prospect. I remarked that the Koran was certainly an odd religious document, in that it prescribed so many literal rules for day-to-day living, rather than concentrating exclusively on the afterlife (though I realized much of the Old Testament did the same). They heartily approved of my comment and leapt in to denounce Mohammedanism and all it stood for. The power of the mullahs and the decrees of the Koran had kept their peoples backward, they felt. Science made religion out of date and nowadays one must believe in science and rationality, rather than all that. The Koran said that a prostitute would give you venereal disease—well, any educated man knew this. Now that they were university students, they saw that religion thrived on superstitions and fears, and they intended to have as little part of it as possible, though they acknowledged that their parents were still for the most part under its sway.

They were surprised when I maintained that science could not serve as a religion, that they must not put their faith blindly in it. This was what the communists did, and it provided a very limited, mechanistic view of life. It was not to my way of thinking true to life.

"What then are we to believe? It is either science or religion. We must believe in science because it is free of emotions and superstitions. It is the educated thing to do."

I could not carry the discussion further, for I sensed that in all probability they reverted to piety when in trouble, though they pretended now to be atheists. We passed on to other topics: their practice-teaching, or part-time teaching in the local secondary schools. Several of them were involved in this activity and hated it, but Ruben said he found teaching interesting, though somewhat distasteful. Just the other day he had had an unusually stimulating period, asking his students what various countries were famous for (it was a geography class in the lower grades). Considerable disagreement had arisen about the United States, and what was my opinion? What was America famous for? Would I agree that Italy was known for its paintings, Germany for music, Russia for novels, England for industry, and America for wealth?"

"Yes, we are now a wealthy country."

"If you are not truly interested in making money," said Karim, returning to our earlier discussion, "you are the first such American I have heard of."

"But don't you think of us as a land of free people?"

"But what is meant by freedom? In a way, all of us here in this room are free," said Karim.

"I mean precisely that in my country a man need not be rich to be secure about his rights. Even the poorest man has no fear that his property will be taken away simply because it is coveted by someone else."

"You live in a fortunate land," said Karim.

I thought of a story I had heard in Teheran, told by some Westerner who had spent most of his life in Persia and who loved the country and its people but was distressed by the lack of developing democratic ideals, the absence of social responsibility or social concerns. He said that after he was dead, if his spirit ever visited the land and noticed that an Iranian whose cart or automobile had broken down and who had found rocks in the ditch to prop under the vehicle—if that Iranian, when he had finished his repairs, removed the rocks from the road in consideration of other travelers, then he would know that a sense of social responsibility was beginning to work in the people. But thus far he had seen no signs. A man was only loyal to his clan, only thoughtful in regard to family and personal friends.

I did not tell my students this tale, for they were quick to agree with denigrating foreigners and were only too eager to confess their failures and be humiliated by them, rather than attempt to remedy the situation. It did seem to me, as I looked about the room, that it was extremely difficult to convey to them the sense of a free society. They were still largely involved in the primitive stages of *getting,* of pushing ahead on the social and monetary scale, each generation advancing, and this was goal enough for them, at the moment. Talk as I might of the concepts of a free society, for them we were attractive mostly because of our high standard of living.

Considering their attitude, how could I recommend the "American way of life" and suggest that perhaps they, too, would someday have all the things *we* enjoyed? My mind boggled at such a blatant endorsement of pure materialism. After three thousand years of cultural history they had an appreciation of life much too subtle, sensuous, and beautiful for me to dismiss this simply. Each society was in need of what the other had: in America the arts of accumulating the means to the good life had reached the point where we were wondering what to do with our leisure, our economically freed lives; Persians, who had so many of the secrets of the art of life, now could only think of standards of living, of acquiring refrigerators and automobiles; they scarcely valued the wisdom of life they possessed.

"But Ruben," I said suddenly, "you did not tell me what Iran was famous for."

"Friendliness—and next, carpets."

"I should think you could do better by the United States than you have. Are we known to you for nothing but our gold?" And I thought of King Xerxes, whose gold flooded Asia Minor to bolster his foreign policy, but whose satrapies collapsed, nevertheless.

"America is also famous for virgin soil and clever minds of men."

"I wish *I* were cleverer—I wish I knew what to say to you right now."

Karim turned to his classmates. "We have made the professor unhappy by all of this talk. Let us think of something pleasant, or be on our way."

"No—don't misunderstand me. I think it is well we get to know each other."

"But there is no use, if it causes unpleasantness," said Karim.

"I do not think he likes the way we speak about America," said Darius.

63

"There is a Persian proverb," began Ruben, " 'Do not fear your rich neighbor. It is the poor one you have to watch.' " He explained that this was why Iran feared Russia, because the Russians had everything to gain by taking over Iran; they even tried to do it when they occupied Tabriz during World War II. The United States, on the other hand, was so rich already that obviously it would not profit by taking over Iran. "So we do not fear the Americans." Ruben repeated many anticommunist views and phrases which he had learned over "Voice of America," hoping that these remarks would please me. Then he concluded by saying, "The Russians want to take away from the rich and give to the poor, but the Amercan way is to have everybody get rich. This is better. We all want to make money—and get ahead. We are capitalists."

"We are all brothers," said Karim, smiling.

6 BASKERVILLE, RUBEN AND OTHERS

FIFTY years prior to my stay in Tabriz, a young American Princeton Seminary graduate, who taught English in the missionary school, became involved in the Persian constitutionalists' uprising and was killed in a skirmish between Qujar dynasty troops and the Tabriz revolutionaries, many of whom were his students. Howard Baskerville was buried in a cemetery located near the present U.S. Consulate, and on the site where he had died a school assembly hall had been built, called Baskerville Hall. The old missionary institution served now as a girls' school. A few of the former revolutionaries have since risen to power and prestige in Iran. One of these, an elder-statesman senator, accompanied me on a plane trip from Teheran to Tabriz, in the course of which we had a long conversation. He could not get over remarking how much I physically resembled Baskerville. He spoke feelingly of those times and how dedicated Baskerville had become to the revolutionary cause, how interested in the students and the ideals for which they were fighting. He wondered if I would not, too, become deeply committed to Iranian life—he hoped I would. When he learned that I did indeed find my visit engrossing, he asked me to consider ways in which my career might permanently flow in this direction, toward Iran and her people. He was sentimental about his own youth, and his eyes misted over as he gazed down those long fifty years in memory to the hopes and aspirations he had fought for then, and was still fighting for.

That spring, on the fiftieth anniversary of Baskerville's martyr-dom, the U.S. Information Agency prompted a commemoration ceremony. Dignitaries arrived from all over Iran and people who had known Baskerville or who had been involved in the Consti-tutionalist uprising gathered in Tabriz. The American ambassa-dor journeyed by rail from Teheran; a reporter from *Time* magazine flew in, a few elderly missionaries held a dewy-eyed reunion, and a large number of Azerbaijan residents solemnly came together. It was a fine occasion for the U.S.I.A. to point out how historically true it was that the United States concerned it-self with the problems of Iran; in the case of Baskerville, he had even given his life.

We assembled in Baskerville Hall to view some old photo-graphs which had been converted into slides: scenes depicting the bloody events of the Tabriz uprising. When a tableau of hanging bodies flashed on the screen, an excited "Ah!" went up from the audience—a current of shock. The man sitting next to me sud-denly clutched my hand, murmuring in agony, "This is the death of my father!" Tears filled his eyes, and I could think of nothing adequate to say, nor was I able, on the spur of the moment, to weep, which would have been the courteous thing to do. After the slides there were several speeches, a little music, and the as-sembly broke up. One local Tabrizi whom I had not met before murmured, "Some people say this is all over, finished—happened fifty years ago—is all past history. But I tell you, it is not over yet." He fixed me with a meaningful glance. "It is not over yet!"

For all the neatness of the propaganda message in connection with Baskerville, I was not exactly pleased to have Iranians draw a parallel between me and that young man. I did not feel myself to be a candidate for martyrdom, nor from the records did it appear that Howard Baskerville had any business becoming one. Repeatedly the United States consul had warned him against in-terfering in the country's internal, domestic problems. As a U.S. citizen his involvement with political issues of Persia could only be deemed inappropriate and unwise. To a certain degree, from what I could read of the case, it seemed that Baskerville had "gone native," had lost his perspective, had overly identified him-self with his students and their country and by bearing arms, invalidated his U.S. citizenship.

66

And yet as the year wore on, I came at least to understand how Baskerville had almost unwittingly crossed over the line and become too involved. Living in Tabriz at the beginning of the century, an area isolated and remote from the West, he must have been forced for companionship into greater and greater association with students. My life was considerably taken up with them, too, but it was by choice. At a moment's notice I could always show up at one of the several very hospitable American households in the city, where everything from furniture and phonograph records to buttermilk biscuits and apple pie would remind me fully of my old self and the reality of my native land.

Perhaps Baskerville had been won over less by the facts of association than by the conditions and nature of teaching itself—especially, I supposed, for a religious man serving as teacher. I didn't learn whether Baskerville had actually won any conversions to Christianity. From my experience, there were very few among the Moslems. Now and then a couple of Christian Armenians crossed over and became Presbyterians, abandoning Catholicism; or disgruntled Moslems would have a fling at the Christian religion as a maneuver in some family quarrel of extraordinary seriousness; but my feeling was that saving souls for Christ had never been a very good business in Tabriz. The city had long been one of the strongholds of Islam.

It seemed likely to me that Baskerville had been seduced by the activity of teaching itself, for in the process of imparting knowledge a personal relationship forms. There is never simply the transfer of information; it is always colored by certain values, moral and ethical. The particular knowledge a teacher possesses must mean something to him before he can convey it successfully to another individual. In this handling of information an intimacy arises between student and teacher, a bond that continually seeks ways of externally defining itself. And so it must have been for Baskerville; dying from a gunshot wound, he found himself at the end of a process that had started with the simple diagramming of English sentences.

I did not wish the same to happen to me. I sometimes found myself deliberately withholding my interest and sympathy, knowing as I did that the first steps lead only to further ones. But I too was continually seduced into caring. Once or twice a week, as an extra part of my job, the consulate arranged for me to deliver talks to students in the secondary schools, where they were just beginning to learn English. Throughout the year I more or less gave a variation of that first talk in Rezaiyeh: I described school life for boys and girls in America, and at the end of the formal speech, questions were asked. In this manner I talked to thousands of young people in crowded, smelly auditoriums. Although the sea of faces blurs in memory, I cannot forget one Sunday afternoon when I made an appearance at Amir Khizi school, located in a poor section of Tabriz and heavily under the control of a severe mullah who preached avoidance of foreign ways and stressed absolute adherence to the teachings of the Koran. The mullah felt, and rightly so, that "modernization" meant a weakening of the force of religion among his people and a subsequent loss of his power. The school was located in an old wine factory that had gone out of business mostly because of the mullah's campaign against it. (Persian wines of antiquity were ambrosial, perhaps; but since the drinking of spirits was proscribed by Mohammed, the faltering wine industry of modern Iran produced only sadly inferior imitation Rieslings and a few red wines, which might bear labels such as "Chato Ikem" for Chateau Yquem, but which tasted harsh and vinegary.)

Amir Khizi school was a public boy's institution for this quarter, universal education being the official policy of the Shah, but it was not in fact free to the public. It still took tuition money to send a child to school, and many did not go at all but worked in carpet factories for five rials a day, in order to help support the family. Amir Khizi was one of the poorest schools, physically, I had seen in Tabriz, and the children seemed quite raw and wild, dressed in little grey cotton uniforms like Chinese communist peasants. I spoke to a class of ninth-graders; they were so small, undernourished and pinched-looking, two and three boys jammed together at a single desk, that I was distracted from the words I was delivering. Their teacher translated my remarks as I went along, which somewhat vitiated the point of my visit, for I was supposed to provide an opportunity for students to test their knowledge of English. Usually they would know enough to grasp the content of my speech. I found myself rapidly revising my set address. What could these ragged, starving children even imagine about American schools and schoolchildren, and what did they have in common? The fact of schooling did not comprise a bond, not when all sorts of other factors were present, and it would be romantic, sentimental and false of me to impute that it did. This was a bleak, cold, December day, but there was no heat in the room and no provision for heat, should the weather turn even colder (as it would in January and February). The three large double windows were thrown open wide for fresh air, and the noises from the play-yard below frequently drowned out my voice. It was a hopeless situation, I thought.

But, during the question period, their curiosity was boundless, their response fervent, insatiable. They wanted to know all they could, and I saw their upturned faces and bright, feverishly intent eyes. They were fixing upon me all the attention at their command. "Where is your family?" "What does your father do?" "Do you have any sons?" "What do you think of Iran?" "What time is it?" "Do you know any Persian?" The squalor in which they existed seemed to force them to live at a pitch of burning energy; despite the unmistakable pinch of starvation in their scrawny necks and taut faces, the diseases of skin on their scalps, the blind clots in their eyes, and their inadequate little prison coats, I never before felt so intensely the will to live, an irrepressible, almost magnetic, sense of aliveness that filled the room. I realized that the children weaker in willpower, the physically less toughly endowed, had long since perished. All of their dead brothers and sisters, from infancy on up, were here this afternoon to haunt me.

When the hour was over, the boys went wild in their good-byes and cheers; gaiety simply blossomed in the room; they stomped and shouted "Good-bye," "Okay," "Good-bye." As I walked with their teacher across the compound to the principal's office, a crowd of thirty or more closely surrounded us, bearing me along in their continuing ovation, as if I were a hero being carried from a playing field. Their teacher was somewhat embarrassed and kept urging them to move a little away so that we could walk. "You see," he told me, "most of them have never seen an American before." From behind I felt them touching my coat, as if I were the Pope; their little fingers kept nudging me. At last we reached the office and the crowd dispersed, but their hands still touch me. And I know very well how it was Baskerville succumbed.

I deliberately tried to cultivate friendships among widely differing types of students. Sometimes the divisions were according to whether they were first-form, second-form, or third-form students, but more often the circles were determined by the interests and beliefs characteristic of them. One set of students had an intense concern for the Persian heritage; they were self-consciously trying to uphold the traditions of the ages, identifying themselves with ancient Persia and defining their characters in terms of the past. This reversion to old ways was scorned by my "scientific" student friends—people like Ruben and Karim, who instead were highly interested in modern times and wished to align themselves with a progressive future filled with the technical wonders of the twentieth century.

One afternoon I was invited to attend a *corsi* party in the home of one of my bright third-year students, whom I'll call Mr. Gadimi. He came from a distinguished Persian family and was fairly well-off, his father being a bazaar merchant. Mr. Gadimi's great-great-grandfather had been Amir Khizi, a prime minister of the country about one hundred and twenty-five years ago. My friends assured me that Amir Khizi had been one of the great men of recent centuries in Persia. He had promoted reforms and accomplished many good deeds before he was assassinated at the instigation of the boy-king's mother, who feared Amir Khizi's rising popularity among the Persian people. Mr. Gadimi was a scholar in French and Persian, had a fine small library of handsomely bound books in both languages and also a few in English—Moscow editions of Russian classics which students could buy in the bazaar for less than one dollar. The Gadimi home was a spacious two-story stucco building, well carpeted and amply staffed. Visiting here, as in so many other Tabriz homes, the guest had little opportunity to capture the sense of the activity of the whole household, for in a very Oriental fashion, doors were always being closed, shutting off corridors and family rooms;

70

once I caught a peep of some children, heard laughter, but this was immediately corrected, and to all appearances my student Gadimi was master of the house; the one or two servants who made their appearance were solely at his beck and call.

The *corsi* most resembled a large round table with the legs cut halfway off; it rose above the floor about a foot and a half high. Glowing charcoal was contained in a brazier in the center, underneath, and a quilt and tablecloth were spread above, covering the structure. One sat with legs extended toward the warm center—a wagonwheel of legs—and the quilt held the warmth underneath; the cloth rim could be tucked under one's chin. There was no other heat in the room. On long winter nights, this was the traditional Persian way of keeping cozy despite the bitter mountain cold. Bolsters and pillows were propped behind us in sultan fashion, for support, and one lounged upon the mattresses for hours, through courses of tea, cakes and other food. The *corsi* was comparable to an old-fashioned hearth in a Western home, where a family might gather for food, talk, warmth and companionship. When sleepy one simply slid down, quilt drawn up; if there were room, one might sleep sideways, the charcoal warmth glowing on one's back. I was told that unfortunately many children had accidentally died from the poisonous fumes of the charcoal, when it had not been properly burned off. Children liked to play games around the family legs and crawl from one side of the *corsi* to the other, from the father in the position of honor facing the entrance to the room, to the mother with her back to the door, and sometimes they stayed under too long and were suffocated.

With my friends, we played some old Persian family games. A ring was passed under the quilt from hand to hand, and the one who was "it" had to guess who had the ring in his fist. When they saw that I was interested in Persian customs and was not ridiculing them for having *corsi* parties, though more modern heating methods were available and could be afforded, they asked me why America had no customs. I told them we *had*, but since we were a nation made up of people from other cultures, many of our traditions derived from the Old World. I told of Catholic feast days celebrated by Italians in Greenwich Village, of Christmas caroling, Thanksgiving dinners, the Fourth of July and New Year's Eve. They were keenly interested, for they were under the impression that the Americanization of Iran meant merely stripping the country of its sense of traditions and imposing a bleak, soulless modernity on everything.

Many of them were devout Moslems, underwent fasts during appropriate seasons, and were strict in dietary observations: never drank or smoked and kept themselves "clean" in all the ways the word is meant in Islam. This was a sincere cast of mind for them, but Ruben and some of my other students were cynical about the motives of these orthodox Moslems and neo-conservatives. Ruben claimed it was primarily to ingratiate themselves into various power groups, get noticed, perhaps receive good jobs; he felt this because he could not imagine how an enlightened student could also go in for the old, debilitating ritual and blind faith in the Moslem religion or any religion.

Later, when I got to know one of the religious students well, Mohammed-Ali, I came to understand the sources of his belief. A young man growing up in Tabriz in these times of trouble was faced with a choice of attitudes toward his future. He could feel there was no use hoping at all (and alas, perhaps there wasn't); therefore he would throw his life away by taking opium or living a dissolute life of sensual indulgence, maybe killing himself when these things failed. Mohammed-Ali, however, was infused with a certain strength because of his belief in God; his heart was at peace. He reasoned that there was no point in giving up one's opportunities, one's hope that a worthwhile life could be lived in this city. He thought the only thing to do was to find those areas where one could accomplish something for one's own advancement or for the good of others. He had solved the conflicts that tore apart so many of the other students by keeping Islam at the center of his being and moving out to consider other aspects of his existence, step by step, from that sure and secure center. I sensed that a good deal of calculation had gone into his deliberate decision to have faith—perhaps this was what some of my other students found insincere about the young orthodox Moslems. They were also too goody-goody for students like Ruben, who

72

once scoffingly commented, "If they saw a naked woman in the street they would turn away quickly and hide their eyes."

Seldom in visits to the homes of students did I achieve the frankness and ease with them that characterized the sessions in my living room with Ruben, Karim, Abbas, Darius and a few others. With them I spent my most rewarding hours. Not merely did I absorb their sense of life and use them as a means of becoming acquainted with Azerbaijan, but they made searching inquiries into *my* thoughts and habits as well. As the poet Saadi once said: "The hunter does not bag shikar every day. Some day it may happen that a panther will bag him!"

Ruben appeared to be more Turkish than Persian in physiognomy, or at least he gave the impression of being a northern, mountain man: tough, resilient, sensitive but strong. He was over six feet tall and robustly built, with black hair coming down on his forehead in a widow's peak—hair that frequently stood straight up in gamecock fashion; indeed, he had many of a rooster's characteristics. Sometimes, unobserved, I would watch Ruben among a group of students; he was always in the stormy center of a controversy, his eyes blazing, his hair on end and some adversary in front of him. I did not judge that he was so much a leader among the students as he was a fighter. Usually by the sheer impressiveness of his physique, his loud voice, fierce aspect and persistence he won the day. His eyebrows were thick and joined; he was clean-shaven but always looked as if he needed a shave. His complexion was high-altitude-fair, with rosy cheeks; his nose was large and slightly beaked.

Ruben's father was a landowner in the region north of Lake Rezaiyeh; the family lived in Khoi but also had a house in the village from which they originated. The principal family enterprise was sugar beet farming, and Ruben's older brother was now in charge of the operation, while a younger brother was attending school in Tabriz, living with Ruben, and doing the cooking, cleaning and other chores around their rented rooms. "Oh to be a dog, rather than a little brother" is a Persian proverb Ruben quoted as he laughingly told how he exploited the young boy.

In Ruben's family's aspirations one saw a rather typical example of the bourgeois attempt to edge slightly higher on the social scale; they were using Ruben as the great hope in their desire for "rising." Although the father was now a small-scale landowner, perhaps the grandfather had been a mere peasant; I was never to know. In all of Ruben's talk about his home, the actual facts of the family situation were closely guarded, out of pride and a sense of dignity. "My father owns a village"—this was the vaguely important phrase many of the students used, when asked what their fathers "did." In cosmopolitan Tabriz, Ruben was rather shy about stressing his Khoi residence, for that town was a step down from Tabriz, which in turn was definitely on a lower level than Teheran. I had no doubt but that, in Khoi, Ruben's family was a reigning one; his people probably looked back on their village origins, as Ruben did, with nostalgia and a sense of pride of living there rather than in the village.

Ruben, the son chosen by the father to become a learned man and add lustre to the family name, was to be a physician, not because he showed scientific talent or an interest in medicine but solely because a physician enjoyed the highest, most indubitable prestige in any community; the doctor earned the most money. Unfortunately, Ruben failed his entrance examinations to the medical college in Tabriz. Students who could not enter Teheran medical school frequently crowded the lists of provincial universities, providing severe competition for local residents. Ruben's study of literature was only a stopgap between the annual examinations; he expected to try again next time, though he was doing no studying for it, aside from perfecting his English. Should he fail again this year, his senior year at the Faculty of Letters, he would have to honor his contract with the Iranian government, which was footing his education bill—he would have to become a teacher. A worse fate could not be imagined, he felt. "Teaching teachers to become teachers to teach teachers" he scoffed. "What is the use of it?"

He often spoke nostalgically of country life, with its simple ways and relaxed, familiar customs. "What is the good of civilization, anyhow?" he burst out one day. I assumed at first that he was thinking about the increased Westernization of Iran—the things he'd seen in Teheran, such as the German department store, London buses, splendid modern homes, and fine restaurants—but I quickly realized that he was contrasting Tabriz life with village life. "Don't you think I am right? The city makes people nervous. They are always hurrying to get some place. And no one knows anybody. Nothing but unfriendliness everywhere. Oh, yes, there are things to do, and the cinema every night. There are bright lights and many people here, but what good is that? Modern life in Tabriz is very bad for people, I think."

Back in the village, Ruben said, the people were poor but somehow content with their lives. They were certainly not stylish in any way; they wore suits that were inferior to what the tailors of Tabriz could fashion. Of course, there were no fancy parties, for which they would have to dress up and hope to show how much wealthier they were than their neighbors. And the men in country towns carried big beads in their hands, strung together on a thick cord with a tassel—the bigger and brighter the better—whereas in Tabriz sophisticated gentlemen carried very small beads, scarcely noticeable in their hands as they purled them between their fingers or nervously threaded them in their pockets. The Kurdish men especially liked very large bright beads. It was always a sign of manhood when a young boy began to walk with his friends and played with a string of beads. But here in the city it was so much harder to follow the old ways; boys grew up and nobody cared; young girls married, but who knew of the celebration? In a village everyone came. Also, there were many feasts and agricultural fairs. Farmers took pride in fattening their best bulls by giving them extra food; then on the day of the fair they pitted their bulls against their neighbors'. Women, children, all the men and boys would go to the edge of the village and watch the fights. "You know a bull, when he sees another bull, he must fight immediately. It is their nature." The winner is the one who chases the other off the field. Bets are placed and the farmer with the winning bull is much honored; good fortune will follow him all year; and, "His wife, she is very proud. Every farmer wants to have the best bull, so that his family wins honor."

There were dog fights and cock fights, also, to please the spectators at a fair, but only in the contest between bulls was any family distinction attached.

"The Kurds are especially fond of wrestling matches, for weddings and any feast day, but we in Khoi did not do so much wrestling. I wrestled when I was a little lad, however."

"Do you wrestle now—in the student competition?"

He flicked his head, contemptuously. "I am an intellectual now. I do not go to the sport room, except to play ping-pong."

"Do you know anything about the *zur-khanes*—houses of strength?"

"*Zur-khane?*" he glanced at me in surprise, as if he couldn't quite believe his ears.

"Do you ever go to them?"

"No, never. That is for a certain—how do you say? Another kind of man. At the Faculty of Letters, nobody belongs to a *zur-khane.*"

"But I understood it to be a kind of social club—a place where members go and do exercises, drink tea, relax." I had in mind a Persian version of the Downtown Athletic Club.

"Well, yes," he said evasively, "that may be."

"Do you know where they're located in Tabriz?"

"I don't think there are any here," he said, eager to dismiss the subject. Not until later in the year was I to know why: *zur-khane* devotees were generally common bazaar laborers, taxicab or droshky drivers, hod carriers and the like. The ritualistic rhythmic exercises were felt to be "old fashioned" or "too Persian," and the existence of these peculiar clubs should, if at all possible, be kept from a visiting Westerner such as myself.

Usually Ruben would be spokesman for his crowd—silent Abbas or smiling Karim saying nothing, while their more aggressive, self-possessed friend carried the burden of conversation. About his career, he had nothing but lamentations—in this, all his friends shared. Here they were in the last year of college at the Faculty of Letters, and upon receipt of their degrees, no one would come to offer jobs. No one would ask them, what is your training, your special work? Only a few lucky students with influence in high circles would obtain openings at Bank Melli or in

one of the departments of government. There were no job opportunities—nothing but the miserable prospect of teaching school
for impossibly low wages in some outlying village. Ruben and
Abbas were considering joining the army, for there at least they
might become officers and have servants—live the life of gentlemen.

The crux of the matter was that by becoming educated and
aspiring for a higher position in life, they were forced into a di-
lemma which could not be solved: it was now beneath them to
work with their hands, as Ruben's brother was doing in man-
aging the sugar beet enterprise on the family lands near Khoi.
Though in fact Ruben preferred country life, there was nothing
he could *do* there. Certainly he could not teach school in Khoi
and have his failure to enter medical school paraded before the
eyes of the world. Therefore, he hoped to get to Teheran, where
he might be lost in the multitudes, or possibly find a teaching job
in Meshed or Isfahan—some far away place; he did not wish to
shame his family. The idea of the future made him melancholy
and sweat would moisten his brow. He felt destiny had been very
hard on him. And wasn't it ironic? That brother back on the
family farms, he envied Ruben for being an educated man! "I am
a failure at life," he sighed, "even though I have scarcely begun it.
I live with my little brother in two tiny rooms. I have little happiness to look forward to. What I need is a woman," he said,
suddenly smiling and rubbing his loins. "What I want is a
woman!"

It wasn't likely he'd be able to afford a wife for some time,
given his prospects. Of course, there was the "bad" street behind
the Hotel Metropole; he tried to keep himself from visiting the
prostitutes there; he always felt so sorry for the girls. Ruben opened discussion of this subject somewhat gingerly, uncertain of
my attitude and fearing approbation. "Prostitution is very, very
bad," he said. "I know that."

"There are whores in every land," said Karim with his charming smile. His friends called him Tony Curtis because of his
striking resemblance to the movie star. "In every age there have
been prostitutes," he said.

"And do you visit them?"

77

He blushed and lowered his head.

"Every man needs a woman," said Ruben quickly.

"I've been curious about some of these friendships between boys. All that hand-holding—what does it mean?"

They all smiled. "Some men and boys prefer to make love to each other," said Ruben scornfully. "And some of the teachers at the university—they are always on the look-out." He named some prominent professors, but he was hushed up by his friends. "That is a way of getting good grades. A well-known way of advancing."

Although the truth about sexual behavior was even more closely guarded in Iran than in other countries (partly due to the nature of the Moslem religion), it seemed that here, with marriage postponed until men were in their middle forties, overt or latent homosexual relationships supplied their emotional needs. It was never a chosen sexual role; each Persian man kept firmly in mind his eventual desire for wife, children and a home, and eventually acquired them with a kind of bisexual ease somewhat baffling to a Western observer. "Boy love," as my students called it, was a taboo among them, however, and even if it were common, was never acknowledged or sanctioned. The pairing off of some young men, their walking arm in arm or with little fingers hooked together was an expression of an emotionally charged friendship. What the physical relationship between them actually amounted to probably varied a great deal. In the Persian language homosexuality was referred to as "the Greek vice," and in the Greek idiom it was called "the Persian inclination." I did not feel that pederasty was a problem among the students, but they were also not innocent of its existence.

Ruben informed me, when I asked, that especially on Thursday evenings the "bad street" behind the Metropole Hotel did a big business. I had noticed that a policeman was always on guard at the entrance to the narrow cul-de-sac; my students reported that the police had to be paid off by the patrons, and the whores paid the police, too, since prostitution was illegal in Iran. "That is one of the troubles with a law that goes against the natures of men," said Karim in his worldly way.

Thursday night was equivalent to a European or American Saturday night; it was an evening of revelry before the advent of the holy day. Many bazaar workers and "most of the men students" visited the ladies of the town, then went to the baths to purify themselves mentally, physically and spiritually, since Friday was the Sabbath. The whores in Tabriz were not a very savory group, Ruben assured me. "They are not girls, they are women. The cheapest costs five tomans (about 70¢)," he said. "But for that little money you get the oldest and most worn out. When a new one comes to town and she is fresh, you cannot get her for less than twenty tomans. Everybody knows when a new girl comes and everybody wants her."

"Where do the girls come from?"

"Most of them are tricked—you know—something wicked happened. They did not know they would end up as prostitutes, but once they are whores there is no other life possible for them. That is why I do not go to that street anymore. I have pity for them."

Abbas murmured something in Turki to Ruben, and grinned. I asked what he had said, and Ruben reported: "He says, in the Koran it is written, a man does a noble thing if he marries a prostitute and delivers her from her fate. But I do not believe in the Koran, and anyhow, I would not like to marry a prostitute. There have been too many others. I will only marry a virgin."

"What if she turns out not to be one?"

"I would kill her."

I believed he would.

"It is best to have a mistress," said Karim. "That is expensive, but it is best, for then you may change women whenever you like." He informed me that the higher class prostitutes had their own homes in the red-light district. An ordinary pleasure-house was run by a madame, however, and you paid her and gave the girl a tip, if she especially pleased you. But that was not obligatory. Each girl was on a weekly wage, and a very low wage, if she was no longer fresh. If a customer wished to stay all night, it might cost him as much as one hundred tomans (about $15), "but only for the most desirable."

I asked Ruben where the girls came from, how they were trapped into white slavery, and he began to relate an interesting anecdote. His family back in Khoi had had a beautiful servant girl, but since there were young boys reaching puberty in the household and it was the custom to dismiss attractive female servants before temptation overcame the scions and an unwanted forced marriage resulted, Ruben's parents served notice; the time had come for the pretty girl to seek another place. She replied that yes indeed, she had planned to depart anyhow, since her mother was forcing her to undertake another line of work. But where are you going, they asked? And she informed them that her mother planned to set her up in Khoi as a harlot.

Ruben's parents were horrified. They made a careful investigation and concluded that neither Ruben nor his older brother had seduced the girl, and, "my little brother, he was still too young." The girl was virgin-pure; but why, then, did the mother have such a strange ambition for her child?

"And where was the family—the father of the girl?"

"Her father was dead and she had no family. Her father had been a good, honorable man; he would not have allowed this bad thing to happen to his daughter."

Immediately Ruben's parents sought a position for her with one of the prominent families of the area. There were several openings, but she would take none of them. She preferred to acquiesce to her mother's perverse command that she become a harlot. "You see, a great deal of money could be made very quickly, right in Khoi, for this girl—she was very beautiful. Any man would give much to have her."

Ruben's parents then tried to arrange a marriage for the girl, believing her to be driven by an unseemly lust. Though the eligible men they proposed to her were attractive enough, the girl refused. Nothing more could be done, and since she was not from a religious family, not even the mullah could be called in to persuade her from folly.

And so her mother set her up in a house in Khoi and acted as the madame, making arrangements with a few wealthy men, who supported them well. It was a local scandal, "and truly I believe the girl's mother was mad—else why would she do such a thing to her own daughter?"

"Before she began as a whore, my mother begged the girl to run off to Teheran, and even offered to provide money. I myself believe she was too much under the influence of the wicked mother to do such a thing, even if she had wanted to. Once the business had started, it was all too late. For two years she took in men, but I do not think the mother made a fortune. The people of Khoi are not very rich, and merchants were angry with her and charged her double the price for things. As a prostitute the fees she earned were little compared to what the girl might have gotten, starting off fresh in Teheran."

In Teheran bevies of harlots could be seen any evening in *Maidan* Firdousi, a main square of the city, soliciting every passing male; in summer, naked under their *chedurs,* they would open their robes to attract business.

"Finally the scandal became so bad that the two of them, mother and the girl, were driven out of Khoi. The mother, I don't know what happened to her. The girl turned up in Tabriz, in a house of prostitution. This was her profession now—what else could she do?"

"And is she there now, in one of the houses?"

"No, she has left. Now I hear she is in Rezaiyeh, but I have no knowledge of her lately."

"Is she a prostitute there?"

"Of course."

"And is she still beautiful?"

"I suppose she is—and will be, for a few years longer. She was only about my age, a little older. She could not be so ugly yet, even if a whole army of men have lain on top of her."

"What is her name?"

"Oh, I do not remember."

"And she's now in Rezaiyeh. Do they have a street in Rezaiyeh, too?"

"Of course."

"But you can't think of her name?"

Ruben glanced at me with a salacious look in his eye. "Oh, sir," he said, putting his hand on my sleeve, "do not bother yourself trying to find her. She may still be a little pretty, but she has lost her fragrance."

7 *PERSIAN CARPETS*
AND H*OSSEIN'S TALE*

THERE is a Persian proverb: "If a man is blind, God provides the lure to catch birds." Many students regarded my presence in their midst for one school year as just such a gift from God—an opportunity of which they might make various uses. They were like blind men in the misfortunes of their circumstances, but also like blind men they had learned to compensate in order to surmount their crippling disadvantages. Throughout the year I was constantly aware of an almost palpable pressure from them for special attention. I could not so much as pay casual notice to one student, in a relaxed moment lest he assume immediately that I was suggesting a further relationship. Since there were hundreds of students, my personal knowledge of them and actual acquaintances among them was necessarily limited. This imposed upon the ambitious pupils a necessity to struggle in order to become among the special few. It was a relentless battle, and all sorts of devices were employed, from the attempt to present gifts to a kind of general hospitality characteristic of Persians, in which friendship and good business were equably blended. In the course of their pursuit of me I learned a great deal about them and their country; in fact, my side of the bargain was the better, and perhaps many of them were deluded into hopes that were far beyond my power to bring about. I sometimes longed for the sensibility of a voyager of another era, who might view the natives with simple, irresponsible interest, who might indulge his thirst for travel to strange lands without a twinge of guilt; an innocent, tranquil time (and perhaps it never truly existed) when no disturbing questions of reciprocity need be raised—when the traveler tasted, smiled and passed on.

Hossein was one of these bright-eyed, overeager young men, so competitive in his attempts to win my attention that I was continually put off by him. One of the very best English scholars, he was attending the British Council classes as well as mine, and he studied with a diligence unquestionably commendable. He led my senior class; he was quite clearly the best. But Hossein was too ardent, and I wanted to keep him at a distance. Although he was usually among the five or six students who came most frequently to my home for tea, I noticed that he was not particularly on intimate terms with the others; they left in twos and threes while he went his separate way. I judged that they resented his insistent egotism. Even in the relaxed comfort of my living room, Hossein was always busily trying to press his interests; he was forever seeking signs of special esteem from me—and perversely, I refused to give him any satisfaction. I could not bring myself to feed his starved ego with words of praise, though as a scholar he deserved them.

He was something of a dandy, on his limited means—very presentable physically, but too much resembling the sugar doll on a wedding cake. He possessed two natty dark wool suits, somewhat rakishly cut in the fashion of Tabriz, white shirts and light-colored satin or silk ties. He was clean, well-manicured, always spruced-up, his hair immaculately waved. He was slim, delicately built, with small facial features, large cocker-spaniel eyes and handsome white teeth. Whatever Hossein learned, whether it be an English phrase or a wayward fact, he never forgot. Obviously he was extremely ambitious, but in what direction it would be channeled, I did not know. Despite my first rather disagreeable impression, I found myself increasingly curious about him; perhaps at last I became convinced that his particular blend of intelligence and drive would amount to something. I did not feel I understood him, as I did some of the others, but he was an unavoidably impressive young man, in Persia or anywhere.

One morning in late December he rang the garden gate bell, and my servant Hassan lumbered down the brick path to let him in. When I had expressed a desire to learn more about carpets the evening before, he had immediately volunteered to visit one or two factories with me. Now this morning when I saw him smiling and bowing I was sorry I'd said yes. It was another cold, overcast day (for thirty days the sun did not shine at all) and I wasn't much in the mood for stirring far from the petrol burners I had lit only with some difficulty. But Hossein kept me fiercely to the bargain, declined to take off his overcoat or settle down for a cup of tea. The time had arrived ("Is it not ten o'clock?") to visit the carpet factories.

As we were walking along the *koutche* outside my garden wall, I began to suspect that Hossein had very little special knowledge about carpets; he was going to improvise our morning tour as we went along. The boldness of his game amused me. When he asked if I had any particular place I'd like to see first, I suggested the Emat factory, generally thought to be the finest in Tabriz by the Europeans. Since it was fairly near the Paulus' home, I had once stopped at Emat on the way to the Faculty of Letters. Hossein covered his ignorance fairly well, but I saw that he had no knowledge of the Emat factory and didn't know where it was located.

I had learned of Emat in connection with the turbulent events of World War II, for Tabriz was riddled with German sympathizers, and Iran would certainly have toppled in a coup if the Allies had not moved in. Prior to the outbreak of hostilities the weavers at Emat had been laboring on a carpet ordered by Adolph Hitler (the Führer's portrait set in a red swastika) and the rug had been sent to Berlin at the peak of the Nazi victories in 1940. No one in Tabriz knew what had happened to it since the downfall of the Third Reich. At first the directors of Emat had lived in fear of having the carpet discovered; they had especially anticipated reprisals from the Russians, who occuped Tabriz. But as the years passed and political fortunes changed, their disquiet vanished. Once again they allowed visitors to inspect the premises and watch the workers at their looms. In individual rooms on the second floor I had seen the master weavers (reputedly the finest in Persia) laboring on scenes from the *Shah-Noma* of Firdousi, or woodland landscapes crowded with flora and fauna—all safe subjects, impervious to politics.

84

Near the *maidan* Shahnaz and Pahlavi, the center of the business district in Tabriz (which was only two blocks from my flat), we stopped at the showroom of the Iran-Fars company. Hossein had often seen me pause at the window on my way home from the university to admire the unrolled carpets suspended behind the plate-glass or piled up deep on the floor. I was presented by Hossein as a customer, and the salesman showed me a great many new carpets of medium quality. They were too brightly colored for my taste, and I told him so. Furthermore, the imported aniline dyes from Germany were said not to last as well as the old-fashioned dyes made from vineleaves (for greens), walnut husks (for browns), pomegranate rinds (for yellows) and madder plant roots (for reds). I preferred old carpets, used carpets, I confessed to Hossein and the salesman. He nodded, having heard this before. Because of the widespread partiality shown old rugs, methods had been devised by carpet manufacturers to seemingly add years to a rug. Aging artificially sometimes meant exposure to the sun, putting it out in the bazaar for pedestrians to walk on, or (as I'd seen in Teheran) flinging the carpets into the street, to be run over by automobiles, trucks, and buses. A more systematic method involved washing down the carpets with a solution of wood ash.

I asked to see typical Tabriz carpets, and to the merchant this meant those carpets *made* in Tabriz. A medallion pattern, supposedly originating from the tooled leather bookbindings of the courts of Samarkand, in light beige, cream, plum and milk chocolate colors, with a good many bright flowers strewn in the "field," seemed to me to be the characteristic Tabriz carpet, but experts usually pointed out that here the carpet manufacturers were famous for their ability to copy designs originating elsewhere. For quality of workmanship there was nothing finer in Persia, but there was no particular design, as in Kashan or Kerman, which was the hallmark of the city's carpet industries.

"And now could we go to see the Iran-Fars factory?" I asked Hossein. Nervously, somewhat brashly, with a put-on authority, he asked the salesman if we might now see the factory where these were made.

He scowled, considered, then gravely shook his head. Impossible. The owners were out of town, and in their absence, no special favors could be granted, no abrogation of the rules prohibiting visitors would be possible. Hossein argued spiritedly for some time, then interpreted the gist of the disagreement for me, though I had already followed it fairly well in Turki.

"Tell him that if he cannot oblige, I am forced to go and visit the Emat factory. At Emat I know I shall be cordially received."

Delighted, Hossein relayed this remark. Then both of us turned and walked toward the door. We had scarcely reached the street when the shop-manager caught up with us, begged us to get into his Mercedes parked there beside the *jube*—and he would transport us, this instant, to one of the factories of Iran-Fars.

On our way he apologized for his behavior, but he was only acting under orders. There had been some difficulty awhile back. Visitors from foreign countries had come to peaceable Tabriz; they were hospitably treated, but then, when they had left the country, they wrote "bad things about us." I pressed to find out just what journalists or other visitors he was referring to, and at last got out of him, what I had suspected from his guardedness: he was thinking of the visit of Senator Ellender of Louisiana, who, after his inspection of a Tabriz carpet factory, made a speech on the floor of the U.S. Senate charging that American taxpayers' money should not be sent to a country capable of such barbaric cruelty to its children. The Shah immediately tried to enforce a law prohibiting labor for children under twelve years of age, but it was ignored by most factory owners. They were just more careful about visitors. Iranians excused and countenanced child labor because the conditions in factories, apologists maintained, were so much better than the children would meet elsewhere. It was better to have them at the looms than cold, hungry and begging in the streets. The urchins of the factories earned highly needed money for their families, and to abolish child labor would mean more starving people. Thus ran the argument, with its devil's logic.

We arrived at the Iran-Fars establishment unannounced, of course, and walked in with all the diminutive workers busily engaged at the enormous looms. I noted surprise and alarm on some of their faces, but since I was accompanied by a familiar official, the normal pace of labor resumed very quickly, and they

86

did not scamper away, as they had been told to do in case of surprise visitors.

I walked slowly up and down the aisles between the giant racks upon which the half-completed carpets were hung. The children squatted on boards suspended like scaffolding. They were tiny, undernourished five- and six-year-old boys and girls, fixed in the traditional tailor's position, knees out; the girls wore little chintz *chedurs,* the boys those grey cotton uniforms I'd noticed on schoolchildren; they were mostly barefooted, though this was December. The room was dramatic with color and quite bright, for natural light filtered down through the extensive system of skylights; the brilliant rugs were like luxurious tapestries furnishing the barrenness of an unheated barn. The looms were about twelve feet high and sometimes nearly twice that in length. Suspended above the racks were skeins of yarn wound on spools, and the pattern of the carpet, worked out on graph paper in pencil, was propped up before the small workers, as if it were their lesson for the day.

An atmosphere of gaiety prevailed, and perhaps that was the most moving thing of all. One felt their camaraderie, their intramural jokes and jibes, their companionship as they worked together, from day to day and year to year—perhaps until their fingers became too large to tie the knots adroitly and with speed. Now their nimble fingers were so quick that though I looked as hard as I could, I failed to discern the actual tying of the knots— their speed was so incredible their fingers were a blur. The best Persian carpets have from forty to sixty or more knots to the square centimeter, all individually tied, and a skilled weaver could do approximately 15,000 knots in a single day. Here they were using the Turki knot, I was told, whereas elsewhere in Iran they tie the Pharsi knot—a technical difference important only to rug experts.

The children were singing or chanting something, and I asked Hossein what it was. I stood there looking up at them, perched like birds on branches. It was a workers' song, the lyrics and music made up as they went along, like the hammer songs of the Negro chain gangs of the South. First a row of little girls would burst out with: "Pass me the blue, oh the blue, pretty blue; pass me the

87

blue, pretty blue, oh, the blue," and down from the spools above came the blue yarn. Then another phalanx of children, boys and girls mixed, would start up with: "Now send me the black, now the black; oh, send me the black, yes the black," and finally in a kind of chorus, they would all join in: "Now the blue, now the black, now the red; oh, send me the black, now the red, now the blue," and the yarn would vibrate through the air in front of the loom, as faster and faster they worked, buoyed up by their singing, making it a game or a race, until they broke down in torrents of laughter—or the supervisor came by and stood sternly below them, scanning the quality of their labor. In the course of a day each child earned about five rials (around eight cents), and sometimes a boy or girl would be assigned to a single carpet for a year or two. The ultimate cost to the purchaser in Iran might vary from $400 to $1000 for the better carpets, depending on the quality and difficulty of design or colors.

Hossein was a close observer of my reactions: my interest, boredom, anger or pleasure. He was disappointed, therefore, and unable to understand why I wished to cut short my carpet factory visiting, why I should abruptly suggest going home. "I have seen enough." I also knew, from this brief glimpse, that I would not buy a carpet; it would be like walking on children's lives. Ilse Koch and her lampshades made of human skin seemed the only parallel I could think of. But my reactions were difficult to explain to Hossein, bright and perceptive though he was. He maintained that he understood my feelings of pity, but I could tell he really didn't. Baffled by my withdrawal, he left me at my door and slunk away, unable to think what it was *he* had done wrong.

News of my excursion spread, and a few days later Abbas and one of his friends, Mir-Mohammed, suggested a guided tour of the carpet stalls in the bazaar. The latter's father was himself a merchant, and the trip would be on an expert level, not the amateur wanderings I had probably experienced with Hossein. They felt I had surely not been able to learn much under his tutelage. Would I not put myself in capable hands and *really* become acquainted with Persian carpets?

I had no objections to a visit to the rug bazaar, the marketplace being something else again; but I told them I had seen all the factories I'd care to. Very well. They were determined that I should meet "the most famous" carpet merchants in Azerbaijan. "Is your father one of these?" I asked. Famous, I assumed, referred to renown for driving a hard bargain; had I been interested in purchasing a rug, I would rather meet the nonfamous, the unknowns.

"My father," said Mir-Mohammed, "is an ordinary carpet merchant. You will see. He is not a rich man, but he will sell you a nice carpet—very cheap." The family came from a small village near Shahpur; they were on the "rise" now, and this son would join the carpet concession in the bazaar upon completion of his studies at the Faculty of Letters.

Mir-Mohammed was a droll, cunning, somewhat phlegmatic-appearing young man, always dressed somberly in tight, severe suits and an elderly, conservative hat. He had a thick, expressionless face, except for his wise brown eyes which showed a smart, peasant awareness of everything going on. "You want to buy a carpet? I get you a carpet," he kept saying, his gimlet eyes glittering. When I found a rug I liked, I should call Mir-Mohammed, and he would get it for me wholesale, far below market price. When I looked dubious, he assured me that his father would seek no personal profit for his role as agent—it was simply to accommodate me. I smiled, nodded, but begged off. Actually, I was quite wrong about Mir-Mohammed, prejudiced merely by his appearance; I later found him to be honest, generous and reliable.

The three of us set off on our excursion into that section of the bazaar where carpets were sold and bought, the center of which was a vast cathedral chamber. Rays of sunlight probed down from the clerestory into the dust-filled atmosphere. The merchants' stalls were like chapels around an apse. Each seller had a particular spot in the great central area, where his rugs were piled, sometimes six feet high. After tea and ceremony in the stall, the proprietor would take the prospective customer out to inspect the stock of rugs, or the smaller carpets would be brought in by flunkies and spread out. Lit with kerosene lamps, hung with the most precious silk prayer rugs and other prime specimens of the art, the stalls were rich in the aura of the ancient Middle East. Swarthy men, sometimes bearded and turbaned, with kaftans and baggy trousers, sat in the rug-draped little rooms beside flickering lamps. Many of these people were mere observers of the transactions, relatives or friends, the whites of their eyes flashing in the gloom, the decorous ceremony kept lively by their darting, expressive glances.

Mir-Mohammed's father reminded me of a lower east side New York tailor. He was grave, hospitable, and considerate as he showed me his wares. After I asked the price of one rug—and he had told me—my reply was *choke, choke,* Turki for "much" or "too much." Thereupon he spread his hands and bowed; "You may have it"—the classic peasant response. Once when climbing Analzanal, the small mountain near Tabriz, I came upon a shepherd with a beautiful flock of sheep and lambs. When I admired them, he too spread his hands and bowed. "Please take any of them, they are all yours." I declined the sheep, and now I said no to the carpet.

Outside the great hall, in one of the regular tunnel-like streets of the bazaar, we stopped to inspect the carpets of a merchant who had a very tiny cupboard, in which he himself sat. He would haul out his small rugs and drop them before us like windowshades. At last he came to his prize possession, a finely woven silk carpet depicting an elaborate pastoral scene. When I asked him the price of it, he looked me up and down contemptuously; then he snarled—50,000 tomans. In other words, he had no intention of selling it, especially to a foreigner. He murmured something else, which Abbas wouldn't translate. At last, when I persisted, Mir-Mohammed interpreted what he had said: "You Americans make big bombs. The Russians make bombs. But we make these! I think you people are barbarians."

After our expedition we settled down in my living room for tea and a discussion of what we'd seen. "Did you not like the carpet bazaar?" asked Abbas. "Is it not so, you are beginning to like our country?"

I nodded but said I was distressed by all that I would never know or understand about Azerbaijan. Carpets I could inspect, from the dying of the yarn to the weaving on looms and the eventual selling of them in the bazaar. But this was such a small thing to learn; there were countless other things which piqued my curiosity. Why was it, for instance, that despite the way most men were Western-style in their appearance, they never parted their hair in the European fashion? They had brush-cuts, or long hair combed straight back, or short hair also turned back; but I had never seen an Iranian with a part on the left or right side of his scalp. Did this bear any relation to the fact that pedestrian traffic on sidewalks was characterized by no "parts" either? You neither kept to the left nor to the right, because there was a constant stream going both ways at once, and you not only collided with people, but with burros, goats, sheep and turkeys.

They shook their heads gravely. And how strange it was, I added, that through these thousands of years of civilization, no Persians had discovered that the way you butchered beef or mutton made a great deal of difference. At the meat market there were no "cuts"; one either got fillet or the other, hacked off anywhere it could be found. Iranians ground their meat (for stuffing eggplant, grape leaves and the like) or charcoal-broiled strips, but they had never gone beyond that to steaks, roasts, or chops—why not?

"We like our food as it is," said Abbas, which seemed a sensible answer.

While we were talking, the doorbell at my garden entrance clanged, announcing another visitor, and Hassan went down the path to let him in. It was Hossein, looking harried, concerned and, as I soon found out, betrayed. He had learned from friends that I had been seen in the bazaar looking at carpets. News always traveled like that—instantly, secretly, in its own grapevine way. He was sorry I had not told him yesterday that I wished to visit the carpet merchants in the bazaar. It would have been a simple matter to go there at once. He was at my service—anything I wished, anywhere I wanted to go, he would escort me. These assurances were uttered in the presence of my guests as if he did not see them at all. Only after persuasion would he sit down and consent to have tea with the others. I was finding Hossein a pretty tiresome young man, but his assumptions of privilege with me, by dint of his being the number one student, also interested me. There was a neurotic feverishness about him that was curious and unexplained.

And so, when the others stepped into their shoes at the doorstep and walked off, and Hossein remained seated, I did not insist on his departure. He chatted about his schoolwork, the books he had been reading, and recounted his labors on the senior thesis; he had just completed the paper, though it was not due until spring, when all seniors were required to submit a thesis in order to earn the degree. Hossein had started early in case his project didn't turn out well. In most instances, for language students, the thesis requirement involved a translation of some piece from Pharsi into English.

"But it is becoming very difficult to find material that has not already been done." The well-known Persian contemporary writers such as Heydeyat had been completely translated into English. In order to have an acceptable thesis, each student had to discover a literary work never before done.

"And who are you translating then?"

"A writer of stories named Sh Patchou."

"Who is he?"

"I suppose you have never heard of him."

"No, I can't say I have."

"I became interested in him because I like to know all I can about writers. Where they live, where they come from, if they are married, and so on. 'And so on'—is that right? Or is it 'et cetera'?"

"Either is all right."

"I became interested in Sh Patchou even before I knew I would write my thesis, using one of his short stories. He is not so famous in the world, but he is known here in Iran very well. He is a communist writer."

"He is?" I suddenly had whole new speculations about Hossein; he noticed my surprise.

"Not that *I* am a Communist. But it so happens, most modern Iranian writers are Communist. However, they cannot print anything, except in secret. Or they flee to other countries—Heydeyat, as you know, died in France. Sh Patchou was put in jail, but he escaped. Nobody knows where he is. Some say he is dead, others say he has gone to Russia, or maybe Iraq, but I do not think so. He has taken another name and is hiding out with friends, perhaps right in Teheran. When I read about him in the papers, I became interested. I want to find the biography of the man, but nobody could tell me anything. So, when I was in Teheran two years ago, I went to the Russian Embassy and asked them if they could tell me something about Sh Patchou."

"You did *what?*"

He smiled and calmly repeated himself, proud of his daring. "Why not?"

"And what did the Russians tell you?"

"I could find nobody who would give me information. But they took me in to see many officials. It is a very beautiful place, with many gardens. I was always interested to see what it was like there. The Russians may have known about Sh Patchou, but they didn't want to tell me. As soon as I left the embassy, I notice this man following me. That was just the beginning. Everywhere I go, there is a man behind, watching."

The way he told it, I saw that he had anticipated this development and in fact had put himself in such a position out of a sense of adventure.

"When they arrested me two days later, they already knew that I had gone into the Russian Embassy to ask about Sh Patchou. How had they found that out? I don't know, but I think there must be spies everywhere in Teheran. They threw me in jail and then began questioning me. 'Are you one of his followers?' they wanted to know. 'Are you Communist?' 'No, no,' I told them, 'I am interested in *all* writers and I want to find out their biographies.' 'But why do you want to know Sh Patchou—why not other writers?' This I could not answer because, in point of fact, any writer I might choose would be Communist, too, like Sh Patchou. At that time I did not think of my thesis, but the next year I thought, I will translate Sh Patchou. The other students do not have trouble; they choose dead men to write thesis on. They take writers who have no political importance. But I think living writers are the most interest. You are a writer, too, aren't you, sir? I know you will agree with me. I did not want to write my thesis on somebody who is no longer alive. At least I *think* Sh Patchou is still alive."

"How long were you in jail?"

"Only a short time. You see, they could find nothing bad about me, only that I had done this thing. And it was no crime to go to the Russian embassy. It was just suspicious."

"But you don't live in Teheran?"

"I do not. I have friends there, however, and they helped me. So I came back to Tabriz, and then it started all over again. Men following me. Here in Tabriz the police finally arrested me, too, and then began to ask me questions about who I knew and what I did. I could not remember. I could not answer all those questions about which day, with whom. For a long time they kept after me; then they had to let me go. I am no Communist, and they could prove nothing bad against me. For weeks and weeks I was in trouble, though. I was followed and watched. At last I think they forget me."

"I'd like to see your thesis—is it finished?"

"Yes, almost. I would be grateful if you would tell me what you think of it. The story comes from a book called *Thirteen Flaming Tales;* or, *Enduring Tales.*

"And what's the name of the one you translated?"

He smiled, pausing somewhat mischievously before he said: " 'Man's Deceiver.' A good title, don't you think? I will go home now and get it for you."

MAN'S DECEIVER

by Sh Patchou

MR. RAHBAN liked to go to his office on foot in the mornings. He was very fond of clean streets with gutters full of running, clear water and trees along both sides the streets which were not crowded; every time that he passed Parvin street which had green trees, he felt joy. He liked this street very much and when he passed it he used to peer at the trees, doors of the houses and balconies.

During these few days there was a china flower-vase full of red flowers in a window of one of the houses. He told himself that the landlord of the house had exquisite taste! One day when he was looking at the flower-vase, as usual, the window was suddenly opened and a young beautiful woman appeared in it. Without looking at the street, she took up the flower-vase and disappeared in the room. Her lovely face and her short pretty colored hair were imprinted in his mind.

Four days had gone by but he could see no flower-vase there in the window. The lady, too, didn't open the window. But on the fifth day, just as he looked up at the window, it was opened and the woman appeared. There was a big red flower in her hair on the left side. It was not clear why she leaned out and looked at the street. Perhaps she was looking for someone. Whatever it might be, by a sudden motion of her head, the flower fell down out of her hair in front of Mr. Magid Rahban. She drew back her head very quickly and closed the window.

It is natural that he picked up the beautiful big flower. He smelled it and felt its pleasant scent. How strange! The red flower gave out a pleasant smell of somebody's odour of sweat. How this scent was exhilarating!

All the way to his office he smelled it and when he got there he was still smelling it. He was very happy and delighted with it. It was as if they had slept together and he was kissing her.

The next day he could see the flower-vase in its place again, and it was there till five days later. In the morning of the sixth day it was not there; but as he was passing the window, it was opened and she appeared. She leaned out to the street, as though she was looking for someone or something. Suddenly her necklace fell down just in front of him. It was a golden chain and in the middle of it there was a golden crescent, and in the middle of this crescent there was a turquoise pendant. He picked it up and looked at the window and showed it to her.

"Excuse me, sir," she said, smiling, "would you mind bringing it up?" The lady didn't linger at all and closed the window.

When he got to the second floor and drew near the semi-opened door of her room, he hesitated and wondered whether he wasn't doing something wrong; but his hesitation didn't take him long because the lady, as her hands were soapy, opened the door widely by her elbow.

"Excuse me, sir," she said happily, "I troubled you. It was very kind of you to bring the necklace to me. Give it to me please."

He stretched out his hand to give her the necklace; and she wanted to receive it by her wrist. As her wrist was soapy, it slipped and fell down. Rahban took it up again. It looked as if she were taking exercises and she, like a happy young girl, said: "How strange. It fell down again. As you see my hands are soapy, may I ask you to put it on the table?" She turned back and went towards the wash-basin. She turned up the tap and washed her hands, then she took the towel. "My maidservant has gone for a long time to buy some aspirins. I have a headache. I was looking out of the window to see if she was coming. I troubled you. Thank you very much for your kindness. Put it on that table, please," she said, smilingly, and turning back in triumph.

Rahban put it on the table and turned back towards the door. He was looking up and down from her head to foot. She was very lovely. "You are certainly going to your office," she said. "I wasted your time. You may be late." She was laughing and laughing.

He went down the stairs. He became giddy. She had squeezed his hand while shaking it, and after drying her hands, she had scented them. He took a sniff of his hand now. He could smell the scent of her body's sweat, too. He remembered that when he had entered the house and stood by her, he had noticed the same scent; but now he could smell the scent on his hand. He was overcome, suddenly, by a feeling of bliss—absolute bliss—as though he had swallowed a bright piece of that late afternoon sun and it burned in his bosom, sending out a little shower of sparks into every particle, into every finger and toe.

Mr. Rahban had been married twelve years, but he had no child. He didn't love his wife but as she was experienced and efficient woman, who used to manage the house as she liked, he had come to an agreement with her. He had not taken any pleasure in the early days of his marriage. In his work he had served eighteen years and hoped he would become the director general, then the deputy, or minister. Poker was his amusement, which he sometimes played in his friends' or his own house.

The following days he could see the flower-vase in its own place. Several times when he went by the window she opened it and poured water into the flower-vase out of a big glass, and, when her eyes met his, she used to laugh. Rahban tipped his hat and greeted her.

So they became completely acquainted with each other. One morning instead of going to his office, he went to her door and knocked on it. She opened the door. "You are late," she said, smiling, "come in please."

She closed the door behind him. She took his hat and put it on the table. Then she led him to her bedroom. She made him room on a chair and let herself fall on her bed. He was looking at her but they didn't touch each other. They were apart as when someone comes into a room and people are self-conscious.

"My maidservant has begged leave to go and see her brother from last night," she said. "I am alone here and I don't feel well. In the morning the heat knocked me over and I had two degrees temperature, but now I have a pain in my back. It was very kind of you to come here, but I expected your coming here sooner than now."

"Sooner than now?" he answered, stammering. "Had you been waiting for me?"

She laughed . . . "Don't be surprised if I say that I had been waiting for you." She said, "I like you very much, not only me but also every woman, with good taste, would wish to have a man like you, once she has seen you. . . ."

Then she looked over his shoulder with a sudden jerk. The back of her white neck was revealed by the action. He felt a new sense within himself. Manliness and dignity must appear in another way. Since she loved him, he had to win her heart.

He peered at everything which was in the room: curtains and pictures on the wall; the flower-vase on the table which he had seen from the street; her bed with white sheets; and

97

her well-built body, which was the most pleasant thing of all. She suddenly turned back and leaned on her elbows. This time she let those precious things shine on her marbly breast. Then she laughed. "Excuse me, sir, for entertaining you in this way," she said quietly. "I will entertain you on a day when I feel well. There are fruits and sweets on the table; get up and serve yourself, please; and make yourself at home."

She saw that the hour of shooting her last arrow of coquettishness had struck, so she put her left hand out to him. "Look here. The heat has knocked me over," she said.

He felt her pulse. Though her hand was warm, she had not any temperature. He wanted to say something but he couldn't. He brought his head near her hand and gave it a kiss. She caressed his face with hands that were so pale a light seemed to come from them. While she was doing this, he could smell the same scent of her body that had first fallen out of her flower. It made him intoxicated. He drew himself near her bed, so that his head was between her hands; he looked into her eyes and put his arm around her. He kissed her lips. He kissed her hard and held her tight and tried to open her lips with his own. They were closed tight. He held her close against himself; as he did so she suddenly shivered. He could feel her heart beating and her lips opened. Her head went back against his hand.

Two hours later they sat together and laughed, for it was as if they had achieved their joint wish. He put out his hands and took hers. He looked into her eyes. "You haven't told me your name, yet," he said. "What is your name, please?"

"Delroba" (charming, in Pharsi), she answered smilingly.

"How beautiful a name! Everything of yours is charming, too, like your name. Do you live here alone?"

"No, I live with my brother and maidservant here."

"Is he now here in Teheran?"

"No, he has gone to Isfahan for several days. He may be back next week."

"Have you any husband?" he said, after a little thinking.

"No, he died two years ago."

"Have you any children?"

"I haven't had any children up to now. I didn't marry after my husband died. My brother took me here in order to keep me from caring for my husband."

"Haven't you a mother?"

"Why not? She is in Isfahan. She insists upon my going back to her. Last week my brother wanted to take me along himself to Isfahan; but I didn't agree, because I wanted to—"

"You wanted to . . . what?"

She laughed. . . .

"I wanted to see you more and more," she said, "from that very day when you brought up my necklace. I liked you and felt that I had fallen in love with you. Every morning when you went to your office I used to look at you through the windowpane, and I was waiting for you to come here. And today . . . it looks as though fate is going to bring us to each other."

"Are you satisfied?"

"Satisfied? More than satisfied. Tell me, are you lucky?" she said, as she put her head on his shoulder.

From that day the course of his life was changed. When he found an opportunity he would go and see her. He was welcomed with great joy. When he entered the room she used to take off his hat and carry away his stick and help him in his undressing. Then she seated him in an easychair and put a beautiful pair of slippers in front of him which she had bought for him. When he wanted to leave her, she fixed a small flower or a bud in his buttonhole.

His pleasure was indescribable. But he didn't let anything be known of his secret love. He went no more to any club to gamble with his friends, but in the excuse of going for gambling he used to spend a lot of his time with her. Sometimes he gave her some cloth or jewelry made out of gold. Everytime that Rahban went to her home—when these two fortunate creatures were together—they forgot everything in the world, even the world itself.

99

One day when he was caressing her he felt that she was growing a little big with child. The discovery chilled him. He suddenly drew back his hand. "Are you expecting a baby?" he asked.

She nodded.

He turned pale. He was unable to speak. He said nothing for a while. "Who got you with child?" said he with round eyes.

She shrugged and set her lips and eyebrows in a way that meant she didn't know.

"Have I got you with it?" he asked again, quietly.

"I dare say, it may be you."

Rahban kept quiet and was absorbed in thinking.

"If it was you, are you pleased?"

"No, I can never believe that it is me. And if—"

"And if . . . what then?"

"And if it was me, I suppose you had a bad intention in this matter, and you certainly were determined to take advantage of it."

Very soon the mood of her eyes changed and turned yellow. She was not the Delroba of a few minutes before. She drew herself backwards and was discouraged. "Don't think at all, my dear," she said indifferently, "it doesn't matter for me if it is you or someone else. I agree, it is my own responsibility and in any case it is my own child. Be relieved. I promise that I will try and not make you trouble, though I know I've made trouble now. You can go and relieve at your own home." Then she got up and brought his hat and stick and gave them to him. "Please, trouble me no more," she said. By saying it, she meant him to go out. He did so, but when he was at a distance of some hundred paces from her house, he felt that he had gone off ungentlemanly.

From that day onward he neither used the street nor saw the flower-vase in the window. But two or three months later a satanic temptation made him walk the street. Her window was closed. He couldn't see any flower-vase there at the window. He wanted to continue his way but the temptation made him go upstairs and he knocked at the door. An old woman opened the door. "Is Mrs. Delroba in?" he asked.

"No, sir, it is a long time since she has gone to Isfahan, to be with her brother."

Though she had gone to Isfahan and he was satisfied with it, he felt that he had lost his love and something else in his life. The following days he was more unsatisfied and was thinking about her and her caresses day in and day out.

When he saw the flower-vase at the window, how glad was he! He was so entirely confused that he rushed towards the stairs, going up them hurriedly, two at a time and knocked at the door. His heart was beating. The old woman opened the door and smiled.

"Has she come back from Isfahan?"

"Yes, sir."

"When?"

"Two or three days before."

"Can I see her?"

"No, I am sorry, she is not in." Just at that moment he heard a crying baby.

"So she is in," he said. "I hear a baby."

"Yes, it is her son."

"Son?"

"Yes, her son. But she, herself, is out."

He was more uneasy. His heart began beating. He stood in the doorway. "Let me have a look at him," he said. He entered the room. The old woman led him to his cradle. He was a beautiful boy, and he was struggling with uneasiness. She stooped over him and changed his diapers. He was uneasy before, but now when he felt that he was no more alone, he kept quiet. His eyes were shining in the daylight. He fixed his eyes upon Rahban. Rahban recognized a resemblance between the baby and himself. Was it his son? There was no doubt of its being so, and every one would see it at the first sight. His heart was beating so that he could hear it. He stretched out his hand and began to play with the baby's exquisite fingers as they shone in the daylight. The baby took his father's fingers and clung to them. There appeared a triumphant laugh on his face. He liked to kiss his son but he was ashamed of doing so. He turned to the old woman. "Thank God, he is a beautiful and healthy boy," he said. "Please give me a glass of water, dear nanny."

She went to bring water. Rahban stooped over the baby and kissed him. He was entirely confused. Those fathers who have no son know what I am driving at. He drank up the water.

"Tell me the truth now," he said, "where has she gone?"

"I told you, sir, that she is out."

"Where to?"

"I suppose she might have gone to the bath."

"All right, I want to go," he said, after a little thinking, "when she comes back, tell her that Mr. Rahban will dine with her tonight."

Delroba opened the door with cheerfulness and love-airs. On seeing him her face lit up. Rahban kissed her hands and face. While he was doing so he felt her hand on his shoulder. They went together to see the boy.

"What have you named him?" he asked smilingly, taking him out of his cradle.

"I have not taken his identity card," she said. "I thought you would rather call him whatever you liked."

This, of course, in his present mood, was very kind of her. He put the baby back into its cradle. "Let us go and have a chat," he said. "I have many things to speak about."

He sat down by her and continued: "I have told you before that I have a wife. You are certainly aware that she knows nothing about you. I am in love with you, especially now that you have born me a son. I have to think deeply on this matter so that all of us will fare well."

"I am at your service."

"What do you think we have to do?"

She looked down and said that his idea was hers. It looked as if he had thought about it long before, because he took a golden wedding ring out of his pocket and wore it next to the little finger of her left hand. "The only thing that we could do was that," he said. "I had bought this ring for you and tomorrow evening we will marry here, after performing the legal formalities of marriage. But I prefer it to be very quiet."

She had achieved what she wanted, so put her head against his breast. There appeared a few drops of tears in her eyes and they rolled down her cheeks. For a few minutes they were busy with kissing each other. They were happy.

"May I ask you a question now?" he said. "I swear you, by God, to tell me the truth: how did you take my heart within your hand? I can't believe that all was by chance. Why did you decide to choose me for yourself as a husband?"

She laughed.

"It is true that this was not by chance," she said. "This was my thought and plan that culminated in marriage. The fact was that I was suffering with loneliness and I didn't want to be a bad woman. I wanted to have a man to be my patron and love me. I wanted to have a home, children for myself, as other women do. At last I chose you among the men and tried to win you."

"You didn't know me."

"No, I didn't know you, but one day I saw that you were passing this street while you were thinking. I liked your figure because it was finely sculptured, so I followed you up to your home. There was a grocery near your house. I asked him your name and your business. Next day I gave your neighbor's maidservant a hair pin which I had bought for fifty rials and in a few minutes I knew a lot of things about your life. When I saw that you had no child, I felt happier and made up my mind to deceive you into being my husband. . . ."

Rahban was all ears. When she said that she had known that she had chosen one of the noblest men, he couldn't contain himself for joy. "Oh, God!" he said in a low voice, "the woman whom I had chosen as my wife couldn't make me happy, but now I see that a woman who has chosen me as her husband does make me happy."

"How smart is this woman," he continued, "who knows how to lure a man! Oh, God, the best trick taught a woman is how to excite a man's silent feelings."

Then he looked at her bright eyes and said: "It is true that a man who has been chosen by a woman to be her husband is luckier than he who has chosen a woman to be his wife."

THE END

When I had finished reading, Hossein, poised on the edge of his chair, asked me: "Well, sir, what do you think?"

"You've done very well in the translating. I mean, it reads quite fluently. There's still work to be done, however. Your pronouns often don't have clear antecedents, and some of your sentences are awkward."

"I have failed then?" he asked sadly.

"No, I'm sure you've done far better than other students in your class could do, most likely."

"I have? Then I am happy."

"It's just that when you try to be idiomatic, you have trouble. And I don't think you ought to have stolen that line from Katherine Mansfield's 'Bliss'—that business about swallowing the bright piece of the late afternoon sun."

"I cannot use it?"

"No, it's already been done. You have to think of a fresh image. Surely Patchou didn't use that very expression, did he?"

"But that is what he meant, I believe."

"As for the story, it strikes me as pretty silly. You certainly don't think this is 'literature,' do you?"

"It is a love story," he sighed.

"A cheap, popular romance, supposed to titillate the readers. He must have written it for money."

"I, too, do not think it very good. It is not the best of his work."

"I hope not."

"But it was one that had not yet been translated by anyone into English."

"Don't misunderstand, I found it fascinating. The way the woman is pictured, for instance—the conniving, assertive partner, whereas the man is passive but drawn in, finally. This would not by the way you'd find it in *True Romances*—in our confession magazines." (U.S. pulp magazines were on newsstands throughout Iran.) "In our romances the man is supposed to do the pursuing. This fellow here seems awfully weak and whining."

"He is deceived, that is all. And at last he comes to understand how it was that it happened. But he is not sad. He is happy that she did it."

"Delroba is sensual, materialistic and practical, she never loses her head. That's the Persian notion of women, isn't it? But Rahban—I wonder about *him*. What if Delroba had given birth to a girl? Then he wouldn't have been interested in marrying her, I suppose?"

"You see, he did not have a son. That was an important point."

"I know—he's really more in love with that child than he ever was with Delroba. Having an heir is all that matters."

Hossein fidgeted nervously with his teacup. "It is merely an amusing story."

"Hardly what I'd expect from one of the prominent communist writers. Unless he intends it as a picture of a decadent society and is laughing at it. But I don't see that the story is meant that way."

"Perhaps the communist part, the serious part, has been left out. After all, I found the story in a book, and maybe the printers wouldn't let him keep in those parts."

"But I can't imagine where any communist doctrine could fit in!"

"Please, sir, do not trouble yourself. It is just a story, it is not true. It is nothing that ever happened."

I saw that he was becoming extremely uncomfortable. "Really, Hossein, you've done a very good job, and your teacher will surely like it. I've noticed you're especially interested in writers and literature. Is it because you hope yourself to be an author?"

"I? Oh, no sir, I had no such thought."

"You don't write poetry, you never have?"

"I am in the Faculty of Letters by accident. You see, I wanted to enter medical school."

"You too? Everybody wants to be a doctor."

"That is true. But only a few will be."

"And when you applied for medical school, did they turn you down?"

"Oh, no, sir, it was not like that at all. Something terrible happened and I did not even get to take the examination."

"Oh?"

"When I graduated from what you call the "high school" before entering the university—did you know I was first in my class in all of Azerbaijan?—the teachers told me I would have no trouble entering the medical school at the University of Teheran. So I went there in spring to take the examinations. I went to Teheran with a boy who was my best friend. He and I—is that how you say it? 'He and I'?"

I nodded.

"He and I were the best friends for many years. Everything we did together, we go everywhere together. We are hand in hand on the streets as we walk. He was number two in the graduating class. I was number one. So in Teheran we are together, too, seeing the city, and the night before the examination for medical school, something terrible happened to me. I did not know what it was. But I woke up in the hospital four days later. I had been hit hard over the head and found in the street. But I had not been robbed, and nothing else was wrong with me. My friend, he was nowhere to be found. Of course he had gone in to take the examination. But I knew, when I woke up in the hospital, that I had missed my chance. The tests are given only once a year. The police investigated. They said my best friend must have done it to me—hit me over the head from behind—and they arrested him. Never would he say he had done it. The police wanted to bring him to me in the hospital, but I did not want to see him. They thought he would confess if he saw how badly I was hurt. But I would not have it. I told the police I did not wish to see him ever again. They didn't mind. They kept him in prison. The newspapers wrote all about it—my name, my picture was there. They thought it was because my friend feared I would take his place and he would not be admitted to medical college, because he would not do quite as well on the examinations as I would. That is what they said. I do not know. The medical school, of course, when this happened—they crossed his name from their list. So he got nothing from it, and I do not know how he could have deceived me that way. My friend's mother came to Teheran and out

106

to the hospital to see me. The family name was dishonored, she said, and it made her so unhappy. Would I not forgive and forget? That is what she said. But that was hard to do, I replied. How could I forget such a thing? And worst of all, I had missed my chance to get into medical school.

"But when the Shah reads all about this, he sends word that he would like to have an interview with me, when I am well enough. Oh, it made me well very quickly! It was almost worth everything—all the pain—to be able to see the Shah himself, in the palace."

"And so you went?"

"Of course."

"I hope he helped you."

"Yes, he wanted to. He is a very kind man—a very great man—but when I saw him I could not speak, I was so full of wonder to be in the presence of the king. He asked me, was there something he could do for me? I could say nothing. I bowed and replied, 'Thank you,' and again, 'Thank you,' and I backed away. That is all that happened. When I was outside the chamber, I remembered—yes, there was something the Shah could do for me. If only I could take the examination for entrance to medical school, if they would please let me take it, though I knew it was late. And so, when I got to see the Prime Minister—"

"Manouchehr Eghbal?"

"That is he. I asked the Prime Minister this favor. I said I would very much like to have it arranged for me to take the medical college entrance tests."

"And did you?"

"Oh, no, sir. The Prime Minister said it was a university business, he could do nothing. It was impossible for me to beg this favor. The examinations had been given already, and nothing at all could he do."

"A Prime Minister could do nothing? You should have gone back in to see the Shah!"

"But I am nothing, sir, a mere student. I was sorry I had not told the Shah, but it was quickly too late and they showed me out of the palace. When I got home I wrote a petition, but it was denied. It was explained to me that once an examination has been given, the questions are known. It would be cheating of me to take the tests, so many days later. Besides, the result had already been announced, and those who got into the medical school had been notified. There was not room for one more. And they could not take the place away from somebody who had been told he was admitted. I understood. It was all explained. Once a year they are given, and that is final. So I decided to enter the Faculty of Letters and try again the next year for Teheran medical college."

"You did that?"

"No, it is strange, but I found that perhaps I am not suited for medical studies. I would rather become a doctor of literature and teach in a university. Perhaps it is best that things turned out this way. I would like to go to Germany or England—or maybe America—for my doctorate."

"What happened to your friend. They let him out of prison?"

"Oh, he is no longer my friend. And I do not know what happened to him, after they released him from jail. I have not seen him, nor do I wish to see him. I try to forget it all."

"Your real-life story, Hossein, is far more moving than this trashy piece by Sh Patchou."

"Yes, but it is sad to think of real life. I like stories, better."

"I can see how you would."

"The worst thing is that now I am lonely. I do not trust to have a friend. I am afraid because of what happened, to trust anybody. The wound on my head has healed, but not the wound in my heart."

8 MR. IVOR'S HAT

ONE winter evening I walked home from classes in the company of several students. We made our way along the crowded streets amid the hawkers of fresh lamb's feet, roasting entrails of sheep, and steaming tin platters of beets, turnips and potatoes. Burros loaded with straw were kept in line on the sidewalks by stick-carrying ragged shepherds who made loud burring noises in their throats, like the starter of an automobile pressed on a cold morning.

"Would you care to stop and meet my music teacher?" asked Darius. "His shop is nearby, and he would very much like to make your acquaintance."

"Does he really want to meet me?"

"I have told him about you—that you love music—and he has said I should bring you around." Darius spoke precisely and somewhat proudly, concealing his nervous disposition behind a deliberately calm mien.

"I didn't know you studied music. Are you learning to play an instrument?"

"Yes, I am taking lessons in the trumpet."

"A trumpet?" It was certainly not the typical instrument in this region.

"I wish to learn to play, for my own amusement."

"Several of you might learn to play together, in an ensemble."

"That is what I hope. It would be something pleasant to do. Here in Tabriz it is necessary to think of interesting things to do."

We elbowed our way through the all-male stream of evening strollers who plied their way up and down Pahlavi Avenue, purling their strings of beads, laughing and conversing with friends, going to the cinemas, shopping in the lantern-lit stalls, stopping in teahouses for refreshment or to smoke narghilas, the Laocoön waterpipes. Darius paused, touched my arm, and pointed to a wooden sign above our heads. I saw in English "Mr. Ivor" and underneath, Pharsi characters, and also the block-lettered squareness of "Mr. Ivor" in Russian.

"Your teacher is a Russian?" I asked. "This is his music studio?"

He nodded gravely. "Would you care to go up?"

"Why not?" I said, parodying one of my students' favorite slang phrases, which they used in place of a simple "yes."

Abbas, with his droopy Chinese moustache, was with us—also, Ruben and Karim. We hauled ourselves up the steep stairs. Steps in Tabriz were normally twice the height I'd been used to, and going up a flight was like climbing a cliff. We arrived puffing at the top and found ourselves in a dim corridor of music studios and professional chambers. I saw a portrait painter at work at the end of the hall, in a tiny open room under a naked lightbulb. Darius, quite excited, stopped before the first door and knocked. *"Salaam. Entrez,"* came a gruff, muffled voice.

Heavy shrouds hung over many Tabriz doors and windows in winter, to prevent drafts and conserve heat. Once past the drapes, we found ourselves in a spare, high-ceilinged room with a lantern and reflector on the wall. The music teacher was introduced to me as "Mr. Ivor," though this was admittedly not his last name. His patronymic was so difficult to pronounce and so hard to remember that he was chiefly known simply as Mr. Ivor.

The Russian nodded uncomfortably, bowed, and tried to smile. He had a thick Slavic face, heavy black eyebrows over deep-set eyes, and wore a dark blue felt hat low upon his forehead. He was tall and thickly built and his rather sluggish appearance was further heightened by the tight black topcoat he wore over his suit. His shirt was not clean and his tie was frayed. It was cold enough in the room to warrant hat and coat, and none of us took his off. I noticed a small petrol-burning stove in the corner, the thumbscrew set so parsimoniously that the silver drop of liquid fell only once in a while. Mr. Ivor was undoubtedly a very poor man.

The first problem was language; Darius realized that I did not know Russian. He told me that Mr. Ivor had no English and only a smattering of French. I said I thought French would be best for us and we exchanged a few pleasantries, Ivor's accent as bad as mine. I should have been able by this time to conduct a conversation in Turki, but I had made limited progress, trying instead to improve my French and learn some Pharsi. I was surprised when Darius said that Ivor would not speak Pharsi. Darius smiled enigmatically, as if he too thought this very strange. His voice firm but gentle, he grasped Mr. Ivor's hand and reached for my right. "You two should be friends," he said.

Abbas, Ruben and Karim grinned and murmured their approval. Yes, the American and the Russian should be friends; it would be good for the whole world if they were. Darius, by holding our hands, seemed to be joining global adversaries and reducing international politics to a simple matter of Persian diplomacy. His esteemed teacher, Mr. Ivor, Darius assured me in English, was a fine gentleman and a cultured person, one who liked music especially. He had learned that I had a phonograph from America with many fine records, which I had played for people. Would I now show Mr. Ivor the honor of allowing him to trespass on my good nature and trouble myself to invite him to my home for a sampling of this music?

Of course, I replied. Any time at all. When this was relayed to Mr. Ivor he broke out in a gold-toothed smile, grasped my hand, and pumped it vigorously. Then he apologized in Turki because he did not have tea ready to serve us. He would be happy to send out to a *chai-khane* for some glasses at once, if we would only please make ourselves comfortable. Darius translated and I responded with appropriate compliments.

It was embarrassingly impossible to "make ourselves comfortable," there was just one chair in front of a music stand; the only other furniture was a table laden with instrument cases and sheet music. We all simply bowed and repeated the courteous words one learns to murmur in Iran on such occasions. Many foreigners were affronted by Iranian flattery and overly gushy remarks, but I recognized, as on this occasion, the usefulness of social patterns which could be employed to grace over what might otherwise have been an awkward situation.

After a number of inquiries about his work, his pupils and his health, I invited Mr. Ivor and all of them to my house. As we walked along the *koutche* Darius proudly turned to Mr. Ivor on his left and me on his right, as if he sought to show us off to the world. Abbas and the others seemed inordinately amused and also somewhat amazed. Passers-by turned their heads, startled. Mr. Ivor peered at me around Darius and began asking questions in rusty French: how long I'd been here, from what city in America I had come, and whether or not there was an opera company there. He loved the opera, but in Tabriz there was nothing. Did I know the work of Verdi, Moussorgski, Donizetti? We conversed in pidgin French. He would name an opera and I would supply the name of the composer; then we would oh and ah and smile and nod as we mentally recalled some of the arias.

Darius was one of my rare students who seemed to truly enjoy European music, who listened and understood; he was very proud now, for unlike his friends, he grasped the significance of the bond between music lovers and had in fact anticipated this development. My other student friends usually listened politely to music from my phonograph, but confessed it would take some time to develop a taste for Bach, Beethoven and Mozart. Did I not find it difficult to understand the beauty of Iranian music? I did indeed. Upon hearing my Vivaldi record, one first-year student turned to the phonograph in amazement, then hastily covered his ears, an expression of pain creasing his forehead.

I had gone to considerable trouble providing myself with music in Tabriz and had deprived myself of other things, in order to ship a phonograph on my weight-allotment. In New York before leaving I had pondered a long time in Sam Goody's record department, trying to imagine the privations of my stay in Azerbaijan and which pieces of music would be the greatest comfort. I guessed that the systematic clarity of such composers as Bach, Mozart and Vivaldi would be the best antidotes to possible excesses of Orientalism in my life. But with the different electrical voltage in Tabriz, the r.p.m.'s underwent a change and Bach came out sounding like any wailing Persian music from a transmitter in Teheran until I took the machine apart and adjusted the speed of the turntable. Luckily, since I lived in the center of the city, I had fairly steady current; in other households lights would dim frequently, as if the power station were undergoing the effects of a thunderstorm.

Arriving at my house, we kicked off our shoes on the Turkey carpet in the foyer, and I started up the phonograph; Mr. Ivor was immediately mesmerized by the music. He drew his chair close to the speaker, and without removing his hat (though he took off his overcoat) he sat and listened. I got the water boiling in the kitchen and prepared a pot of tea, while the students chatted among themselves and ate nuts. Mr. Ivor paid no attention to any of them; he listened with complete absorption to Heifetz playing Beethoven's violin concerto. He was utterly still and oblivious to everything but the music. He ignored me when I offered a cup of tea. Abbas and Ruben nodded at each other and began to snicker about Mr. Ivor's queer behavior. But when they saw tears running down his cheeks, they were immediately sobered, for Persians are always in awe and fully reverent before any show of emotion.

When the record had to be turned over, I pushed the teacup toward him again. *"Chai?"*

He took it and gulped the brew gratefully, but his fingers trembled, and all of us could see that he was still caught up in his feelings. Darius, I noted, had a wise look on his face as he watched us both.

"Permettez-moi, s'il vous plaît," I said, reaching out and almost touching the brim of his hat, *"votre chapeau ..."*

But he jerked his head away, neck and cheeks flushing, eyes sullen and suspicious. *"Nyet, nyet."*

"What's the word for hat in Turki, Darius?" I thought Ivor had misunderstood.

"I do not think he will remove his hat," said Darius. "He never does."

"Why not?"

Darius shrugged. Immediately a cacaphony of Turki arose from the students as they began urging Ivor to uncover his head. Their behavior toward him was a curious blend of ridicule and respect. I felt that they would pursue their scorn until a gesture from him would put them in their proper student places once again. He was, after all, an older man in his forties whereas they were young upstarts; but Ivor ignored their gibes.

"It is not proper to wear a hat in the house, is it, sir?" asked Ruben.

"Never mind. Let's go on with this Beethoven."

When the music started again, Ivor drew up his chair to within two feet of the speaker and sat there, hunched over, like his Master's Voice. The others—except for Darius who also listened closely—were bored and began to ask me questions or talked among themselves. When the Heifetz was over I put on Maria Callas singing arias from *Norma*. Her voice seemed to leap out of the speaker and strike Ivor between the eyes. He was so visibly shaken when it was over that he staggered getting up. He had forgotten in which direction the door was. He could only bow repeatedly to me, grasping my hand, and say over and over again, *"Merci, merci, merci!"*

He spoke further to Darius in Turki and this was relayed to me. "Mr. Ivor says he is very, very grateful for this wonderful evening, and if it would not trouble you too much, he would like to come again."

"Tell him I enjoyed having him, and we must do it again soon."

Shortly afterward, everyone left, the students in formation behind Mr. Ivor. They walked down the steps into the garden as if they were small birds harrying a clumsy crow.

Next day after class when I saw Darius alone, I asked for particulars about Ivor. Aside from being a violin and trumpet teacher, just who was he and how did he come to live in this city? Did he have a family here? Was he an Iranian citizen? Why did he refuse to speak Pharsi?"

"Ah, it is a very interesting story," began Darius, his beautiful white teeth flashing, "a very tragic story, however. You see, it happened like this: the Russians came into Azerbaijan one morning. I was just a little lad, but we awoke to a noise like thunder. There were tanks and big guns on wheels going through the streets, a red star painted on every one of them. 'It is the Russians,' my father said. 'We shall all be killed.' But we were not, and the Russians stayed here for several years. That was the time of People's Democracy. They also started the Faculty of Letters and made some paved streets; but other than this, I do not think they accomplished much because the people hated them. We lived under fear, always, and the soldiers, it was said, were very cruel. We were sorry the Americans had not come up from Khorramshahr. When the war was over, the Communists would not go until the United Nations made them get out. Therefore, we in Tabriz believe in the United Nations.

"Well, it so happened that Mr. Ivor was a soldier here in the Russian army, but when it was time they must go, he hid and was left behind. It is said he was in love with a woman—a bad woman—and he did not want to leave her. They did not marry, but he lived on the street where women of that kind are, you know, behind the Hotel Metropole. I do not know if there is truth to this story, for of course I was not old enough to know him then. Some people say he was in love with a good woman but for some reason they could not marry. In any case, he cannot go back to Russia. He is now an Iranian citizen, but he refuses to learn the Persian language. He's very stubborn. He is Russian."

"So he's an exile here."

"Of course he has friends, but perhaps no girl friends anymore. I do not know. He speaks Turki because that is what he always spoke where he grew up, in Russian Azerbaijan. Music means a very great thing to him. You were kind to let him come and listen to your phonograph. He would certainly like to come and hear more of your records."

"Bring him again."

"I shall see to it. Would tonight be suitable?"

"Tonight? You mean now? Well, I suppose so." I was not sure I wished a routine to develop; if he expected music sessions every night of the week, it would be difficult to stop once he took them for granted.

But I agreed, and Ivor came, as well as Darius and his friends. Abbas, Ruben and Karim drank tea, ate pistachio and almond nuts, and talked, while Ivor absorbed himself in the music. This evening, too, he refused to remove his hat. The students began making remarks about his gross behavior, which I was sure Ivor overheard, though he pretended to ignore them. Finally I told

115

them to stop bothering the man about his hat; if he wished to keep it on, let him.

The following Sunday while out walking, I paused to study the display on a movie marquee of a Fred Astaire film which had just arrived. *"Bon jour. Bon jour, Monsieur,"* said Ivor, coming up behind me, bowing and smiling. He thought the cinema attraction looked very good. Would I not join him?

I begged off, but Ivor found my reluctance incomprehensible. He was very lively and genial, quite different from the person I'd known before. Here was an American film in technicolor, he argued, filled with pretty dancing girls. *"Toutes les jolies jambes!"* he winked, pointing to the advertisement. I was astounded by his different manner, his engaging, suddenly free, behavior. The truth of it was, I had a tentative appointment in about an hour, but my French was inadequate to explain the matter fully—or he refused to understand me. Taking me by the elbow, he urged me into the lobby, where he bought two loge tickets, the most expensive in the house. We found our reserved seats in the very last row. I wondered if he had arranged for this particular spot because here he could keep on his hat. I noticed, however, that many other men in the audience continued wearing their hats, as this was the custom in public places. Perhaps, I reasoned, there was nothing extraordinary about Ivor's hat behavior, after all.

At the beginning of the show, the Shah's picture flashed on the screen, accompanied by the militant national anthem. I stood up immediately, along with the audience, as if there were bayonets at our backs. But Ivor refused to budge. I urged him to rise, but he kissed the air in that inimitable way, which meant "No, damn it!"

Noisily, the crowd settled down in their seats and the Fred Astaire picture began. Before my eyes I saw a New York never-never land in glorious color, a paradise city of dazzlingly beautiful buildings, happy, well-dressed people, pretty girls; music and bird-song filled the air. Ivor nudged me and pointed to the audience on a level below us: it was indeed disgusting to see all these men *sans les femmes*. What ignorant, contemptible people they were, what a stupid lot, to come here to the cinema and eat away

116

(here his hand motions substituted for the missing French words), while the women were left home behind doors, veiled in *chedurs*. He obviously wanted me to join in denouncing them all; but at that point Fred Astaire made his appearance, speaking a dubbed in, mellifluous Pharsi, and we turned to watch.

Now and then I asked Ivor to explain what was happening (only once during the film was there any possible doubt), in order to show my interest in the entertainment. Usually he would shrug his shoulders, spread his hands, and confess that *he* didn't know what the figures on the screen were saying. The Persian language he did not know and didn't care to understand. What gave him pleasure was the dancing, the music and the girls. Was it all not wonderful? And when Fred Astaire danced around on top of the Washington Square Arch, Ivor was blissful. The grace, the daring! Fred Astaire was surely one of the world's best circus acrobats. In Russia there were many delightful circuses; he was confident that in America there were circuses too, and that was how Fred Astaire received his training.

When the film was over we strolled along Pahlavi Avenue slowly, Ivor's arm linked in mine in the customary way. I knew by now that it was too late for my previous engagement, so I did not break away. Repeatedly Ivor bowed to acquaintances ambling by; it was the evening hour for men to take walks with their friends, up and down Pahlavi and Shahnaz streets. I sensed that Ivor was not only proud to be seen in public with me but this was a coup of some sort. Indeed, inhabitants of Tabriz rarely witnessed a meeting of Russians and Americans. Officials of the U.S.S.R. board of trade in Tabriz, whose positions roughly correlated with those of the U.S. consulate staff, did not mix with Americans at official functions or social gatherings. It was a ruling made by the Americans and observed faithfully by their Azerbaijani hosts. One American, Roger Thompson, explained the chill to me this way: complete severance of social relationships was the only proper and honorable course for Americans to follow, since the Soviet men in the city were "only spies, here to keep an eye on what's happening. They're in close contact with the Kremlin." (As if he himself were not in direct communication with Washington.)

We stopped in a shop where an artisan was mending one of Ivor's violins. While we waited I asked my host how many students he had. He replied: three violin pupils, two accordion, one mandolin, one *santor,* two harmonica, and one trumpet. Darius was the only trumpet student, I asked? And he nodded. It seemed a very feeble accounting of a man's daily labor, for how could he make a living from the fees these poor students paid him? Had he no other occupation I asked? No, he gave lessons, that was all.

I pondered as we waited there in the dusky shop, the lamp light gleaming richly on the polished woods of the music instruments. Ivor with his hat low on his brow began to look rather sinister to me. Could it be, I wondered, that his being "left behind" in the arms of a mistress was merely a clever Russian way of planting an informer? His real funds for living might very well come from the U.S.S.R. As an inconspicuous music teacher, he would be in an ideal position to keep in close touch with local political developments, especially since it was among university students that rebellions in this part of the world so frequently began.

Ivor wanted to stop in a *chai-khane* where a ballad singer was entertaining with renditions of Firdousi's *Shah-Noma,* but I felt I ought to be getting home. I thanked him for the afternoon and bid him farewell with a hearty handshake. Just as I was turning away I said the only Russian I knew, *"Dost-devanya,"* "goodbye," which had been taught me by the Russian-born messenger boy of the U.S. consulate.

A look of alarm crossed Ivor's face. He turned to me abruptly and put his head close to mine. There was not a trace of the phlegmatic Slav in his manner as he gripped my elbow. *"Nyet, nyet. Dos vidanya. Dos vidanya!"*

I repeated his correct pronunciation, but he did not smile. He was terribly alert, trying to catch whatever implications might be forthcoming. We stood there, the echo of this word passing around us. Those peering black eyes of his seemed to be asking, who are you anyhow? What are you up to? I wondered the same of him.

Once started with suspicions of international intrigue, my imagination was aided by movie memories of "The Orient Express" and "The Third Man," as well as countless spy novels. Tabriz was obviously the proper setting. Was Ivor the likely villain? Quite aware of my tendency to whip up an atmosphere of suspense far beyond what the realities of the situation suggested, I was nevertheless astonished a few days later when Madame Lydia of the Faculty of Letters, the Russian teacher, for the first time made friendly overtures toward me. In the faculty room we chatted amiably in French, whereas previously she had given me only hostile glances and had ignored my presence as much as possible. Of course, it was highly unlikely that Madame Lydia, though of Russian birth, was a Soviet spy; given the rigorous communist-hunting activities of the Savak, the secret police, a teacher of Russian would have to be especially circumspect. And yet, there was no denying, Madame Lydia had never before been so cordial.

Several times in succeeding weeks Darius brought Ivor to my house, and record by record we listened to my whole collection. The tiresome controversy about whether or not he would take off his hat was always introduced by one of the other students present, and it was a source of amusement to them. Darius did not approve of their ridicule, but I felt his attitude was also somewhat inscrutable. He may have been putting Ivor and me together in order to watch possible fireworks, once the music stopped. Ivor never removed his hat.

Then for weeks in the middle of winter I did not see Ivor nor did Darius mention him or bring him round for a session of record-playing. When I finally asked Darius about this, he replied: "Oh, he does not wish to trouble you."

"It wasn't much trouble. I guess I don't have any new pieces for him to hear."

"One can listen to the same music many times and never tire of it."

"True. And are you still taking trumpet lessons from him?"

"Of course."

"Could it be that Mr. Ivor got tired of the way he was always mocked for keeping his hat on, in the house?"

"That might be. I do not know."

"Is there some reason why he refuses to remove his hat? Is he bald and ashamed of it?"

"I do not think it is quite that."

"Do you have any idea?"

Darius thought for a moment, but not about possible motives; rather, he seemed to be considering whether or not he should disclose his special knowledge of the case to me. Finally, confidentially, he began: "I believe Mr. Ivor is a very proud man, and he does not want anyone to know that he has the sickness."

"Sickness?"

"The sores, the sickness on his head, in his hair. You have seen it, have you not?"

I nodded. In the schools, on the streets, I had looked on countless festering, wormy scalps, saw bald spots on close-cropped skulls, scabs and scales on many shaven heads. "He should not keep the disease covered up, if that's what it is. He should go to a doctor and have it taken care of. What's the matter with him, anyhow? I thought he had some intelligence."

"I do not know for sure it is the sickness on his head, but that is what I have heard. That is what people say."

"I don't understand. Why doesn't he go to a doctor?"

"Mr. Ivor, he is a very proud man. It hurts him to have this disease. He is ashamed."

All of Ivor's small arrogances, the things he said to me in the cinema, his contempt for his neighbors—how degrading for him, who considered himself a European, to fall ill with one of *their* diseases! Though Russian by birth and training, he was doomed to live out his life among these people he considered inferior and uncultured. How could he ever admit that he partook of their diseases, that he had succumbed in such an intimate manner to their way of life?

9 HOUSE OF STRENGTH

MY CATEGORIZING student friends liked to point out that England's national sport was soccer, France's racing, Spain's bullfighting, America's baseball, and Iran's wrestling. One Thursday evening a local physician, house doctor for the event, brought me to the semifinal wrestling matches for Azerbaijan *Ostan* (province) in the annual competition. The winners of the bouts, which were held in the *Golistan* sports' building, a field-house in the middle of the Tabriz city park, would go to Teheran for the contest to determine which athletes would represent Iran in tournaments with Pakistan, Russia, Japan, and other countries.

My host, whom I shall call Dr. Faroosh, was a tall, beak-nosed opportunist who had come to my house to attend a tea given for Tabriz teachers of English; before I realized that he was not an educator, he had firmly established himself, wife, brother, and several cousins as regular visitors to our sessions of English conversation, much to the annoyance of the teachers. Soon to depart for Europe to intern at a Danish hospital, he was anxious to perfect the little English he knew, since he had studied no other foreign language. Not a sportsman himself, he was an avid spectator, and from the time of his youth had followed statistics of wrestlers' wins and losses, their weights and their monetary fortunes.

The spacious field-house contained bleachers on three sides; the customers streamed through a side door, paying a couple of rials to the gatekeeper and scrambling up to perches on the boards. Although there was no heat in the building, the seven hundred men and boys who assembled soon produced a permeating body warmth heavy with odors of garlic and sweat. The patrons were of the laboring class, males of all ages, most of them in dark, shabby suits; the keenest followers of the sport were boys in their teens.

After the bright lights over the mat area had been turned on, Dr. Faroosh and I walked somewhat ceremoniously to a bench on the sidelines, directly opposite the judges' table. Looking up, I noticed a small room set above the bleachers, with windows partially painted over but with a long transparent expanse, where secluded observers could take in the scene below. Gentlemen of importance, generals, government officials—perhaps the Governor-General himself—could come here to watch the wrestling without having to mingle with the steamy, smelly mob that filled the gymnasium.

Tall chromium poles with green, white and red lights affixed to the top were on three sides of the mat. The judges, seated at tables on the dais, had switch-panels before them which they used to signal shifts in the rounds of the match and, later, to announce the winner. Since the national colors of Iran were green and red, one contestant wore a green ribbon, the other a red, tied to the left ankle. At the start of the first match, the wrestlers came out of their corners and after shaking hands grappled standing up for six minutes. Points of advantage were duly noted by the judges, then a white light bulb flashed, a bell rang. The referee walked over to the judges' table and took from them a small metal disc painted red on one side, green on the other. He flipped it high in the air, and it landed with the red showing; this meant that the green opponent would have to be "under" for the next three minutes. Then he would have his chance on top, for three minutes.

The four judges scrutinized the proceedings very closely, now and then jotting down notes. During the last three minutes the wrestlers again stood up and encountered each other, at the end of which time they marched in a soldierly fashion to a spot before the judges' stand. They untied their ribbons and slung them over their right shoulders; the referee stood behind them, body at attention and eyes up, looking at the light bulbs which would announce the judges' decision.

The contestants were the last to know. A roar went up from the audience; the referee snatched the ribbon from the shoulder of the winner. The athletes turned to confront each other, the loser to grasp the proffered hand of the victor. At this point there was a mutual movement toward an embrace, but the announcer, who sat at the judges' table, sternly admonished them over the loudspeaker: "Do not kiss! Please do not kiss!"

Kissing between men, Dr. Faroosh explained, was not an admirable custom; it just wasn't good. Of course, it meant nothing when wrestlers kissed, other than an affectionate concern, a friendly gesture, but when these contestants became national champions and traveled to other countries, their kissing was misunderstood; wrestling audiences might laugh and ridicule them. And so a new ruling was to be enforced: athletes were not to kiss. "Many of the wrestlers do not like the rule. They do not want officials to say what they should do or must not do. You see, it is for the spectators this rule is made. Men should not kiss each other, they should kiss their wives."

As the next match was prepared for, with the contestants dancing in their corners and kneading their muscles, Dr. Faroosh explained to me that there were eight divisions of competition, according to weight; we would progress from the flyweights to the heavyweights. At the end, with the big men, I would see some wrestling! We were now in a medium-weight category; one man was a taxicab driver, the other an army sergeant. The wrestlers of Tabriz were exceedingly loyal to one another; they formed an elite group among the commoners of the city and enjoyed special privileges accorded them by a grateful following. "In their lives wrestling becomes the main thing. These athletes, they are like a profession—they wish fame and money, and the people who are weaklings, who will never be strong, look up to the famous wrestlers and love them."

The cab driver and sergeant were dressed in wool caveman-type loincloths, one strap over their left shoulders. Under this garment they wore boxer shorts of the kind frequently seen on the local market, rather billowy blue and grey striped or flowered trunks. The contestants had just begun to lock their heads like stags in combat when a drunk in the grandstands began to shout and lunge about at various people. One frequently saw sleepy-eyed dope addicts, but drunks on the streets of Tabriz were less common, the rules of Islam still holding sway, and the present outburst in the bleachers caused a sensation. Several indignant spectators tried to throw the man out of the auditorium; a general free-for-all began, everyone shouting, whistling, laughing, and joining in. The poor wrestlers, heaving and straining in battle, glanced wild-eyed over their shoulders. No one paid any attention to them. The contest proceeded according to the duly set time pattern as the melee in the corner grew louder and louder. The drunk was at last shoved outdoors by a band of police who had arrived. Dr. Faroosh shook his head and looked at me, a half-apologetic smile on his face. By this time a large portion of the audience had streamed outside to watch the drunken man in his ravings.

When the wrestling match was over, only a handful of people were on hand to applaud the victor. I could tell that curiosity was consuming Dr. Faroosh; he wanted to go outside, too, but being an official, couldn't. "You get up, if you wish," he said. "Perhaps there will be an injury. Then you must tell. I would come to help."

I'd just stood up when a throng of men began pouring through the small door. They were in stampede-haste to return to their seats, and once they were all in again, I saw why: a larger force of police had turned upon the mob and was even now driving the last stragglers back inside the auditorium.

In a boisterous mood, the crowd began shouting for the wrestling to continue. Two athletes stepped forward, entering the padded arena. "Ahmad! Ahmad!" the audience shouted, hooting and catcalling. An enormous, mushroom-headed fellow in a green moth-eaten loincloth raised his hand and acknowledged their tribute. "Ahmad! Ahmad!" the cries became louder.

"Is he the champion?" I asked.

"No, no, he is poof! Like wind—oh, so big, but that is the trouble. His name is not Ahmad."

"Why do they call him that?"

"You did not see the film at the cinema? Not long ago, perhaps last week, there was a film about a big, big man, a—how do you say?"

124

"Giant?"

"That is right! A giant named Ahmad. He was so strong he could crush the little people."

The loudspeaker urged the crowd to quiet down, but this only roused them to greater frenzy. "Ahmad! Ahmad! Ahmad!"

The match started, and as the big man lumbered forward, reaching for his adversary, a roar went up from the crowd. Their Ahmad was clearly a half-wit; for all his massiveness, there was the inert, fleshy quality about him of the glandularly overdeveloped. At the end of the first six minutes, when it was obvious to everyone, even the fool himself, that he would lose, his opponent (a swarthy, lithe young man with glistening-coal eyes and a flashing, white-toothed smile) reached out and hugged the giant, kissing him on both cheeks.

Angrily the loudspeaker chanted: "No kissing. No kissing. You must not kiss." Further admonitions were lost in the deafening clatter and shouting from the crowd.

The red and green disc was flipped, and the next phase of the match got underway; Ahmad lost the spin and he was "under." The tumult from the bleachers grew steadily worse; Ahmad was becoming so upset that he lay back upon the mat, shaking his head and muttering. He was giving up the match. The referee called a halt; the giant wandered off, forgetting the ritual before the judge's stand. The referee urged the swarthy victor to untie his ribbon and place it on his shoulder, so that it could be snatched away. This was done; the winner's hand was raised. Then both men went off quickly to find Ahmad, who by this time was confusedly wandering among the benches behind us, tears streaming down his cheeks. The stomping of feet, the shrieks and hoots, made a bedlam of the field-house. The black-haired, victorious wrestler threw his arms around the giant and began kissing him heartily, all over his face. The audience thoroughly approved, and the simpleton's face broke out in a smile. Obviously winning the match was not so much his concern as being reassured that he was liked by everyone. He threw his arms in the air and acknowledged the applause; then he looked around to return the embrace of his benefactor, who had already gone. The loudspeaker warned, solemnly: "Do not kiss. Please, do not kiss."

"This is a very strange wrestling match," I told Dr. Faroosh.

"You do not like?"

"Oh, no, I wouldn't have missed it."

"Tonight, these things—it is not always so—not this way. You must come again sometime, when the crowd is more serious."

The next bout proved to be a superb demonstration of Iranian wrestling and Dr. Faroosh kept turning to see if I noticed the adroit way the offensive and defensive maneuvers were employed. "They are national champions. Can you see?"

I nodded, but although I had one of the best seats in the house, their tactics were executed so swiftly that it was hard to catch what was happening until it was already over. "Wrestling is only partly with the body. It is mental skill, it is wit that is needed!" He tapped his head. "You see, they are equally strong. Nothing would be done by force alone. The best wrestlers are also the smartest."

The wrestlers were locked in their struggle, with every thrust meeting a parry, every tense contortion matched by a muscular lever that counteracted it, and I felt I was watching a single organism possessed by a conflict with itself. The audience was hushed, gripped by the drama. And at last, when the ribbon was snatched from the victor's shoulder, it was the loser, for his valiant struggle, who got the greater applause: the defeated had also triumphed because the test he had posed made the winner that much stronger for future matches.

And then we had another odd bout. Two rather inexperienced wrestlers were pitted against each other, and when a murmur went up from the audience, Dr. Faroosh explained that everyone realized the bad luck of these two friends. Neither wished to have his status changed at the expense of lowering the record of the other. Here for the first time in their careers they were seeded together and now, surely neither wanted to win. "This will be interesting," said Dr. Faroosh. "*Very* interesting. You watch."

I did, but there wasn't much to see. Most of the time was spent in a kind of limp sparring. The body holds lacked conviction; the hammer locks became bear hugs. The audience was deeply touched; here was friendship locked inextricably with fate. Although one of the wrestlers was finally declared the victor, it was almost by default; with the match over, they shook hands warmly and walked off laughing, as if it had all been a lark.

The last event, involving two heavyweights who had been national champions in previous years, got underway with a promising clash of sinewy arms and beefy hands; both men were well over two hundred pounds and impressively developed. Dr. Faroosh told me that they had wrestled on Iranian teams in Russia and Pakistan; they had been in training together in Teheran; they were good friends, magnificent fighters. They set about racking up points in a thoroughly professional way, at least during the first six minutes. As the match proceeded, however, I noticed a curious absence of aggression; it was finally not even simulated. "They are about even, I think," said Faroosh. "It is wonderful. Look how he locked his leg there. See? Now watch him turn." The red-ribboned champion clearly had his way with his opponent "under" him; they reversed positions. The green-ribboned athlete seemed not quite as adroit in his offense as his friend had been. They reached a stalemate. Then a curious thing happened: the red-ribboned wrestler, whose right hand was free, though the rest of him was thoroughly rigid in combat, reached up painfully from his position under the green-ribboned wrestler and slowly adjusted the knee-band of his adversary, so that it fitted neatly over the kneecap. Then he tried to do the same for the other knee—the pad having gone awry there, too—but he didn't succeed. Ungrateful Green, sensing his advantage, quickly shifted positions, thoroughly pinning his adversary, and the referee threw up his hands; lights flashed on. The match was over, one wrestler having "given" it to the other. The applause was enormous.

"Magnificent! Did you see that? Did you notice?" asked Dr. Faroosh. "What heartbreak for those two! That is the trouble with sport contests. Someone must lose—yes?"

In photography shopwindows of Tabriz I sometimes saw portraits of Iranian men which showed a three-quarter view of the face, with a cartoon-blob just behind the ear—a little explosion of space—in which was set a miniature snapshot of the man in gymnastic trunks, his biceps flexed. I always fancied I was looking at someone contemplating an idealized image of himself; and in a way, I wasn't wrong. Body-building, weight-lifting and physical culture enhanced the Persian male's natural narcissism, allowing him to preen over his physique, or hold "in his mind's eye" a photographic impression of himself as Hercules.

One evening in the company of a British physician, a lecturer at the medical college, and his pupil Behrooz, I visited a *zur-khane,* a house of strength, in my neighborhood. "We are just in time," said Behrooz, a pale-faced, almond-eyed intellectual, no proud specimen of a former house-of-strength devotee. "When young I used to come here often, for I was sickly. But now I am too busy." Actually, I already knew that students considered the *zur-khane* a typical example of the lamentable rites and customs of the centuries, hung like an albatross around the neck of Iran, hindering the country's development, its movement into modern times. Most university students would have nothing to do with these quaint ways. For months my pupils kept protesting that no thing so old fashioned as a *zur-khane* existed in Tabriz.

We descended a series of cobble steps to a second basement, where we entered a dome-shaped room with a skylight high above, as if we had come upon the apse of a buried cathedral. Behrooz was our forerunner, our magic messenger, whose open-sesame was necessary before we could trespass in this private, ancient, Persian male club. In the wooden-floor pit, set four feet below the circle of benches which formed an arena, a few men were doing rhythmic exercises, swaying from their hips in unison, like reeds in a wind. Other young men were taking off their clothes in the rear and getting into their *zur-khane* costumes. Twilight filtered down from above; a few low-watt lightbulbs dangled in dim arches.

We were introduced to a burly athlete who took our hands in a fierce grip and pumped once, as if opening the latch of a heavy door. His bald, glistening head rose above his powerful body on a columnar neck; his ears were like baby feet. There were garlands of welcoming phrases: we were bestowing much honor and extreme pleasure upon his humble self by our mighty presence in this place, this scene of lowly but honest activity. Muttering the words rapidly in the Turki dialect, he bowed slightly as he spoke, his obsequious language in strong contrast to his sinister appearance. His beard was black with a four days' growth; his mouth glinted with gold-capped teeth; his breath reeked of garlic; and he fixed his glance upon one with a frank, fearless expression, as if it were his right by dint of his strength to examine anyone who came before him—and to toss the intruder away, if he failed to meet with approval.

Speaking gruffly to a boy behind him, he ordered glasses of tea to be brought from the *chai-khane* on the street. And now if we would please excuse him, the time had come for him to change clothes for the event. His company of men had arrived and were waiting for him. He put his arms around Behrooz affectionately, remarking that once Behrooz had come regularly to the *zur-khane,* but now alas he had forgotten his old friends. The medical student protested and affirmed his loyalty and devotion, pleading the difficulty of his studies, the hours of work at his books. "No, no," said our host with a genial laugh, "no longer do you remember us."

Behrooz, greatly touched by the reunion, showed us to our seats, promising that we would have a chance to talk further with the athlete after the performance.

"Are you sure it's all right we've come?" I asked, noticing that no other spectators were present. Just as mosques were not to be defiled by Christian feet and the baths were a place of prayer where only Moslems assembled to clean themselves spiritually and physically, so the *zur-khane* was not intended as an arena for amused, casual spectators. Except for the elaborate *zur-khane* of the Bank Melli in Teheran, which was a tourist spectacle, the ritual rhythmic dances were private.

"Do not trouble yourself with doubts," said Behrooz. "I only pray you will not be disappointed."

As we waited on a wooden bench above the pit, I noticed that every available space on the wall behind us was adorned with artifacts of the muscle cult. Mostly there were enlarged photographs of mustachioed athletes holding rigid, frieze poses, dressed in their ceremonial *zur-khane* uniforms. These were knee-length trousers of satin or silk, richly embroidered in peacock hues. Though most were naked to the waist, some wore leather harnesses with metallic clips and helmet headdresses, which gave them a Genghis Khan appearance. A rather dusty, used-looking, very old ceremonial costume hung on the wall, but obviously an athlete inside was necessary to make anything grand of it. Behrooz told me the official uniform was never worn here, nor did any of these men aspire to such finery. "They are too poor."

"Can anyone belong to this club?"

"Of course. The fee is only four rials [about five cents] each time, and almost anyone can pay that. It is not too dear."

"Could I belong, for instance?"

He laughed, assuming I was teasing him. "Yes, of course, but why would you? It is enough to see once, and I dare say that is all. These boys and men come every day, sometimes morning *and* night. You see, they have nothing better to do."

In a rear alcove containing weights, bar-bells, handsprings, and other gymnastic equipment, the club members were draping themselves in maroon and blue plaid towels called *longhes*. One often saw these yard-wide scarves drying in the sun on clotheslines, hanging like pennants outside *hammams,* the Persian bathhouse.

The drummer boy, aged about eight, sitting like a little tailor on a raised platform (he also collected the price of admission from each arrival), began warming up by giving the drumhead a few rat-a-tat-tats. His sticks were a couple of sheepshank bones, and the drum was hide, stretched taut over a wooden hoop, open at the end, so that he could lift the instrument up and bang it like a gong. With an impish pleasure in his power there on the throne above the ring, the boy pounded away, calling the performers into the pit. Most of the athletes were teenagers, some as young as twelve or thirteen, putative mustaches shadowing their upper lips. I also observed that the drummer boy had some sort of fire going under a pan set close beside him, and I assumed he was roasting pistachios over a bed of charcoal. Then I smelled a strong, pungent odor, clean in the nostrils, and realized that he was deodorizing the gym with aromatic weed seeds. The air had been rank as a goats' cave, and the acrid fumes now cleared away the stink.

The master of ceremonies, that bald-headed djin who had greeted us upon arrival, strode into the pit wearing his *longhe* tightly girded about his loins; he began doing kneebends as he walked, a broken-legged shuffle that he managed to make graceful. His yellowish-tan body, hairless, save for the muzzle of his jaw and thick eyebrows which projected like feelers, was armorially developed. He did not have to beat his breast and bellow at his herd of men; they accepted his superiority and formed a circle around him, imitating his slow, elegant kneebends.

The drumbeat now became the call of the dance, and as they began to bow from the waist, offering obeisance, dipping lower and lower until their foreheads nearly touched the floor, they were perfectly synchronized acolytes humbling themselves before the high priest. They rose, flinging out their arms like the unfolding of a bud, and as they began to undulate slowly, the design of the ensemble was that of the sunflower, ancient decorative motif of the Achaemenian kings and still to be seen in the ruins of Persepolis. And then, issuing out of the center of that pulsating flower, came a deep, anguished voice: the leader had begun his chant.

"What is he saying?" I whispered to Behrooz. Perspiration moistened our guide's brow, and he was transfixed, staring at the spectacle before us.

He turned slowly. "It is from the *Shah-Noma*. Do you know it?"

I nodded, having read an English translation of Firdousi's long epic poem of the deeds of the legendary kings of Persia. (Matthew Arnold's "Sohrab and Rustum" is based on the *Shah-Noma*.) "The lines," began Behrooz, "say things about bravery, about strength. You notice how they are moving, coming low to the earth—that is the way it has always been done in the *zurkhanes* of our land. Each generation teaches the next. And always they sing the *Shah-Noma* while they do it."

The athletes had now become a dance corps. They began to move in a circle, stepping backward, forward; they were chanting and half-singing the poetry, following the beat of the drum. At the end of this phase they fell forward on their hands, arching their backs like tigers about to spring; then they collapsed. The drummer paused while the men picked up hand bar bells, instruments which looked as if an iron bar had been squeezed so hard it had ballooned on each end. With these they began flailing the air, dancing back and forth to a new rhythm. Gradually a change came over the men, as if they drew upon the mysteries, receiving sustenance from the *Shah-Noma* ritual, which provided an authentic connection between themselves and the glorious days of the hero kings. Absorbed, caught in a filmy trance, their eyes were glazed over; they had lost their paltry, unrealized day-by-day existences and were alive at last.

"What are the words?" I whispered to Behrooz. The sing-song Pharsi was muffled, the emphasis distorting it.

He told me not to try to hear whole stanzas from Firdousi. Only certain phrases were picked out by the leader, just a few lines. Now they were repeating over and over again, "We are strong as lions, brave as bulls. Our children will be brave and strong. We are strong as lions, brave as bulls."

Possessed by their movements, a kind of revival-meeting euphoria filled the air. Now and then a young man would cry out to Allah with a sobbing wail; another would shout in painful bliss. Every calisthenic routine was pushed to the limit, and if a mood began to wear thin, if the men seemed weary or about to drop out, the leader would shout commandingly, drawing their attention to a new variation, which he executed for them to behold. Soon all would be doing the same maneuver, whether it involved a highland fling step demanding precarious balance or a flat-footed, primitive, African stomp-stomp. At one point they were grouped in a phalanx, swinging their heads and grinding their shoulders as they pawed the floor with their feet, like rams in the rutting season or bulls about to fight. Mythological creatures seized and transfigured them, and in one gallop around the ring they were centaurs on a romp, Sagittarius in the center, his arm an arrow.

During an interval when the spell had diminished, three performers picked up battle shields shaped like great flat-irons and manipulated them fore and aft like beating wings. They rolled on their backs on the floor, the shields hovering, waving back and forth, like the flutter of dying lunar moths. Again the drummer boy rattled out a command for the troops to resume their positions; huge Indian clubs were introduced, and the men worked them under their arms, flipped them in the air, turned them over their necks, and exchanged them with each other, under their legs and over their heads—miraculously avoiding collisions, never dropping them.

The performers frequently worked together in twos, perhaps paired off according to friendships; and often they engaged in mock combat. When they faced each other arms outstretched, feet wide, simulating a struggle, I was reminded of a favorite emblem of the Shah of Iran, taken from the stone jamb of a portal of the *apadana,* the great hall of the palace at Persepolis: the king, Xerxes, engaged in conflict with a winged lion on its hind feet; royal animal and royal man, destined for a partnership that could not end. Locked in their immortal embrace, man and beast seemed transfigured into dancing partners, and here in the *zur-khane* the dance of kings was re-enacted.

At last each man took the center for his solo, and with shouts of encouragement from his teammates, demonstrated his skill at a wild, improvised dance that consisted of high, arching leaps and ended with a whirling similar to the dervish's mystical spinning in order to attain union with Allah. Faster and faster the athlete would twirl, until he literally flung himself away like a gyrating top suddenly released, and his friends had to catch him or he would crash into the wall of the pit. It took a while for the athlete to recover, and not only physically; from the absent look on his face it was as if the essence of his being had been cast away, and now he must try again to collect himself, what was left of him. "Allah! Allah! Allah!" cried the performer in the ecstasy of his dance.

Then it was the leader's turn; surely, if he could not clearly outshine every one of them, he would have to relinquish his authority. He hauled out a greatly enlarged, mythological version of a hunter's bow. Shaped like an upper lip six feet long, it was solid as a steel beam and weighed a couple of hundred pounds. The leader's iron wrist upholding it was rigid as a girder. The "bow-string" had been strung with metallic chips and sharply notched pieces of left-over tin and copper, tightly packed together, the way red peppers were strung in necklaces across the apertures of vegetable shops. As he moved, the jagged discs, some the size of half dollars, spun on their axes, becoming the teeth of a saw. No arrow would spring from this deadly weapon, it was a hero-king's instrument of war; the danger was that a presumptuous would-be hero might not be up to its challenge—in which case he would be lacerated by the bowstring and crushed by the enormous weight of the bow.

Feet wide apart, he moved with a Neanderthal step; the bow was held horizontally above his body, the metal discs whirling ominously close to his bald head. Then he tilted back his face, and with increasing grace, manipulated the weapon as if his body were to become the arrow, as if he would string himself upon the metal rope and shoot out of the pit, soaring through the skylight of the house of strength.

Above the pounding beat of the drum and the chant of the men, his "Ugh! Ugh! Ugh!" accompanied each shift of the bow. He brought it abreast of his body; he held it parallel in front of him; but his favorite position was that of exultation, as it was pushed high in the air—high as he could reach—and in this position he danced the hardest. Around and around the circle he moved, as if the bow were made of balsa, the string gossamer, and finally he even leapt, shouting as his feet left the floor, bellowing when he landed.

Then he gathered strength for the final demonstration, the climax of his rejoiceful ordeal; he shifted arms, and I saw that he was going to show how close he dared come to wreaking destruction upon himself. His arm supporting the bow began to sway; the knife-edged teeth came nearer and nearer. With his face tipped back, he did not take his eyes from the flashing, rattling discs; he did not blink. Awed and entranced by their master's self-imposed test of courage, the troupe murmured a melodious prayer and swayed in their stances, as if fearing that a single break in their rhythm, seen out of the periphery of their leader's hypnotically staring eyes, might throw him off, cause him to lose the delicate muscle control he was exhibiting, and send the metal chips across his eyes, blinding him.

He quickened the pace of his dance about the pit, the metal pieces shaking over his ears like the warning sound of a rattlesnake. His arms moved up and down with the bow, a piston action, and the saw teeth swept closer to his black, gelid eyeballs;

134

his glare was as transfixed as if he were mesmerized. Up and down, up and down, and with each enlarged cycle the whirling metal plates came nearer his face. The danger of the dance was given voice in the drumbeat, throbbing with suspense; at last it could beat no longer, being merely expressive of the anxious heartstroke of mortals, and the leader was alone with the legendary rulers of ancient Media—and his own matchless courage. With a cry from the men, he raked the metal as close to his eyes as possible, then joyously lifted the bow high—shouting! The dance was over.

The men filed out of the arena, tired but exhilarated; already I saw a new group of *zur-khane* advocates with their leader descending the stairs and going into the far corner to put on their *longhes*. For many of them this was their mosque, and I learned from Behrooz that the mullahs condemned the houses of strength because they usurped the province of religion, even to the point of holding their pagan sessions at sunrise and sunset, when the muezzin call was sounding from the minarets.

Some of the athletes continued to exercise with weights in the rear of the room, patiently lifting the pendulous bars, as attentive to their muscular development as if they were nurturing plants in a garden. The bald-headed master, now in shirt, trousers, and felt hat (there were no showers) came over to our bench disconsolately. To our effusive compliments and words of thanks, he only glumly nodded. Did we get our tea, he wondered? Bah, it was cold. He would send the drummer boy for more.

We persuaded him not to, since we had to leave very shortly. There were a number of questions on our minds, however. How long, for instance, had he been a leader? What was his work, his occupation? When had he learned Firdousi? Were each day's sessions much alike, or did the program vary, according to the calendar, the weather, or some such thing?

Behrooz restated our queries in fluent Turki, but the athlete did not respond; he was like a great hulk becalmed in a glassy sea. I guessed his recessive mood was the natural antithesis to what he had just gone through and offered him a cigarette, which he accepted. Clasping my knee, he vowed that we should become fast friends. The British doctor, was he truly a physician,

135

a medical doctor? He wanted to be sure, for he knew that many university professors were called "doctor" but they were actually of little help to a sick man.

My friend explained that he was a dermatologist, a skin specialist; with this news the athlete looked more and more gloomy. He moved closer, his odor overwhelming, and bearing down on my thigh with his hand as he leaned over to speak to the doctor, pledged eternal friendship. He was unspeakably honored by our presence, and we must not leave him. I was feeling extremely uncomfortable and tried to edge further along the bench, suggesting to Behrooz that it was time for us to depart.

No, no, we must not go, our host insisted. He wanted to have a long, medical talk. With a forced, weak smile, he confessed to the doctor that he was in desperate need of advice. Why was it lately that bad dreams afflicted him, allowing him no rest? Could it be connected with his diet? That was what he had thought at first, but the dreams kept on, even though he had stopped eating onions and cucumbers. Now he was exhausted; he felt miserable, every day. What could be the matter? He looked down at his body as if it had become some foreign thing, exceedingly troublesome.

The doctor suggested he have a medical check-up, since it would be impossible to guess what might be wrong.

This answer only made him more insistent. I am not a young man any more, he said in Turki. Would you believe it, I am forty-eight years old?

We expressed our amazement.

Oh yes, he bragged, I am stronger than all these men put together. But lately—lately, these bad dreams come. I am tired all day long and eager to get to bed. And yet at night, no sleep.

The doctor said it might be merely overfatigue. How often did he perform at the *zur-khane,* putting himself through these strenuous exercises?

At dawn and sunset. Twice a day.

But if his body had to work this hard at the end of a full day's labor (he hauled carpets on his back in the bazaar), it was very likely that he was suffering from overfatigue. Only a thorough physical examination would tell, so why didn't he go to a doctor?

The athlete smiled a flash of gold. That was why he was so grateful we had come; now the doctor must diagnose the trouble. Surely it did not seem feasible that being overtired would prevent sleep. A man sleeps all the sounder, if he is tired. No, such a theory simply did not serve. He himself had another idea. Could it be that he was having intercourse with his wife too frequently? How often was permissible and when was it dangerous? How many times?

The doctor laughed, and we got up to leave.

But, insisted the athlete, at least you could say how many times I should sleep with my wife! Why do you not answer?

"For a healthy man, the frequency varies. It is not a matter of medical concern unless one is sick. If sick, a doctor should be seen at once."

The athlete sank back on the bench, shaking his head. Why do you not answer what I ask? The Koran says a man should visit his wife once every four days. But I . . . I have been more frequent than that. Is this bad? Should I stop? I tell you I cannot sleep. I am now forty-eight years old, and my woman, she is old, too. My children are grown and some are gone. I should perhaps behave like a man who is getting old, but I cannot. I am like a lion. I am strong as a bull.

He lifted his arms in a pose reminiscent of his performance in the pit and repeated the phrase from Firdousi: I am strong as a lion, brave as a bull.

10 THE WASTEFUL SAVERS

I LIVED on *koutche* Ark, in the home of German-born Mrs. Nadjmi. It was a whitewashed adobe building, formerly the Turkish consulate, set in a deep garden with a small pool in which geese swam; the French windows of my living room looked out upon unkempt beds of flowers, straggly fruit trees, and beyond the high mud walls I could see the ruins of the fourteenth century citadel, the Ark, which was shaped something like a barge (though Mt. Ararat was nearly one hundred and fifty miles away).

I was the first tenant. Mrs. Nadjmi, widow of a prominent physician, had been forced by financial straits to rent out half of her home only recently. Before the year was out she had also sold most of the garden, where a big modern house would be erected. Clearly she had fallen upon lean days. A wide veranda was located between the Nadjmi living quarters and mine; the exposure was south, and I frequently lunched there in the warmth of the winter sun. Even when snow lay deep on the ground, out of the wind at noon I could sit comfortably in T-shirt and shorts.

The nights in winter were sharply chill, and so were the sunless days. Both the living room and bedroom had small iron potburners, the intensity of the heat depending upon the frequency of the drip from the fuel cans connected to them. I bought "petrol" (actually kerosene) from Hassan in large red containers and spent much of my time during winter refilling the small tins affixed to the stoves, sending Hassan out for more fuel, paying him, and reviving a stove that had gone out. In the kitchen I cooked on the one functioning burner of a Coleman stove. Mrs.

Nadjmi installed a stone sink at my request, with one faucet. Water out of the tap was unsafe for drinking; I boiled up a supply now and then and stored it in empty whiskey bottles.

The living room was furnished with an oak dining table and chairs having padded seats of blue cotton plaid. A makeshift divan in one corner was actually a mattress on a wooden platform, with a pleated skirt, rag-stuffed bolsters, and blue cloth tacked on the wall behind it. I had a fine Empire-style desk, and I placed in the two French windows a couple of three foot high kerosene lamps with baroque trim, which the late Dr. Nadmji had picked up in Samarkand. White cotton curtains were swagged across the windows; red, blue, and white village carpets covered the floors.

A third window, to the south, gave out upon a roof, and in good weather I would climb out and sunbathe there. At other times cats of the town, who were always parading about on top of walls, respecting no privacy and heeding no barriers, would frequently pause at that window to gaze in at me. They were "Persian" cats, long-haired, yellow-eyed, and so powerful was their mysterious cat-presence, that even while working at my desk, back turned, I could tell when one of them had come to look.

My daily life involved a certain amount of exchange with Mrs. Nadjmi, for she was in charge of the servants, Hassan and his wife, and would direct them in tasks I requested. She was also the intermediary for the shopping list, which I would write out in German on a piece of paper. Hassan would take the slip to Mrs. Nadjmi, who would translate it into Turki; when he returned from market, she sometimes inspected his purchases to see if he'd gotten a good price. Usually I went for beef myself, to the only beef butcher in the city, located down a narrow dirty *koutche* which led toward the poorest, most backward section of the city. Since there was no refrigeration or aging of meat, butchering was done in the early morning, and the bloody wagons with the carcasses would wind through the streets like a cortege, from the packing plant to the butcher shops. The beef wagon was fly-encrusted and stained a rusty, purplish color. Little ragged boys, butchers' apprentices, bearing the usual pitiful afflictions of sores and scabs, their hands and clothes grimy, would industriously handle the critters, hauling them into the shop, where the proprietor would sling the beef onto meat hooks. I usually ordered a kilo of fillet, which cost about sixty cents, and often I'd have him grind it for me. The butcher and I had a falling out, however, because I insisted on having it ground twice to make it a little more tender. At first he grudgingly performed this task, but finally he became stubborn and would not. We had words. I did not go back, but sent Hassan. Gradually I came to rely more and more for meat on the canned goods shipped from Teheran, various fish, ham, bacon, Spam, and supplemented my diet with occasional orders of fresh mutton.

Mrs. Nadjmi was delighted to have the "Herr Professor" in her home, but I wondered if my presence were not also somewhat socially embarrassing, since it was a convincing sign to the world that she was poor. However, my rent provided her livelihood, enabling her to make much needed repairs, such as replacing the kitchen pipes; and she probably put savings in the bank. She was a shrewd Iranian in business dealings; at other times, a sweet little Freiburg widow in black, sad-eyed, trying to cope with a tempest of troubles.

I learned something about her background one afternoon when I entertained a group of English teachers. Among them was Ahad, a nephew of the late Dr. Nadjmi; he arrived as my other guests were leaving (I was told later that he had crashed the party, for he was not a teacher at all). When calling upon the Nadjmis, he had noticed Iranians sitting down to tea with me and decided to join them. Once we were alone, he told me that his uncle, Dr. Nadjmi, had gone to medical school in Germany, and there he had met a girl whom he wished to marry. He brought her back to Tabriz, where in the course of years he was successful in his medical practice and his wife bore him six children.

"Six children?" I asked, astonished. "But where are they?"

"Yes, there were six, I believe. Four sons and two daughters. All of them but Jaleh died."

"But what did they die from?"

"They were in childhood," he replied, as if it were a disease.

"How strange! I'd imagine a doctor, of all people, might have been able to save them."

Ahad said nothing further, gave no more details. The fact that children were always dying seemed no news that needed explanation. He was pleased to have so strongly engaged my curiosity, and his delight was almost childishly apparent. He had a clown-comic face, sad but also faintly risible. When he smiled the tip of his chin trembled as if he were about to cry. He had a pointed jaw and a funny carrot-shaped nose. "Do you see Jaleh, my cousin, Jaleh, do you see her very often?"

"Oh, now and then."

" 'Now and then,' that is very nice. Did you know that she is marrying?"

"No, I didn't."

"I believe it is now official. There was a big party, to tell it. I was invited, and this gave me much pleasure. I wish Jaleh married my brother. My older brother he is captain in the army. He loves Jaleh and wants to marry her, but she says no, it is not good to marry a cousin."

"He must be sad to hear she's marrying somebody else. Who *is* she marrying?"

"He is in medical school. You do not know him. His father is very rich."

"I see."

"My brother married someone else from a very good family."

"Oh? I understood you to say he was still in love with Jaleh."

"He may be, I do not know. I am in love with her, too. She is very beautiful, don't you think? I am glad she is my cousin because I can come to see her often, and no bad talk is said about it."

"Do you have other family members who visit the Nadjmis?"

"They are all in Mahabad, not here. My brother now has two children and he lives in Mahabad, too. Excuse me if my English is so poor. I cannot help it. I have very bad teachers. Mr. Fanshawe, the Englishman, he is the worst."

"I should think you could learn a lot from him."

"I cannot."

"He expects you to work and he is right. That is the only way to learn a language."

I poured fresh tea in our cups and Ahad continued: "Students all like me and laugh, even Mr. Fanshawe, though he failed me last year and I fear he will fail me again. He says I am 'blissful.' I know what that means. But I am not 'blissful.' Really, I am very sad." His chin trembled; he was on the brink of laughing or crying. "I told Mr. Fanshawe that what we were reading was too hard for us."

"Did he agree?"

"No!"

"I shouldn't think he would."

"I suggested other texts, easier things. But Mr. Fanshawe he scolded me. He says a teacher knows best, knows better than the student. He is that kind of man, he gets very angry."

"I think a teacher *does* know, better than the student."

"But you see, he is English. That is his language."

"It's mine, too."

"No, yours is American. It is different. We can understand that. But he is English, and he talks so fast. Oh, he is very stern and nobody likes him. Everyone is very unhappy. But you, sir, are not like him. Everyone loves you. May I come to your house again?"

"But since you're a relative of the Nadjmis, you must have been coming to this house frequently. How is it I haven't seen you before?"

"I do not know. Perhaps because I have not come around 'to knock you up.' That is the phrase, isn't it?"

I nodded. "You have learned more from Mr. Fanshawe than you think."

At a later time Mrs. Nadjmi told me that Ahad was indeed her nephew, and Jaleh affirmed that she was very fond of her cousin. But something in their manner suggested that they regarded him lightly, as a bit of a fool. He was not, however, stupid; and the day I first met him and we chatted in my living room, I sensed that he perceived how curious I was about the Nadjmis. He was only too happy to be the betrayer of family secrets. He told me all.

The doctor had died of a "bad stomach," a euphemism Ahad used for opium addiction. In the last stages there had been trips to Europe to try to bring about a cure, Dr. Nadjmi borrowing heavily from friends; when he died he had left his widow deeply in debt. She discovered that her chief creditor was a man who had been a life-long friend of her husband. But business was business and he could not forgive the debts. To help pay him off, Mrs. Nadjmi had sold much of the large garden. It so happened, Ahad informed me, that the boy Jaleh was to marry was the son of this man, and thus by entering the family, the Najmis' financial difficulties would finally be arrested.

But was Jaleh really willing to offer herself in sacrifice in what appeared to me to be a caliph and harem-girl situation?

"Oh, they are in love," Ahad assured me. "The boy is handsome and he is rich. He is going to be a doctor. Jaleh is pleased. After two years or more they will be married."

"Two years?"

"Not before."

I knew that Mrs. Nadjmi would miss her daughter, for they were constant companions. A few German friends living in Tabriz would come for coffee now and then, but the big reception room in the center of the house was only used for one party during my stay. Mother and daughter sequestered themselves in two or three simple rooms, and they sewed, hour after hour, working on Jaleh's trousseau. Occasionally, I heard a Brahms lullaby or other German lieder sung in duet, often in accompaniment with a record on the phonograph. Later in the year Jaleh's fiancé was frequently about, the duenna-like mother always present.

On Saturdays, according to our arrangement, the Nadjmi women visited my *hammam*—the bathroom—for which in exchange I could use their Kelvinator refrigerator in the china-decorated dining room, any time I wished. Significantly, Saturday was bath day rather than Thursday, despite the fact that Mrs. Nadjmi and her daughter were both Moslems. When I observed through a window the Christmas Eve candlelight celebration in their rooms, I could only conclude that Mrs. Nadjmi was Christian some of the time.

The parade on bath day would usually begin with Hassan, who filled the kerosene can and lit the boiler under the shower; he also brought in a small stove to heat the cold, stone room. The shower bath was a clever contraption resembling a man-sized samovar. Fuel dropped down a tube to a wick (actually a piece of clothesline) and burned there under a boiler shaped like a doughnut. When this jacket of water was hot and ready to use, the bather turned on the intake faucet and cold water entered from below and forced the hot water out of the shower nozzle. To regulate the temperature of one's bath, there was also an independent cold water faucet which fed into the stream of hot water. Usually one used up the whole tank and had a long shower, since it seemed so wasteful of hot water not to do so. The tank took about two hours to heat up properly, and the Nadjmi women, when the time was right, would troop into my flat wrapped in terry cloth robes, bathing caps on their heads. The *bodgee,* Hassan's wife, would follow with towels, soap, cologne, and henna pots (both of them dyed their hair, because it was healthy for the hair, according to Mrs. Nadjmi). Jaleh was very beautiful, even in mourner's black, which she mostly wore. She had a pleasant disposition, a brilliant smile, and a full *mädchen* figure. Her mother was short and dumpy, but in her youth had probably been as blooming as Jaleh; now she no longer seemed to care. She wore her auburn hair straight over her ears, without a wave in it, Buster-Brown fashion.

Often on *hammam* day the *bodgee* would clean my room, while her mistresses were laughing, chattering in German, and splashing about in my bathroom. Both of my large rooms had glass double-doors leading to the foyer; when the cleaning woman was working in one room, I could be in the other. This was necessary, to keep from suffocating. The *bodgee* would stir up clouds of dust by switching the carpets with a small weed broom. Although the windows were flung wide and a certain amount of dust drifted away, most of it settled down inside after the woman had gone. She would also wash all the dishes I had stacked in the sink, air out the bed, run a dust cloth across the wooden furniture and scrub the foyer floor. During the week she did my laundry, usually returning it a piece at a time on whatever day she managed to finish it—a couple of handkerchiefs, one undershirt, a pair of socks—presenting them to me with arms outstretched, like the gift-bearers approaching the throne of King Darius. I think she thought the oftener she came to me, the more impressed I'd be with her industriousness.

Despite the fact that I soon knew about as much Pharsi as he did, Hassan was thoroughly amused by my inability, at first, to speak or understand Turki, and he never stopped talking it to me. Over and over he would repeat what he had to say, for it was inconceivable to him that any grown man who seemed to be intelligent could not comprehend the simplest Turki phrases, words that his five-year-old son immediately understood. With his genial disposition, his pleasant, kindly ways, he would persist, his voice rising in volume, until I either got it, or in desperation we would adjourn to Mrs. Nadjmi's parlor, where she would translate what he said into a torrent of German. Given my limited knowledge of German, it never resulted in total enlightenment. By the time the year was out, I came to know household Turki, much to Hassan's satisfaction and thanks to his persistence.

Hassan's duties for me were very light; he would cheerfully do whatever I asked. On days I had students in, or other guests, he would burn off charcoal, stoke up my samovar, and have it boiling and whistling by the time the visitors arrived. Mrs. Nadjmi kept him on a round of tasks, but he had plenty of time to doze in the sun and contemplate the fountain that sprayed up from the center of the pool, or sit musing on the front steps below the veranda. In the evenings he called the chickens to their roost with a melodious whistle, a vibrating, lulling sound. *"Nina, nina,"* he murmured, tenderly. *"Nina, nina"* (Turki for "nest") and the whole flock would walk into the coop as if mesmerized.

I thought Hassan an old man because his beard was grizzled, his walk slow, his face lined; but once or twice I saw his two sons, the elder aged eight or ten, the younger five, and I realized that he only appeared to be old. He wore a dark, much-used Western-type suit on his ordinary work days, and in winter a black, thick overcoat, also badly worn. His shirt would always be buttoned to the top, and usually he had on some kind of vest and wore a floppy Western hat. Like country peasants, he did not shave; instead, he kept his beard trim by using a scissors whenever his whiskers became long enough to snip. His wife was never without her *chedur*, flying like a sail-cloth about her body as she moved, but in the house her face was uncovered. She was so shy about this exposure, however, that whenever I looked directly at her, she instinctively drew up the *chedur,* the hem in her teeth, so that only her black eyes showed. Under the skirt which came down to her knees, she wore black trousers and sandals—or went barefoot. Hassan and his wife left for their own home in the evening and returned shortly after seven o'clock next morning. I never knew them to have a whole day off, though on Fridays they apparently had half a day. Mrs. Nadjmi ruled them firmly, and they were happy.

The Iranian ingenuity in economizing never ceased to amaze me. Every piece of goods was put to use in a rather simple and obvious way. Yesterday's newspaper became the sack in which Hassan brought home my eggs. An empty spool of thread served as the draw-pull on my cotton bedroom drapes; the cord was made up of bits of saved string. Even Hassan's shoe soles appeared to have once been pieces of an automobile tire, and probably his shabby suit had originally belonged to Dr. Nadjmi. Everything was put to use several times; it was easy to trace the identity of parts, to understand how everything worked, where every item had come from.

My students frequently surprised me by their ingenuity and thrift, their habit of making do with highly limited capital, their clever notions of converting durable goods into something else, also useful, parlaying the life of all commodities. They in turn were occasionally surprised by my casual, seemingly wasteful attitude toward *things.* And I had so much! Gazing at the array of commissary goods in the kitchen, shipped by rail from Teheran, they marveled at the extent of the hoard and said: "You could open a shop!"

I remember, on one occasion, a student asking, "Sir, what is this?" He stood over my wastebasket, pointing down. "Surely you are not throwing *this* away?" At first I could not understand what he meant, until he fondled the garland of excelsior I had discarded. "What is it?" he asked.

I explained, but inquired, puzzled, what use *he* had in mind for it?

These wonderful, delicate coils of wood were soft but springy, he pointed out, and far better than the stuffing Iranians ordinarily used for mattresses and upholstered chairs. I assured him that he might have it, and he reverently gathered it up in a paper sack, which I also supplied. I felt somewhat disturbed that such a lot of fuss had been made over a basket of excelsior. I understood his high valuation of it, but I was bothered by the impetus behind his interest. Coming from a throw-away economy, where there was something almost purifying about discarding used-up commodities, from automobiles to Sunday's newspaper on Monday, I found the preservation of some excelsior a misplaced concern. Why weren't Iranians interested, instead, in how to make something new? I was, I began to see, incurably American.

As the months unfolded, the interest of the Persians in what I had to throw away began to work upon me in a strange fashion. Of course, I felt humble and unworthy, having so much of everything, but there was no simple means of salving this guilt, except in small ways: the ocean of want around me was too wide, too deep; and yet, it was there.

One thing became clear: I could not really dispose of anything, and I began to feel hemmed in, denied my rights to get rid of whatever I wished. At first there was a sense of bountifulness in the realization that my discards made someone happy, but this was true only when I was aware of what I was discarding. It made me uneasy, otherwise. My sense of privacy seemed invaded and I felt picked over. My most immediate adversary in this respect was Hassan, who came each day to remove garbage. I prepared my own meals, and the fact that I did not use Hassan's wife as cook baffled and amused the household and made them curious. Hassan was always absorbed by what he found in my garbage pail, as if he would figure out how I managed by examining the leavings.

I would watch him from the window as he shambled along slowly, poring over the treasure trove for the day. His wife, swathed in veils, would fly from the house to help him, like a carrion bird whose mate had found a choice morsel. Often Hassan would shoulder her aside angrily and make his way alone past the little chicken coop and dog house to a spot almost out of sight. Then he would begin his excited perusal, lifting out the burnished Tuborg beer cans as if he had found miniature bronze samovars. The foil packets which had contained Lipton's soup were delightful surprises—and, at first, quite baffling—both as to what I had used them for and what use he could make of them now. The malleable metal strip from a coffee can lid (minus the key, which I had carefully saved for possible future emergencies) could be twisted and looped. Hassan would sell this to a droshky driver for one and a half rials; it would be an admirable device for holding together a broken harness. I saw that I was introducing into Hassan's life a modest source of capital, an American aid program on a diminutive scale.

Since Hassan and his wife were reading my character by my trash, and I didn't want them to regard me as utterly extravagant, I had to be careful to cook only as much rice as needed; if a handful were left over, I gave it to Boppe, the dog, at night when no one was looking. I was also careful to make my apple and potato parings lean. If they got the idea I was a spendthrift, I'd be fair game, and all of Mrs. Nadjmi's careful training would be eroded, their honesty perhaps imperiled.

One winter morning I felt sure the avalanche was beginning. Hassan charged me a strangely high price for a bag of oranges I had ordered. I protested in the usual way, murmuring *choke, choke,* that wonderfully apt Turki expression for "too much." Later, in the street, I stopped a fruit peddler and inquired the price of oranges. Much as I suspected, they were half the price Hassan had said and they looked much better than the scruffy oranges he claimed had cost him close to fifteen cents a piece. In order to fill out my five-toman note, I ended up with a larger sackful than intended. Once home, I peeled an orange and immediately realized my mistake. These were pulpy and so bitter I could not get them down. I had been caught, but the problem was: how could I get rid of the evidence?

The oranges were inedible, but I allowed them to remain a few days in my larder, though I knew that this stalling was no answer. If I did not throw them out until they spoiled, Hassan would be horrified by my profligate ways. If I dumped them out now, when they looked tasty, he would be even more astonished and prompted to try one immediately. Once he discovered I'd been duped, he would begin to work upon me in almost any way he chose.

I considered carrying the bag down the street and casually dropping it in the gutter, although I realized that as a conspicuous American, my unusual action would be spotted and widely remarked upon—and would eventually reach Hassan's ears. I finally squeezed the oranges into a bowl, looked with distaste at the yellow bile I got for my trouble, poured in a mound of coarse-grained sugar, with water, stirred everything up, and tried to drink it. Impossible! I gagged and threw the stuff into the sink. It gurgled and disappeared. The orange rinds in the garbage were noncommittal evidence of my folly.

But more and more often the basic problem posed by this situation was repeated. Mrs. Nadjmi at Christmas presented me with certain varieties of local cakes which were dangerous to eat, especially those filled with a creamy custard made from the highly lactic-tasting milk of the water buffalo. I could only gratefully accept these goodies; I did not dare throw them out until they had decomposed beyond recognition. Boppe, unused to sweets, wouldn't touch them.

Wastepaper presented still another problem. I ripped letters to shreds before consigning them to the trash, knowing that school children in the street would eventually try to make out the English words and show the scraps to their teachers of English. Pieces of my letters were blown all over town by the desert winds, and once, while visiting a high school about a mile away, I noticed a bit of familiar blue airmail stationery drifting about the volleyball field. I picked it up and tore it in half again and saw the tatters float away in the breeze. But was that really the end of it now? No, in this land it was never the end.

I confess I even saved some especially personal letters and, crumpling them up in a hammered-brass, Isfahan bowl, I lit a match. The blaze leapt surprisingly high and lasted a long time. American paper was made of good sturdy wood pulp, I thought, with patriotic satisfaction. Then I noticed Mrs. Nadjmi, highly agitated, running from her wing of the house. In a gabble of German she asked me what in God's name I was doing, setting the house on fire? I apologized, poured cold tea on my bonfire, and gloomily stirred the charred remains before throwing them away. Even now some of the pages were legible. American paper was *too* good.

I willingly gave many items to the rummagers, but seldom with the sort of charitable feeling in my heart one has when extra household junk is carted off to the Good Neighbor Society. Azerbaijan life was too voracious for such luxurious gestures. I was pleased, however, to realize that Hassan's wife would be delighted with the stack of American Christmas cards I had received. Later, she was even wearing one of them. She was enchanted with the gift-wrap paper and colored ribbons and probably resold them. Sometimes for Hassan I obligingly set aside an empty olive jar or a neat little mushroom tin; after all, he should know that I knew what he was doing.

In some ways a squirrel tendency began to develop in me, and I hesitated over everything before attempting to discard it. All kinds of string were wrapped into balls; my closets began to fill with empty boxes and odds and ends, such as the metal bands which had bound the commissary shipment. This was provender stored up for the future. The empty Hollandia butter tin became my nail container, and the cardboard wedges in a shipment of phonograph records from Sam Goody's became mats for some drawings I tacked upon the wall. For a while, I saved used razor blades and once or twice caught myself long-pondering their possible usefulness.

I was becoming conditioned by Iranian economic life. Each day on Pahlavi Avenue as I walked to the university, I would pass a squatting merchant on a blanket, his wares before him, chanting to attract business. He had for sale thirty empty Carter's ink bottles; it was puzzling to imagine where he had gotten them. Farther along the street a man specializing in art objects was selling a page from an old copy of *The Saturday Evening Post*. It was a four-color advertisement for Hotpoint, and now it was handsomely encased behind glass with a gold, ornate frame. A father, mother, and two crisply dressed daughters were smugly regarding the legend in needlework on the wall behind them: "Bless Our Happy Hotpoint Home."

On the surface of the economy there was a hustling and crying, a certain busy-ness. One saw wooden trunks veneered with patches of Snowcrop orange juice and Blatz beer cans; tables were made of packing crates, dyed mahogany. In a way, all of it was a credit to human invention—as the phrase had it, "Persian version." A few things were produced, carpets, crude oil, ornamented brass and copper ware; but American Pepsi-Cola was still the biggest success story in Iranian business. Most people were concerned with reworking some product already in existence. Every piece of goods, therefore, was like something thrown into a deep sea, where scores of creatures scavenge and have their chances at it, each in his turn, as gradually it falls deeper and deeper—perhaps never reaching the silt of the bottom, as nothing I threw away ever had an end.

The refuse cycle went something like this: from me to Hassan, then often to his wife; what neither of them wanted was taken to the street, where burnt-faced, whiskered beggars waited with sticks to poke around in the trash. And after the men came the ragged children, some of whom were doing it merely out of curiosity. After the people left, the dogs had their day. They were mangy animals almost the same dun color as the refuse, which they worked through with a slow purposefulness, like the worms of decay. Eventually the city workers hauled what was left to a dumping spot near the slaughter house, where wolves came down from the mountains at night and fought over bits with the wild dogs. In the daytime buzzards and vultures lazily wheeled in the sky, looking and looking. Was this, then, the end? Not exactly, for peasants would make use of the compost for their fields, and slowly the cycle of life would begin to swing upward.

One day in spring when Hassan's little treasure room near the chicken coop happened to be open, I peered inside, and there in an enormous heap was what he had collected from me—at least, what he had not yet sold or disposed of. It seemed indecent that I had consumed enough canned food to have left this tremendous pile. And most disturbing of all, I saw many little things that I had not been conscious of discarding: bottle caps, empty folders of matches, underwear buttons, and a used kerosene wick. Next to all of this was a round, somewhat dusty red ball; had this, too, once been mine? I found that it was made of wax and for a moment I could not imagine what connection it had with me. And then suddenly, as if it were a waif to whom much had happened, I recognized it despite its changed form: this was the red wax outer layer of a few Dutch gouda cheeses I had eaten.

Despite all their concern for carefully preserving things, Iranians throw away with the profligacy of kings what other people consider valuable: time, energy, purpose—and so many, many human lives. I told some student friends that I was overwhelmed by this latter, more serious kind of waste. We were walking along Pahlavi Avenue on a mid-week morning. I happened to see a grey long-haired cat climb a poplar tree above the flowing *jube*. The cat scurried along a limb toward a large crow's nest, and a flock of angry screeching crows immediately descended to attack. I turned to my students and noticed that we were being jostled by a sizable crowd which had suddenly gathered. Hastily, I counted seventy-three men and boys, and more were coming. All of these idle, poor, disease-ridden people had come to witness the battle between the cat and the birds. This to them was an amusing way to spend the morning, one of the diversions available to help get rid of empty time, a way of wasting a day. I realized that what I threw away and forgot—what I wasted—was nothing compared to this.

11 SKIING IN SHIBBELEH PASS

"You must come skiing on Fridays," said Abbas. "All the students now go skiing in Shibbeleh pass. The winters are terrible in Azerbaijan as everyone knows, but it is not so bad if there is snow and we can go skiing."

When the first snows began in December, the packed-earth surfaces of many of the sidewalks turned gummy, the consistency of pigsties, and that was how they remained all winter; but the mountains rimming the city became hoary, and their sudden whiteness seemed to enlarge them—or it was as if they had moved closer.

I had no skis or poles. Where could I get equipment? At the local sports shop, they told me; Abbas, Mir-Mohammed, Darius, and Ruben escorted me to the store, which turned out to be one of the three importing establishments, selling everything from Danish hams to French trout spinners. I inspected a number of handsome German and Swiss skis; all of them much more expensive than I felt I could pay at this stage of my interest in the sport. I told my friends that I had had very little experience; I wondered if it were possible to buy second-hand, inexpensive skis in the bazaar, until my pleasure in the sport was confirmed.

"I have some skis you may use. They are not very good," said Darius, "but I have used them two years now, and they will do."

"Have you another pair for yourself?"

"I shall not be skiing for some time," he said, with his usual formal dignity.

"Thank you for the offer, Darius, but I couldn't possibly accept and prevent you from skiing."

"But that is not the case," he insisted, and sweat glistened on his brow. "My sister is making me a sweater. Until it is finished I shall not go skiing. You are welcome to use my skis, though they are very poor skis, I know."

His friends assured me that Darius was telling the truth, though none would say just why the sweater was so necessary. "Perhaps I shall not ski this season at all, if she does not finish."

The following Thursday Darius delivered his skis and poles to my house; alas, he could not come to Shibbeleh pass to watch me ski, and Abbas, too, was busy. Mir-Mohammed would be my guide and host. He came later in the evening to be sure I understood that he would call at a very early hour, before Hassan and his wife had arrived, before the Nadjmis were up. As we talked I learned to my surprise that he did not intend to ski; he admitted having skied now and then, but "not recently." I recalled Abbas' joking remark that his friend had "grown too fat to ski." Mir-Mohammed said there would be many at the mountain pass merely watching. It was the place to go on Fridays.

Next morning when he came for me he was dressed like a businessman, his neat topcoat buttoned tightly across his portly figure, his felt hat low on his brow. "Are you ready? Have you been up a long time?" He rolled his eyes and was as droll and enigmatic as ever.

"Let me get my lunch," I said, starting for the kitchen.

"Never mind, sir. I have provided for that." He carried a large blue plastic airline satchel in one hand.

"I've already fixed some sandwiches. I'll put them in with your food."

"We shall have a picnic," he smiled.

"Hardly the time of year for *that*."

"A picnic can be at any time. We shall have a picnic in the snow." His smile was inscrutable, and his small brown eyes, deeply recessed, glittered amiably.

We proceeded by foot to the intersection of Shahnaz and Pahlavi, where a large crowd of students were queued up before two waiting buses. The captain of the university ski club, a professor of English, came over quickly to welcome me officially. The loading took some time, since every piece of gear had to be strapped on top of the bus. Painted in the garish colors of a juke box, the bus had been "made" in Tabriz; that is, a blously streamlined body had been constructed on top of an automobile or truck frame. I found, when the journey began, that the seats were child-sized and set close together; it was impossible for me to sit any other way than with my knees under my chin. As the bus lurched around corners and bounced over potholes everyone was shaken up, but a gaiety prevailed as if this were a carnival ride, meant to terrorize.

We were in the bus carrying medical students, and they were all good friends. Their leader, Paulo, a handsome young man with black curly hair, stood in the aisle just behind the driver and faced his men. His even white teeth, good color, and sturdy physique bespoke a healthy diet since boyhood; even if he had not been wearing a bulky-knit Norwegian sweater and grey flannels, one would have placed him as a member of the privileged class. Whereas I had tried to dress warmly for the occasion, without regard to fashion, these students were in stretch-pants, Austrian and German windbreakers, beautiful sweaters, Polaroid glasses, and they carried the best European ski equipment. It appeared as though we were headed for a luxury resort in the Alps, not a barren, undeveloped mountainside in a desolate region of Iran. Now I understood why Darius preferred to remain off the slopes until his sister had finished knitting his sweater. I felt rather shabby in my Levis, orange-colored insulated boots from an American hunting outfitter, a green Navy watch-coat over my sweater, and a knitted shepherd's helmet from Khoi in the natural colors of the sheep, brown, tawny-grey and white.

Paulo came down the aisle to welcome me aboard. He spoke French rapidly and none too accurately; the other students turned to watch, proud of him as their spokesman and representative. He headed this group with just the proper mixture of authority and bantering good will. They were a noisy crowd, each one trying to get Paulo's attention. The shouts of "Paulo! Paulo! Paulo!" filled the air until we had begun the long continuous climb into the foothills; then some of them began to sing,

Paulo starting them off in a clear, melodious tenor that hushed them immediately.

When the song ended, amid much applause, Mir-Mohammed turned to me and said: "They are happy, very happy. It is too bad you are not acquainted with any of them. The students you know are in the other bus. It is a poorer bus, not as comfortable as this."

"I see," I replied, rubbing my bruised knees.

"The medical students always have the best," he said.

"No wonder everybody wants to enter medical school. Are these students mostly from rich families?"

"Not all, but most of them."

Laughter exploded up front, and we contagiously smiled. "It's good to see some light-hearted students, for a change," I said.

"At the Faculty of Letters," said Mir-Mohammed, "the students are poets and always sad. They are always trying to tell you their poems. Here they joke and enjoy themselves. They are happy fellows."

"Is it because they know they're fortunate?"

Mir-Mohammed repeated the word "fortunate" very slowly, rolling it on his tongue to extract the full meaning. "Of course they are fortunate, so why should they complain? Everything is good for them. Only they must learn their lessons and graduate from medical school. They will be rich before long, they will be doctors! Do you wonder why they laugh and joke?"

Suddenly from the rear seat a student began a tremulous solo in a loud baritone voice, quavering the half-tones as if his vocal chords were made of split reeds; he slid into falsetto. The busload of students hushed; when it was over, they applauded vigorously, stamping their feet and clapping their hands.

"That sounded like a sad song," I said, "was it?"

"In a way. The singer I believe is from Resht, and he is home-sick for his people. That song comes from Resht; it comes from those people who work in the rice fields near the Caspian Sea. They sing in the fields as they work. The song says: 'Do not be sad, my dear, winter will soon be over. The spring will come, the rice will be put out, and everything will grow. We shall be happy together, my dear. We shall be happy then.' You may think this song is sad, or perhaps not. It is life. It depends on how you look at it."

A festive mood swept the passengers when a boy with a mouth organ began a lively tune; there was hand clapping and swaying of shoulders as Paulo began to dance in the aisle, clinging to the metal seat handles for balance as the bus jolted along. He had a good sense of rhythm, though he was constricted by the narrow space, and after a short time he tired of the activity and fell into a seat between two friends.

Now that we were some distance from Tabriz, the vast emptiness of the country was making itself known. We passed through great desolate valleys, seeing only a man on a donkey or smoke from a hovel set against a mountainside ten miles away. There was occasional traffic, since we were on the main route to Teheran, but the highway was only a narrow ribbon of the twentieth century winding through a landscape unchanged for centuries.

I began to take note of the peaks: the highest, Sahand, was over twelve thousand feet, but many nearly as high were ranged nearby. One felt that if one looked hard enough it might be possible to see the stars deep in the intense blueness of the heavens. Since there were no trees, except for a few thickets along streams, the colorings of the rocks dominated the scene: reds and purples, at other places sandy brown or light grey (much depended on the quality of the light and manner in which cliffs were exposed). Sunlight fell upon the countryside like a warm golden mesh. There was almost no wind, and the altitude gave an intensity to the sun's heat, which came upon one with a friendly invitation to be still, to sit peacefully, to bask, or to stretch out and accept the living moment, Persian fashion, relishing and praising the present.

As we neared the top of Shibbeleh pass, frequently snow-blocked in winter, a long gasoline truck impeded our further progress. It was stalled on a hairpin curve, and its wheels were spinning deeper and deeper into the roadbed. Ahead of us several autos and trucks were stopped, and it was apparent that no one would move until the gasoline truck extricated itself from what appeared to be an impossible position. I got out of the bus, along with Mir-Mohammed and some of the others. A number of students, eager to reach the slopes while the sun was high, were trying to persuade their friends to walk up the mountain, the ski area being no more than two kilometers away. But the driver did not want to unpack his carefully arranged load on top of the vehicle and he refused to allow these eager skiers to pull their poles and skis from the rack.

I noticed, in the line-up ahead of us, an orange American pick-up truck, and, I recognized standing beside it the American road engineer privately employed in Iran for various construction projects. I had encountered him in Tabriz now and then—I shall call him Hawley—a Southerner with a loud mouth, a drill-sergeant's sarcasm, and an attitude toward Iranians closely akin to his feeling about Negroes in his native state, Arkansas. Hawley loved to hunt, drink, play poker, bully people, and create a little kingdom around himself; he enjoyed the challenge of looking out for his interests in any situation, the rougher the better. He was a red-necked Southern hill-man, as tough as the razor-back hogs of Arkansas. "What the hell are you doing here?" he said when I came up.

We talked a little about the stranded truck. It seemed to have *him* stumped, as well as everyone else. The driver had gunned the motor in panic and had dug himself down close to the axle. The drop off was about one thousand feet, and the trembling, tubular truck appeared to be edging closer and closer. Hawley went up the road to the cab of the truck, his interpreter following at his heels. "Ask the driver what the hell is the matter with him. Tell him to go straight on."

"*Che khabar ast? Rast buro.*"

The small, frightened Iranian behind the wheel said: "*Hanooz mashin ra durust nakarde-am.*"

"For Christ's sake, what's he say?"

"The driver says he has not put his machine right yet."

"Hell, can't I see that?"

"*Rast buro. Rast buro,*" said the interpreter. "I tell him to go straight ahead."

"That's right, now you're talkin'."

Then the driver said that the curve was too snarp—he wasn't able to make it. Hawley listened to this, when it was translated, but merely asked again: "Tell him he's got to get this friggin' thing out of here. We can't wait around all afternoon for him."

Hawley seemed almost amused by the impasse, and now and then he looked down the road at the traffic piling up. He scratched his beer-belly and spat. "I'll be damned. I'll be God-damned." Then he started to needle the driver again, urging him to *rast buro*, otherwise he might find himself over the cliff in a minute or two.

The driver was rapidly panicking under Hawley's persistent comments, and all he could shout in reply was a Pharsi phrase meaning, "No, it cannot go. It cannot go."

But as we stood there the truck suddenly moved, like a great beast coming out of a hole, and soon it was lumbering and groaning up the mountainside. Hawley turned to me with a contemptuous smile and said: "These people are the God-damnedest liars in the whole world."

The bus soon arrived at the top of the pass, and we all piled out and retrieved our skis and poles from the luggage-carrier. Since there was no ski lift, most of the students began herring-boning their way up the white mountain slope. I skied on a lower run, the beginners' area, but fast skiers from higher up would frequently sweep through the valley, shouting warnings and scattering the neophytes in a mica-dazzle of snow. The surface was powdery, the underlayers firm. The skilled skiers, black against the glaring snow, were flies crawling to the top; then they became swift linedrawing figures as they swept in and out of one another's path in the moment of action after the long climb. There were no trails, no pattern to the sport. As the day wore on, the mountain swarmed with students, and there were frequent collisions. An ambulance drove up and stood waiting for victims. The previous week a professor at the medical college had broken a leg; there were always one or two who were taken to the hospital on Fridays.

A number of townspeople arrived, especially the physicians who taught at the medical school, their wives and children; also, most of the Europeans who resided in Tabriz: the French consul, the British Council man and his family, several Germans. On the beginners' slope I encountered the only female student skier, a member of the medical school. She was a midwife trainee, and she must have been a feminist as well, to venture out in a sport so strictly identified with male students. They treated her courteously but appeared to have little to do with her. Friendships among the skiers gave the sport the aspect of a team activity.

At no time was the *esprit de corps* more evident than when we all retired for lunch at about two o'clock in the mountain tea house down the road. The *chai-khane* was a ramshackle one-story building with a small deciduous grove behind it. "A good place for our picnic under those trees," said Mir-Mohammed. But first we went inside to get warm.

A mountain tea house in Azerbaijan is a combination inn, restaurant, and way-station. Crude tables and benches filled the front portion of the interior; the exposed beams and pillars were smoke-charred, and the woven reed roof was sagging. Dingy carpets were tacked to the walls and strips of carpet had been used to upholster some of the benches. Draperies hung in the doorway to the cooking area, and a large bronze samovar was steaming and rattling, as in the best Russian novels. Several framed steel engravings of Victorian ladies were also on the walls, and, oddly enough, a tapestry of the Madonna and Child. Toward the rear a pot-bellied stove was glowing; behind it was a raised platform thick with carpets and comfortable bolsters. There one could lie down and rest, and we all scrambled for a place in the dark loft. First we took off our boots and left them in a heap below the dais; then we crawled up. More and more students sought places around the stove, and soon we were packed together, stretched out lengthwise or hugging our knees. The sudden warmth and comfort was enervating and delicious after the cold. Some of the livelier ones wrestled together, the drowsy play of bear cubs, but most of the skiers were too tired to do anything but lie inertly.

A couple of grey-coated boys with shaved heads passed up glasses of tea in metal holders. Coins were sent along to the child-waiters; there was a steady traffic in glasses, saucers and money. A number of skiers ordered lunch, and when it came I was invited to dip in, though Mir-Mohammed made it clear that we had our own lunch and would very shortly retire to the grove behind the *chai-khane* and have our picnic. Two large tin bowls, one of mutton stew, the other of puréed egg flavored with garlic, were set before us and we communally scooped up the food with wedges of the delicious unleavened bread, *nun.* A flap of this bread looked like a giant unrolled crêpe suzette; it was chewy and had a nutty wheat flavor. One frequently saw people walking home from bakeries in Tabriz, long rags of *nun* hanging from their forearms, where the baker had placed it.

The heat from the stove made me sleepy, but after a while Mir-Mohammed roused me. His cousin, who had lived in Hamburg a number of years as a student, was joining us in our repast. I realized that since Mir-Mohammed was my host for the day, I was obliged to show enthusiasm for his hospitality but it took a lot of will power. The frigid air outside the door seemed to strike to the bone at once; I was racked with a chill that made my teeth chatter. The day had clouded over and the wind was rising. From inside we could hear the buzz of conversation and occasional bursts of laughter; loud music from a portable radio added a further festive touch.

Mir-Mohammed introduced his cousin, a swarthy, somewhat sullen young man in a ski sweater and knit cap. He began testing out a few phrases of German, hesitantly, until he sensed his superior knowledge, and then he was suddenly quite the man from foreign parts. His face shone nostalgically as he told me of his student days in Hamburg, especially the girls—they were what he missed most of all—those blonde German girls. We proceeded to the grove, crunching across the snowbanks, and Mir-Mohammed spread out his blanket, then unfolded three camp stools. I guessed that he had invited his cousin in order to have someone help keep me company, since he did not like to talk very much. He was now busily uncovering the lunch, which was kept in metal containers stacked Chinese fashion, one on top of the other. I was not very hungry but I knew I must eat with gusto. Surreptitiously, glancing over his shoulder to be sure that no one was observing us, Mir-Mohammed brought out a bottle of vodka and poured it like water into tumblers for each of us. Since students on skiing expeditions were forbidden to drink, I saw another reason why the idea of having a picnic in the grove had such magnetic appeal. We ate the food with our vodka: lamb cutlets (more or less), heavily breaded, a cooked cheese and egg mixture wrapped in a pastry crust, some delicious spiced rice, raw onions, fruit, and nougat bars. Soon the bottle of vodka was empty and we were finishing off the cognac I had along. We were all quite suddenly rather drunk. My hands were numb from the cold, but my teeth were no longer chattering and I assured Mir-Mohammed that this was the finest picnic I had ever been on. The cousin from Germany, his diction slurring more and more, continued to talk about the yellow-haired girls—how he had kissed and loved them! How he missed them! To come back to Iran, after having experienced that! Life was intolerable here once a man realized what he was missing. We sat agreeably in the snowbank for some time, until the icy wind again made itself felt; then we went back inside the *chai-khane*.

We could scarcely force our way into the room, there were so many people. The portable radio had been turned off, and the music was provided by a couple of bongo drums made from two large tin cans put together, with hide stretched across the top. One member of the student combo plucked a string instrument which looked something like a guitar; another beat upon a board with his knuckles. The rhythms were infectious, and I sensed a heightening suspense as the pace increased. There was a good deal of shouting in the rear of the room, behind the stove. Gradually a small space was cleared on the dais, and a student stepped forward, dancing. He was too self-conscious to stay the center of attention long, and he quickly fled to a corner, amid shouts and handclappings. Then the audience began entreating another student to perform. As the drums pounded they chanted and clapped hands, until, by pushing and pulling the next reluctant dancer, he was finally forced on stage.

After three or four had performed, the crowd began shouting "Paulo! Paulo! Paulo!" He was blushing and trying to hide behind some friends, but they wouldn't let him get away. Once he was in the clearing, however, and definitely "on stage" he took up the dance with complete authority and devotion. His skip-step was intricate, what could be seen of it, but the most difficult aspect of the dance was probably the counterpoint movement of his upper body. His hands were uplifted in the classical positions of the Indian dances. His fingers snapped in time with the rhythms

162

of the drums, and his lean hips were swiveling in the traditional bumps and grinds of the Middle Eastern belly-dancer. I had seen this same animated pelvic action watching the belly-dancers who nightly performed in the basement dives of Teheran's Lalazar street, but it was strange to see a young man impersonating a woman this way. Paulo kept going: his head was high and his eyes were rolled slightly back, ecstatically. In addition to the circular female motions, he began adding sudden forward male thrusts, as if—since he danced without a partner—he were enacting both the man's and woman's part. Round and round the clearing he danced, possessed by a frenzy that the music enhanced, hips swinging convulsively until he gathered himself for a forward plunge. Although Paulo was masculine in appearance and manner, in the womanly part of his dance he was supple and female, coquettishly holding his head to one side; but then he would suddenly assert his maleness, drive the other image away with a linear surge of his lower body, his muscles taut and biceps knotted. To the audience it was simply the usual dance done superbly well by a favorite fellow student; but to me it seemed that these bisexual displays were only another manifestation of a culture which had shut up its women or excluded them from full companionship with men.

The afternoon was rapidly waning, and the ardent skiers were beginning to be restive; soon everyone was scrambling into the pile of boots (they were now quite mixed up). We left the tea house and ascended the mountain for a last hour of skiing. Then, at about five o'clock, the buses loaded for the trip back to town. A Pepsi-Cola stand had been set up along the road, and it was being heavily patronized by the skiers. Somewhat dehydrated from the drinking in the grove, I downed one twelve-ounce bottle quickly and took another with me into the bus, though it was difficult to manage the thing without getting my teeth knocked out. Most of my fellow passengers were swigging Cola, too, but with miraculous ease, despite the jolting bus.

The way home seemed faster, the spiral down the mountain faintly soothing, a progression that suggested settling down to rest. The tired skiers lapsed into silence and stared at their countryside. All along the way the scenery was splendid, and familiar as it was, they were spellbound. Nothing seemed deeper in the Persian than his love of nature, however nature was found; he had a reverence for it that years of urban living could never remove, or perhaps at heart they were all country people. The brilliant white snow on the purple and red mountains began to take on a blush of rose from the sunset, and then the sky turned a deep azure as dusk descended. A white, naked full moon hovered in the east.

Two or three Fridays later—toward the end of January—I arrived home and found one of my students, whom I shall call Mahmoud, waiting to see me. In my absence Hassan had let the student into the house, for the boy had asked to wait on the veranda outside my locked door. I discovered him there, pacing up and down the rough cobbles; Boppe the dog, normally so fierce toward strangers, was calmly gazing at my guest from the garden.

"Ah, at last you come home! I have been waiting a long time for you." The criticism in his voice was surprising, since I scarcely knew his name and had made no appointment to see him today. "I have been waiting almost an hour."

"You should have come some other time," I said irritably, setting down my heavy skis and poles and unlocking the door. I was stiff and tired and longed for a hot shower.

"You remember me, of course?"

"Yes, yes, the evening class. You're . . ."

"Mahmoud," he said at once, guarding against the possibility that I might not know. "I could not come another time because I am not in Tabriz every day. I go back soon to my village—the place I teach."

"Now I remember." He had first come to my attention in a newly formed evening school section of first-year students because he had asked a special favor. Since he taught school in a distant village, there would be days when he could not attend my class. Would I please make an allowance for this and not mark him absent? Although the excuse seemed valid enough, I could not make special concessions without immediately encountering similar requests from others, equally valid. I stuck to the firm policy announced at the beginning of the term: when I called roll, students were either absent or present, and that was as far as my responsibility extended. All other matters regarding excuses had to be taken up with the clerk of the Faculty of Letters. This question of attendance was vital, since permission to take the final exams and thus receive a grade in the course was only granted if a minimum attendance in class had been achieved.

Mahmoud had impressed me as a potentially brilliant student, and he had a physical presence that was arresting. His eyes were exceedingly alert; he was full of zest and eager to recite. He was fairly short in stature but powerfully built; I learned later that he was a champion wrestler in school competition. When he spoke, his voice was loud, clear and authoritative. Normally students showed no respect for one another during class recitations. They talked or laughed when one of their number tried to answer a question. I judged that this lack of manners came about because they saw no reason to respect a fellow student, who after all had no more authority than anyone else. They only showed respect and obedience to someone who had a recognized higher position. But when Mahmoud spoke (and at first his English seemed exceedingly poor) there was an immediate cessation of chatter. I could not tell if they respected him, were afraid of him, or merely curious about him.

"I would like now to see you," said Mahmoud, coming in the door after me. "Is the hour convenient?"

"Come on, I'll fix some tea."

"Thank you. Thank you very much." He slipped off his shoes as I unlaced and removed my boots.

I showed him into the living room, saying "Let me take your overcoat."

"Do not trouble yourself, sir," he said, throwing it on a chair. He looked around my quarters with a somewhat falsely assumed air of confidence, as if he were inspecting an apartment he intended to lease. He looked longest at my desk and typewriter, the many papers and books stacked there, and asked if this was where I worked. He seemed heartened by this actual evidence of my industry; perhaps it somewhat offset the frivolity of my having spent the day skiing.

His black suit was a sharply tailored whipcord, and he wore a white shirt and a satin, custard-colored tie; despite the urban costume, he did not seem a city man, nor properly outfitted in these tailored, zooty clothes, though he was dressed in acceptable Tabriz style. He had a big peasant head with a lot of sandy, close-cropped hair, blunt features, and coarse, heavy hands. The overly sharp tailoring emphasized his powerful torso; he had a thick, sinewy neck that strained against his shirt collar and his face was flushed, as if he were being strangled by the thing. His loud voice had the careful clarity of a man used to speaking in the open air, or in crowded, noisy rooms. When I left to put the kettle on, he followed me into the kitchen and surveyed my arrangements there with an ingenuous curiosity. I lit the kerosene wick under the shower tank, and he expressed interest in the commode and my toilet articles arrayed on a stone shelf. This easy intrusion into my intimate life seemed to inflate him with a sense of power over me, as if, like an aborigine, he were used to employing talismanic devices to get his way.

Perhaps what was most unusual about Mahmoud was his bantering, familiar air, so unlike the formal reserve and cautiousness I had experienced with other students. The protocol and politeness sometimes became a screen before me and my Iranian friends, but I had become used to it and now noticed its absence in Mahmoud's manner. His faintly derisive or mocking tone might have been accidental, but I didn't think so. We went back to the living room with the teapot and cups, and I turned on the phonograph. After a few minutes he said he would like it so much better if I would turn the machine off.

"Don't you like music?"

"Oh, yes, *Iranian* music. But that . . ." He snorted noiselessly, tossing his head in the kiss-the-air gesture of contempt.

So I shut off Beethoven. We discussed the types of music, for a while, somewhat artificially; I saw that his English was becoming lubricated. I sensed that his book-knowledge of the language was quite extensive, but his practice was slight. He listened regularly to Voice of America, hoping to improve his English, but they had no program in English, only in Pharsi or Arabic. "I listen to Radio Moscow. They speak very good English. Have you heard?"

166

"No." At that time I had not yet heard a Moscow program. But where is your radio, he asked? And when he learned that I had none—just a phonograph—he was puzzled. He knew where he could get a radio for me very cheaply, would I like that? When I insisted that I didn't want a radio, he was baffled; he gazed at me long and deeply, then settled back in his chair.

Deliberately, he set about being charming: he wore a wide grin and adopted his best social manner as he discussed the English language. Did I know how many irregular verbs there were? Did I? And when I said I didn't know, off-hand, he shook his head with a smile, admonishing me. "Ah, sir, I thought you were a smart teacher."

He had all sorts of odd facts of grammar and I wondered if he had boned up for this meeting, especially to display his knowledge to me. I tried to explain why someone whose native language was English might not know certain oddities of the language that a foreigner would see. Mahmoud's face was an impassive blank, as if he were not listening at all. We dropped the subject of grammar.

Last summer in Teheran, he told me, he had had an American teacher at a summer session in English sponsored by the Iran-America Society. Mahmoud told me the man's name and asked if I knew him. I didn't. This American was a "very nice man," and upon conclusion of the session Mahmoud had given him a book by Karl Marx. "I found that he knew very little about Marx. He gave me Alexander Hamilton. Which do you think is of greater value? Is that right, 'greater' not 'greatest'?"

I nodded. "For any student of history, it would be valuable to know *both*."

"Ah, I see you are a very clever man. Do you have a copy of Marx here?"

"No, I don't."

"I shall give you one."

"But I've read him, even studied him in college."

"Oh, are you a student of Marx?"

"It isn't necessary to give me his books."

"But I would like to."

"Forgive me, but I know that teachers earn very little money. I would be unhappy if you gave me such a useless gift."

" 'Useless'—is that what you think?" He seemed more amused than angry. "Tell me this, sir, have you been to Russia? Have you seen what the words of Karl Marx have become?"

I told him I hadn't been to Russia but hoped to go. At travel agencies in Teheran I had investigated the possibility of going into the USSR from Baku. A passenger boat sailed from Pahlavi on the Caspian Sea, and Intourist of Russia allowed Baku as a port of entry. I had discovered, however, that the trip would be very expensive.

Mahmoud was amazed that I felt I could not afford to travel in Russia. He had not been there himself, but he was sure that if the Russians knew who I was and that I wished to study their society, they would make it easy for me. He thought it highly important that I see the Soviet Union for myself, then make up my mind. He remembered the Russian soldiers when they occupied Azerbaijan during World War II—they were brave, courageous, and strong. Especially, he admired their strength. "American men I believe are weak," he said. "They may have better minds than the Russians, but they do not have as strong bodies. That has been my observation. It may or may not be true."

I argued the matter with him, particularly trying to get out of him a clear statement of value on the question of strength. He did not understand what I was driving at. The strongest man is the best man, in the wrestling ring or in the world; it was as simple as that, and there was no reason to talk about what was "good." It was best to be strong. The Russians of the Great October Revolution were strong and they were good men. We got off on the topic of "the Great October Revolution." He maintained that "Great" was part of the noun and as much an integral factor as "United" in "United States."

Facts and figures began tumbling out of him. Did I know that Lenin's brain weighed 2.9 kilos? After Lenin's death they had weighed his brain—yes, this was a fact. The average man's brain weighs a little over one kilo. "Therefore, it is scientifically true, it is a proven fact, that Lenin was over twice as clever as other men."

"Where do you get all this—from Radio Moscow?"

"I learn what I can," he said, sipping tea.

168

I offered him a cigarette. No, he did not smoke. He did not drink, either, and he had sworn not to marry until he had reached his middle forties.

"For health reasons?" I asked, smiling.

"No, for political reasons."

"Just what are your plans?"

"I am a student. I want to learn and study. That is why I am happy to be in your class. I wish to learn everything you can teach me. I promise not to forget it. Do you know where this comes from?" He began reciting a passage which he later, after much teasing delay, identified as from Dostoevski's *Poor Folk*. Had I read *Poor Folk*? Did I not agree that it was a true story of how terrible life was under the czars? He proceeded to illustrate his memory of other books, and to my astonishment he even began reeling off a speech by Dwight D. Eisenhower. At last he came to the point of his visit. He had heard that I had been making speeches in secondary schools of Tabriz. Would I not come out to his village and talk to his pupils?

His town (I shall call it Hakhapur) was located a half day's journey away by bus. "I would have to stay overnight," I said.

"Yes, of course. You will be my guest. I am a poor man. I have nothing, but what is mine shall be yours. If you will come I'll make room for you. You have not yet seen a village, that is to say, you have not *lived* in a village?"

He did not have to persuade me long. I accepted, but I did not know when I could make the journey. There was a movement afoot to organize a big game hunt, and I had agreed to join the hunting party. I didn't want to miss it, and my share was promised in the expenses. In the meantime, while waiting for a suitable date for me to visit Hakhapur, Mahmoud said he would like to come to my home many times. We should get to know each other. He understood that I was a writer and he was, too. He wrote poems, and some of them had been published by journals in Teheran. I requested to hear one. Yes, of course, he knew them well and could say them for me. "But they are very revolutionary," he warned.

"I'd like to hear a revolutionary poem—go ahead."

169

He recited in Persian, then tried to translate; but he found it difficult. "It's about a man, a very, very poor man."

"Yes, I caught the word *faqir*."

"You know Persian?" he asked, startled.

"A little. But I couldn't follow your poem."

"This poor man has no house, no food, nothing at all, just his one little son. But the little boy takes sick and finally dies. The body is taken away, leaving the man completely alone. The last line tells: 'I cannot be helped, for all is terrible.'"

"A very sad and tragic poem, but I don't see that it has much to do with revolutions."

"Do you think such things would happen in Russia? A man so poor as that? Now listen to this next one, it is *more* revolutionary. Then you will understand." He recited very loudly, with considerable emotion; when finished, he asked if I knew what he said. I shook my head and urged him to translate. "*Na.* You should know Persian to know my poems."

"I wish I did."

"Tell me, why do you not know Persian? I know English."

"Well, I know some French and German, and I'm studying Pharsi and Turki. I understood your poem a little."

"'A little!'" he scoffed. "'A little' is not enough. I can speak Russian, Arabic, Kurd, Gashghai, Turkish, English, Persian, and some others."

"I envy you."

"I have studied hard, and I continue to study. I am interested in politics, in governments, in people. But here in Iran they will not let you study. They do not want the people to know about these things. At the University of Tabriz they do not teach political science. The government won't allow it and yet this is the subject all the students wish to study. In Baghdad there is a great teacher of political science, a great man from Russia, and he is teaching the students how to think."

"No doubt!" I laughed.

"And what is *true.*"

"You mean, he's preaching communism. Yes, I've read about him. But you seem to know a great deal about the theory already. Why is it you wish to study under him?"

"Because he is wise and very great and very famous."

"Are you a Communist?"

A mixture of amusement and surprise crossed his face. "No, I am not Communist, I am not capitalist, either. I am interested in all ideas. I study Marx, Lenin, Stalin, Washington, Lincoln. I read what they have to say—I want to study." He got up and put on his topcoat. "I shall tell everyone in my village that a great man from America will be our guest. We shall have much to learn from you about your country, about capitalism. You must tell them the *truth,* always the truth. Now I shall go. I thank you very much." He shook my hand and laughed. "Do not look at me with such a puzzle on your face. I am just a boy and study is best for me now. I want to learn and read and study." He started away, down the steps into the garden. "Good-bye, sir. Good-bye."

The sound of his voice did not soon die away; it echoed again and again in my consciousness. I knew that his arrival on my doorstep, like a telegram found upon one's return from a party wedged under the door, meant that reality was about to intrude upon my travel idyll. But I still tried to fend it off, postponing my confrontation of Mahmoud's significance by telling myself that there were other things I wanted to see and do in Persia before I had to ask the ultimate question of why I was there at all and before I could answer such a query.

12 THE HUNT FOR MOUFLON

ON BARREN Eshek island in the middle of Lake Rezaiyeh, according to tales of shepherds, mouflon (wild sheep) abounded in such numbers that the fresh water supply from one trickling spring was woefully inadequate. With vegetation sparse and no predators to thin the herds, the animals were dying from diseases, starvation and thirst. For three years Eshek ("sheep" in Turki) had been closed to hunting, following a much publicized safari of thirty-two Americans, some arriving by seaplane from Teheran, who had slaughtered the mouflon in a no-rules hunting orgy that inflamed the Iranian press. I had seen pictures of the returning hunters on their rented barge, crossing the great salt lake with the horned heads of mouflon mounted on the gunwales like trophies decorating a Viking ship. But, through the influence of the Azerbaijan transportation chief, a Mr. Haleh, who had been invited to the U.S. the year before to study the railroad system and whose daughter had been awarded a Fulbright grant, Roger Thompson received special permission for a February hunting expedition and for four hundred tomans rented the lake steamer *Pahlavi* to transport us to the island.

Our party would include a German doctor now a resident of Tabriz, who had "discovered" the island and paid frequent visits there hunting for the tomb of Hulago Khan, grandson of Genghis Khan. According to old records, he had been buried somewhere in the region of the lake with a Mongol treasure hoard and twelve live virgins. The foundation of Hulago's palace could still be seen on the edge of Tabriz, near the new university site; but as with so many other historic buildings and famous mosques of Tabriz, the combination of earthquakes and invaders had obliterated almost everything. The German did not plan to hunt mouflon, but we expected to draw upon his extensive knowledge of the island, and particularly, his help would be necessary in guiding the *Pahlavi* into the proper channel for our landing.

The French consul was to join our group at the jetty near Azarshahr. Also, there would be two American road engineers, a twelve-year-old boy, and two American Army sergeants. The latter were stationed in Tabriz, showing the Iranians how to use the military equipment sent from the U.S.

Thompson had hoped that an American colonel, an experienced hunter, would head our party, but at the last minute he couldn't fly up from Teheran. Therefore, with the exception of the road engineer, Hawley, and Thompson, none of us had hunted mouflon, reputedly one of the world's cleverest game. They were surely not dangerous beasts, yet it was the element of danger which had quickened my blood, had gotten me interested in hunting. During the depths of winter when forage gave out in the mountains, wolves sometimes descended into the streets of Tabriz looking for food in garbage dumps. My students told me a child had recently been attacked by a wolf and had had its arm torn off. Of course I had no gun, nor was there any likelihood that the Iranian government would grant me a weapon permit, since I was not accorded the privileges of the diplomatic corps. Normally I was seldom concerned about personal safety, but one particular January moonlit evening, well after midnight, when I was forced to walk home after visiting Persian friends living some two miles from my flat in *koutche* Ark, I heard in the distance an eerie howl and felt the hairs on the back of my head stir. There were no taxis coursing the avenues, no droshkies lumbering along and not a single pedestrian. Because of the late hour, the street lights had been extinguished, and the silvery moonlight fell upon a totally deserted walled city, a Jerusalem of the Sunday School books. I remembered the rumors about the wolves running with the feral dogs. I recalled the tales describing the peculiarly long fangs of the Caucasian wolves, their monstrous size. These were not the dog-creatures seen in zoos or heard in the timber regions of northern Minnesota, Wisconsin and Michigan; Azerbaijan wolves were deep-chested, rangy beasts, strong enough to topple a horse. Some were said to be as large as small burros. With all this lore in my head, I walked rapidly down the snow-crusted boulevards, nothing but a flashlight in my hand, knowing full well that if I encountered a wolf, I'd be helpless against its attack. Each time I crossed the opening of a *koutche* I glanced nervously down its shadowed, moonlit depths toward the garbage bins but I saw only a few wild dogs. By the time I reached my garden door I was fully possessed by the danger of the hunt, on quite a different basis from my boyhood excursions against rabbits, squirrels, and pheasants. I felt a stirring of the blood that seemed a refreshing change from the overly protected conditions of civilized society. I thought of tiger hunts, which would take place in spring in the mountains along the Caspian Sea. I envisioned tramping through a bog after wild boar. And now I contemplated a variety of encounters with packs of wolves. Walking home, however, I did not have to defend my life; when I opened the creaking garden door and entered the secure confines of the Nadjmi dwelling, even the dog Boppe, who was unleashed and prowling, did not snarl and bound menacingly toward me; he wagged his tail and snuffled my trouser-cuffs. I had arrived home safely, and I was almost disappointed.

The chartered lake steamer was to carry us from a jetty on the eastern shore to the island, and remain anchored in the bay of Eshek until we were ready to return, at one o'clock the following day. Thompson picked me up in his Land Rover at ten; he was well equipped with camping supplies for the two of us, and he had offered to let me use his 30:06 rifle part of the time, while he took pictures. It was mid-February, and I wore wool longjohns, sweaters, and a cashmere Khoi shepherd's cap. The German, who taught at the medical college, was in the front seat, dressed in a soft grey felt Swiss mountain hat, white turtleneck sweater lined with satin at the throat, and a waterproofed, insulated storm-coat. He appeared to be about sixty, with beaked nose, firm and well-tanned flesh, white hair. He wore expensive, very smoky dark glasses. Referred to as an "Austrian doctor" by the diplomatic Iranians, his past was highly mysterious. Rumors persisted that he was an escaped Nazi war criminal who had fled Germany when sentenced to five years' imprisonment. No one knew for sure. Speaking English with a strong British accent and looking ahead at the road, he lectured on his favorite topic: the terrain, the history of the region, the ages past, the flora and fauna of Azerbaijan, and especially of the island Eshek, his bailiwick.

I sat in the rear with road engineer McCaffrey and his son, Bud. We were fascinated by the spiel from the German, who did not let the talk lapse. The unique feature of Eshek, he stated, was that there were no predatory beasts—no wolves, no bears—to prey upon the mouflon and smaller game. "They die of old age on that island. You will see the skeletons of mouflon lying peaceably where they dropped. And sometimes at the bottom of the steep cliffs on the northern side of the island, one finds the bones of young lambs, harried over the precipice by the eagles and then pounced upon. Yes, eagles hunt the young mouflon that way—I have seen it. But nothing else disturbs them."

"And so man becomes the hunter," said Thompson agreeably. Thompson had been an Army officer in the Italian campaign in World War II, and his intellectual positions on the questions of life were always highly pragmatic. With a nondescript, smooth-planed, Dick Tracy profile, he seemed to me to be the kind of man the United States has in tight places. Tall, loose-jointed rather than muscular, with a somewhat boyish face, his mild physiognomy belied his actual toughness.

"Have you hunted on Eshek?" I asked the doctor, hoping he would also mention his treasure search.

"No, I do not shoot guns or take away game. I go to the island for scientific reasons—to observe. It is very, very interesting." The isle had been created, he believed, some twenty million years ago, though it was not volcanic, as was Koin, the biggest island in Lake Rezaiyeh, which actually belonged to the chain of mountains that included the 12,138 foot Sahand, as well as the peaks across the lake in the region of Kurdistan. Originally Eshek must have been connected to the mainland by a narrow strip of land, which could still be detected about three meters below the lake surface at many points. These islands formed stepping stones across the glassy, heavy-with-salt sea, and of course, the whole region had once been a part of the Mediterranean and Caspian before the Iranian plateau emerged, in the days when the sea reached all the way to the Himalayas. The mouflon on Eshek had apparently been trapped when the neck of land connecting the islands went under water, presumably during an earthquake.

"How often have you gone to the island?"

"Fifteen or twenty times—perhaps more." As often as possible he had crossed the stretch of lake in a small row boat, his wife and children tugging at the oars in Teutonic cooperation; recently he had purchased an outboard motor, which made the voyage easier. He had to pick the season and hour of sailing very carefully, when the waves were not likely to swamp the skiff, when the conditions allowed for a return trip either the same day or the one following, though once or twice the family had camped on the island for an extended period.

"It must be pleasant on Eshek in spring and summer."

"No, in summer it is really terrible. Spring and fall, yes, when there is frost, that is best. The insects are gone. But in summer the flies are abominable; they crawl into your mouth and eyes, go up your nose, and are constantly riding in your hair. It is not pleasant, I assure you."

"I understand you've been digging for buried treasure?"

Behind the steering wheel, Thompson shifted uncomfortably when I said that; I gathered I was not to have divulged what he had told me.

"What's that?" The German turned.

"Isn't this island supposed to be where Hulago Khan was buried?"

"*Ach,* that is not so. Believe me, I have traced through the records and if Hulago Khan is buried anywhere, it is on the bluffs overlooking the lake, not on an island in the lake itself. Some years ago the Chinese Ambassador to Iran came up to Azerbaijan looking into the matter. He returned to Teheran, convinced that no Chinese treasure was here. Would he have done that, *huhn,* if there had been a chance? As badly as the

Chinese need gold and jewels these days? No, there is nothing to the story, and I am tired of hearing it."

Road engineer McCaffrey, to change the subject, pointed out to his son that we were passing a flock of sheep and goats on a hillside, with several men in attendance and a number of vicious-looking sheepdogs. They were big, lean animals, rather like a Russian wolfhound gone to seed, with an odd coil of the tail, a high body, a Weimaraner head. Shepherds clipped the ears of their dogs so that the wolves couldn't grab hold of them in a fight. Despite the surveillance of men and dogs, wolves were known to attack in broad daylight if they were starving. They swooped down in packs, leaping upon horses or burros as well as sheep, and by cooperating managed to drag off a carcass or two before the shepherds and dogs could counterattack. To avoid this ravaging of their flocks, shepherds in the region of Lake Rezaiyeh transported many of their animals to the safe islands for winter, where, with melting snow and occasional pools, there was enough water for survival; then in spring the sheep were removed in barges to the mainland, for the greater wealth of forage and more plentiful water supply.

The day was bright, sunny and very cold, and as we traversed the flat irrigated agricultural plain the heat on the roof of the vehicle warmed us pleasantly, giving us the illusion that spring was nearly here, though the mustard-colored earth showed no green. The snows of December and January had all melted; the desert, however, gave no sign that it could ever burgeon with life. The ferrous hills, in gaudy vermilion and purple, seemed outcroppings on a landscape of the moon.

On the way we passed the parked pick-up truck of road engineer Hawley; he and his two Army buddies were sighting their rifles, aiming at rocks and tumble weeds. Some distance farther, we took a side road to investigate a bubbling hot spring the German doctor knew about, whose waters he believed to be medicinal. Were this an enterprising, civilized country, a fine spa could be established, of profit and benefit to everyone. He shook his head philosophically.

The area of the spring was now fenced off, since it was located just inside a new Iranian military encampment which featured a rifle range and mortar targets. Immediately we ran into trouble with the guards, who stood solemnly before us, guns *en garde,* fingers lightly stroking the triggers. I looked at my watch and saw that we barely had time to reach the jetty by one o'clock; at my suggestion, we retreated, without so much as a glimpse of the "healthy waters" where now, even in winter, said the doctor, moss and verdant grasses thrived along the edges. A small column of steam rose like smoke in the near distance.

We drove over the crater rim of the lake basin; the vast body of water, inert and silvery, lay like a pool of mercury in a saucer. The road to the jetty led into another military post; we passed through the barbed wire entrance and drove down to the pier. A dismal squad of Iranian troops in ill-fitting brown wool uniforms, all tanned and young and rather dull-witted in appearance, were doing their washing. Some of their garments were drying in the sun on the rocks; surprised by our visit, they were curious, giggly and disorganized. Climbing out of the Land Rover, I looked at the lake steamer at the end of the wooden, rickety pier, which extended a quarter of a mile into the sea, since the shores were so shallow no ship could come closer. Then an Iranian officer in a black overcoat and visored cap low on his forehead came strutting toward us, two frightened orderlies behind him.

No, no, he began at once, pointing to our rifles; you are not allowed to take guns to the islands, since there are domestic sheep and shepherds out there. Furthermore, this was a military zone, close to the Russian frontier, and no unauthorized personnel were permitted weapons of any kind. The German doctor, who knew Pharsi best, began arguing; he looked so much like a Field Marshal in disguise I failed to understand how the Iranian was not intimidated. When I got a good look at the Persian officer under his warbonnet, I realized he was thoroughly scared; blindly, he stuck to the ruling because this was how military commands worked. He had received no different instructions in regard to our hunting party, and he feared he would get into serious trouble if he made an exception on our behalf.

"I'll phone Haleh," said Thompson. *"Telefon. Kojah mita-vanam telefon konam?"* Then, turning to us, "But I want this joker to come along and hear the word from upstairs with his own ears—otherwise, he'll never let us board that ship." The *Pahlavi,* a diesel-powered vessel, standing hugely out of the water (it was one hundred and forty feet long) gave a blast on its whistle.

While the rest of us waited with our gear piled on the wharf, the French consul drove down the slope into the compound in his small French army reconnaissance vehicle, the celluloid side-flaps tightly buttoned. He was in full military regalia: puttees and brogans, heavy olive-drab overcoat that came over his knees, muffler, and a leather field helmet that snapped under his chin, as if he had a toothache. He had a couple of bottles of Beaujolais in his knapsack and a double-barreled shotgun; he came striding toward us, as if ready for his part in a Jacques Tati film.

About then, Hawley and the two sergeants arrived, climbed out of their truck, and came over. Hawley had a short red beard, a good color contrast to his blue eyes. He wore a red and black checked wool shirt, high, laced boots with stockings folded over the top, blue jeans, and a floppy felt guide hat. When apprized of the situation, he rolled his small eyes and scratched his belly meditatively; these God-damned Varsees (his name for the natives, since their language was Pharsi) had better not scoot around in front of us too long, or there'd be trouble!

The French consul decided to have his lunch, in the course of which he offered Hawley a drink of the Beaujolais, apologizing that it was too cool; it was so much better when a little warm. Hawley picked up the bottle. "What's this stuff, anyhow?" He scrutinized the label and shook his head. Go ahead, try it, urged Monsieur M., with a smile, for he saw that Hawley thought wine a dubious drink. "I don't take things like this," Hawley insisted. "You know my liquor? Can you understand me? Bourbon, that's my liquor. Whiskey!"

"Viskee? *Non, Monsieur, je n'ai rien. Peut être . . .*"

"Oh, hell, I'll try it." Hawley tipped the bottle above him as if he were guzzling Pepsi-Cola, then set it down, wiping his lips with the back of his hand. "Man, that's pretty good stuff, after all. It won't make me sick, will it?"

The German crossed the barren parade ground to announce that both the transportation director and the governor general had been reached: permission was granted. We piled our gear on a flat handcar, which rode an extension of rails part way out on the pier, and soon Thompson joined us; we were all set to depart. Shoving from behind, we rolled the little trolley down its Toonerville track. When we reached the portion of pier extending over the water, I became aware of the flimsy poplar planks under us, many of them missing; the poles supporting the structure quivered as we moved. At any moment it seemed we would go crashing through the matchstick foundation and into the three feet of water below. The rails ended far short of the ship; we carried our equipment the rest of the way on our backs, along a boardwalk swaying over the sea, until we came to a narrow gangplank which angled up to the ship's deck like a chicken-run, with latticed ridges spaced every two feet for footholds.

The *Pahlavi* had a rusty, unseaworthy, makeshift quality, as if it had been constructed out of scrapped Lend-Lease vessels, the odd pieces not quite hanging together, the paint chipping. It got underway almost at once, shaking itself loose from the mud and vibrating free, into the deeper waters of the lake. Then the land receded and the waters seemed to extend. The illusion of foreshortened distance we had had from land was replaced by a graphic sense of the true size of the salt lake. We stood aft in groups and looked out across the miles of water to the hills of Eshek, and to some cliffs on the left, part of a group of forerunning islands, extraordinary in color. The red was dried blood, the greens mold, and dusky shades of purple dripped against the white cliffs, softened and blurred by the distance.

The German got out his hydrometer and tossed a tin can overboard, to get samples for a saline reading. With a scholarly, scientific mien, he held up the test tube, squinted. I asked him the results, and he reported that we were traversing a liquid which was 22.5 per cent salt. Sometimes freshwater streams from the mountains flowed over the heavy saline water, and then he might get a reading of only 8 per cent. Once the salt concentration had been as high as 28 per cent. Nothing could live in such a solution of sodium chloride except a few hardy shrimp, not edible. The shores of Lake Rezaiyeh, he went on to say, sweeping out his hand as if it were his kingdom, had such peculiar climatic conditions and such odd chemicals in the soil that some forms of life existed unknown elsewhere on earth. "There is much to study, if I only had time."

Hawley interrupted, extending a bottle of bourbon for us each to take a swig; the doctor declined with a withering hauteur lost on Hawley and packed away his hydrometer, back turned. Hawley rejoined his lusty cronies amidship, where the talk was randy and plentiful, full of bravado. Hawley could do anything: lick anybody, drive any machine, fix anything, seduce any woman, hunt the fiercest game—there was nothing he was afraid of, no challenge insurmountable. The wide-eyed Frenchman followed him about mouth open in amused surprise. Clearly, Hawley was stranger to him than any Persian he'd laid eyes on.

Nearing Eshek, the doctor went up to the bridge and stood near the captain's wheel. We skirted the shafts of rock comprising the fore-islands, which had long since lost their spectacular colorings, and entered a protected half-moon bay. The *Pahlavi* trembled, lumbering its way along slowly, like a whale in a river channel by mistake, past many precariously balanced rocks, some the size of houses. The sea had washed away most of the supporting foundations, leaving them delicately on tip-toe, sculptured smooth at the base by the heavy water. Their craggy mass, suspended above the water, set an awesome mood for our arrival.

The anchor, a cluster of rocks in a rope net, was thrown overboard, and the lifeboat which had been bobbing in the wash of the screw was hauled alongside and a portion of our gear was stashed into it, though the bottom was filled with water. Having no dock for mooring, we would have to establish our beachhead by shuttling back and forth in the lifeboat, a few men and a pile of equipment each time. Hawley had been pacing the deck, his cleated boots ringing on the metal; the confinement of two hours on board had begun to unnerve him. Now he was the first into the lifeboat, with the fair-haired, nondescript sergeants, alike as Joe and Jim. "Okay, shove off!" shouted Hawley to the Iranian oarsman. His voice fell into the silent pocket of the protected bay; even *he* did not seem a big enough or loud enough man to crow over this demesne. Bobbing over the lake in the stubby, awkward boat, sitting in the prow and stern, rifles at alert, they were a sinister bunch. The quiet sunny bay, the eerily empty island, and our nefarious purposes all reminded me of piracy. I mentioned this to the doctor, without at first realizing that he in his quest for Mongol treasure more than any of us filled the role.

"Ach, pirates there have been here. You are quite right. For many years the only human life on Eshek was a band of pirates who made raids on mainland villages. This island was their lair. At last the citizens of the mainland got together, attacked the bandits in their island hiding places and killed every one of them. Now on Eshek there is nothing but mouflon, hundreds and hundreds of mouflon."

"But how do all those animals manage with only one little spring?"

"Ach, they don't—as I have said. But what moisture is there, they find: dew on the leaves of bushes, pools in the rocks after rain."

My eyes were lifted as he talked; we stood leaning on a parapet of the bow. To the west the flat rampart of a mountain curved around, high above the horn-shaped bay. On the beach the surf bubbled white, a disappearing scarf; the roiled shingle glistened in the sunlight. Our first wave of men were tramping through the grasses above the waterline, slow in their labor, as if their feet were in quicksand.

"What is that on top of the palisade?" I asked Thompson, just as he was descending the rope ladder into the lifeboat.

He shielded his eyes with one hand. "Those're mouflon, I think. Wait'll I get my binoculars." He alighted in the boat, drew out field glasses from the case slung around his neck and adjusted the sights. "Two rams! Big ones, too. I've always known 'em to do this. They keep scouts; there must be a herd in the valley just beyond that hill." The Iranian crewman dug in with his oars as the craft pulled away, but Thompson kept the black binoculars to his eyes. In his Eisenhower jacket and overseas cap, he looked like a general in charge of strategic operations.

I was in the last load for shore, with McCaffrey and his son Bud; the clumsy, heavy boat was frosted with salt, and it wallowed in the trough of the waves like a piece of driftwood.

The scrawny Persian, dressed in a grey denim proletarian coat and trousers, leaned with each pull, all the way back, then forward, as if a whip were cracking over his shoulders in a slave galley. He headed straight in, and when the scrabble sounded under our feet, I leapt from the prow, rope in hand, and dragged the thing onto the beach. After we had unloaded, we pushed our boatman off again, and he laughed cheerily, wishing us good hunting.

That poor devil had had a workout, I said to McCaffrey.

"What do you mean? For a whole day the crew will lay up, doin' nothing out there, while they wait for us. This is a vacation for 'em!" He shouldered his duffle bag. "But not for us," he laughed. "C'mon, Bud." The two of them went up the embankment to set out their camp: father and son on an outing. Last fall they had hunted boar in Kurdistan; they had brought down a few ducks and geese on the marshes near Tabriz. But they were not devoted hunters, they just didn't want to miss anything their travels had to offer. In the Caribbean they had been deep-sea fishing and skin diving; while on a road-building project in Spain they had become bull-fight *aficionados;* in Greece they had studied the ruins of Mycenae. There were a lot of countries ahead of them, still to be lived in, pleasures and sights to be discovered, odd foods to be eaten. Meanwhile, McCaffrey built his bank balance in the United States, in anticipation of his retirement from road construction; then he hoped to open an inn in Guatemala.

Thompson called me over to his camp site, asking if I were hungry. It was after three, and we'd had no lunch. I was ravenous. He opened several cans of Army C rations; the consulate was stocked with supplies, in case of emergency, and periodically the tins had to be replaced. After our meal we set up canvas cots and flung out the Arctic sleeping bags, never before used. We had no tent, but in the protected cup of the bay, no wind blowing, and the sun mantling our shoulders, sleeping *à la belle étoile* seemed a feasible prospect. The French consul shook his head when he saw our naked beds. He and the German had already erected a neat white pup tent, which they planned to share, in true Common Market friendliness. The doctor's equipment included a small West German foot-pump, which he used to inflate their air mattresses. "Are you going to hunt now?" asked Monsieur M., glancing at Thompson.

"Look at those mouflon up there."

"Those are mouflon?" He shielded his eyes. "I think they must be shepherds, no?"

"No. Here, have a look through my binoculars."

"I see! I see!" One mouflon was posed sideways; even the unaided eye could appreciate his beautiful, linear proportions, a form which so attracted primitive Iranian potters that they etched the animal on their crude pipkins.

"You think those sheep can't move?" said Thompson. He sighted through the telescopic 30:06, freezing over the barrel, the padded stock lodged against his shoulder.

Monsieur M., smiling nervously, fastened the strap of his helmet firmly under his chin, as if for blast protection. "You will not shoot from here? Is it not too far?"

"Of course. I was only kidding." He put down the rifle. "And remember, we're only allowed to take home one male apiece. I wouldn't want to bag him now. What would I do the rest of the time, till you guys got your limits?"

We turned at the sound of raucous laughter coming from the high-poled field tent erected by Hawley and his cronies. It was about fifty yards away—an extremely big, black, waterproofed army-maneuvers tent. McCaffrey laughed and said: "What the hell's a hunting trip for, if it don't start with a little booze?"

I saw that Thompson was rather annoyed. He spoke of the necessity of unified action against the mouflon, but he doubted if he could ever get Hawley into a serious discussion of how to proceed against the game. "It's those sergeants with him! They're like a bunch of city duck hunters on vacation in the north woods. They didn't come to hunt."

McCaffrey and his son had finished setting up their camp; we'd all had something to eat except the doctor, who refused to join us in our repast. A short time later I noticed he was nowhere around, and nobody had seen in which direction he had gone. Thompson pointed his thumb at the army tent: "To hell with those guys, let's go for mouflon."

He set the pace for the rest of us; the McCaffreys, Monsieur M. and I were strung out behind as we attacked the steep yellow clay mountain side, fighting our way through scrub brush, clambering up rocky slopes. We zigzagged our course, digging boot-toes into outcroppings wherever they could be found. Now and then I paused, leaning flat against the mountain, spread-eagled, as if to stop a landslide. With each level of altitude gained, the harbor below looked more beautiful. The rusty ship was orange in the waning sunlight, the bay Aegean blue, and the wide reaches of the lake spread away to the nibbling sandy edges of the eastern shore, beyond which the mountains began, snow-capped Sahand in the distance.

Keeping up with Thompson's brutally swift gait, we arrived puffing at the crest, where we immediately turned down a sheep-path worn through the mountain gorse. He had the rifle and camera—and binoculars; but the Frenchman with his naked eye first discovered the herd of mouflon streaming out of a gorge below us. Because their tawny color was almost exactly the hue of the terrain, they were scarcely visible until they moved, and then, running together by the hundreds, they were as liquid as a brown stream. I looked through Thompson's binoculars: they appeared to be the size of deer, and some of their horns made complete circles, coiled like the giant seashells in which one hears the ocean roar. Their heads were narrow and long, like a collie dog's. They were rampaging now, beautifully bounding, a rhythm that did not seem staccatoed by hoof-beats on the ground. Thousands of the creatures, but how would we ever get a shot at them? I realized now the full difficulty of our expedition; probably Thompson did, too, for there were no more boasts about bagging our limits too soon.

The island was veined by two valleys; numerous dry, steep gulleys cut into the mountains and gave on to the central ravines. With so many hiding places and visibility unimpeded by trees or sizable bushes, the hunter could spend torturous hours getting into position for taking aim, only to discover, once he peered over a mountain rim, that the sheep had all emptied out of the valley long since.

"The herd will break up now," said Thompson, "but probably re-form tonight or early in the morning. I'd hate to louse up our chances for tomorrow since we don't have many hours of light left. When the mouflon start to scatter we have a chance of getting close to a couple of them. There aren't enough leaders to guide the herds and watch out for their safety, so we can probably find an isolated group without a leader, without scouts. And since this is an island, there's no place for 'em to run, but back down one of these valleys, where a few men should be posted." He decided to go north along the ridge in the hope that part of the herd had fled in that direction. The plan was to deploy against the game, spreading out sufficiently so that if we stumbled upon stragglers and didn't make the shot, the mouflon would run past other marksmen. Unfortunately, none of us knew the exact topography of the island. Monsieur M. went off toward the south with his double-barreled shotgun, which he must now have known was a hopelessly inadequate weapon. McCaffrey dropped down the mountain slope, directly to the west; his son and I (the boy had a good rifle) found a path descending the hillside toward the southwest.

As we sank lower from the spine of the mountain, we encountered foothills which became extremely deceptive: again and again we fancied ourselves almost at the floor of the canyon—and expected mouflon to be quietly grazing there. The false-alarm tension, as we mounted each hillock only to discover another empty ravine before us, a little lower down, began to prey upon our nerves. We talked in less than moderate tones and allowed stones to spill away from our footsteps. To the west we suddenly saw, a couple of miles in the distance, still another herd of wild sheep, jumping over a ridge and disappearing in the cleft of a mountain. "I'm going to shoot. I know it's too far," said Bud McCaffrey, watching their arched, gazelle-like leaps, "but I'm going to." Flat on his belly, he took aim and fired.

"You might as well be shooting at the sky." If the mouflon were now aware of us, there was no way to tell, since their swift, panicky escape could not have been stepped-up. The sharp crack of his rifle rang metallic on the rocks, but the sound was quickly absorbed in the small gulley where we lay and perhaps had been scarcely noticeable on the other side of the mountain.

Bud's father had not been far away, however, and with a clatter of small stones he slid down the slope and came up to us. "You shooting at them things way over there?" he asked, with amused tolerance. He was a tall, handsome man with a quick smile. "Don't you know bullets cost fifty cents apiece?"

The boy said nothing. Then McCaffrey remarked that his thighs and calves were aching from the climb; he was going back to camp, since the light was growing dimmer; once the sun set, he mused, evening would descend quickly. Bud replied that he wanted to hunt a little longer, and I went with him, not only because he had the gun, but in order to reach the valley floor and explore to the south a bit so we might get our bearings more readily next day.

Wild pistachio trees, gnarled and twisted, their grey trunks satiny, grew here and there beside porous yellow rocks. The central corridor of the ravine proved to be a pebbly, gutted, flash-flood river bed, where walking was easier since the surface was mostly level. The sun was already behind the ridge, and a purply evening dusk emerged from the coulees, making uncertain visibility for game. We encountered the Frenchman on his way back to camp; he reported having scared up three rams and several ewes, which escaped up the eastern mountain slope—not farther away into the valley. Had he the proper gun and were it not sundown, he would have tracked them; as it was, he was heading for camp. Since Thompson, on his trek to the north, would eventually swing around and follow the central mountain spine down the center of the island, putting him near us, though we were located in the valley, I thought we should wait for him before going after the mouflon. I hoped to have a chance with his rifle.

While Bud and I ambled along in the valley, we noticed a black goat perched on a ledge. Could it be a wild mountain goat? Neither of us had heard of such animals in these parts, and yet this creature's spiky horns, its size, and its shape all told us it was indeed a goat. "Must be a domestic goat, belonging to the shepherds on this island," I said.

"Let's watch it, anyhow."

The animal did not move. Bud squatted, rifle aimed. "You'd better not shoot—you might hit it," I said.

He didn't fire. A few minutes later we heard a shepherd calling from the mountain, frantically waving one arm. He scrambled down the embankment with the alacrity of a mountain goat and ran up to us, saying we must not shoot his *buz*. No, no, we assured him, his *buz* on the ledge was safe. I gave him a candy bar, and we became friends. His visage was creole-brown; an adolescent beard and mustache grew freely but sparsely on his face. He was about fifteen, just a trifle older than Bud. They made a fine contrast, standing there. Bud noticed that the shepherd carried a bony, new-born lamb around his neck, holding the two foreleg hooves in one hand—it was why he could only wave to us with one arm, on the hilltop. "Is the lamb dead?" Bud asked.

"*Murdeh ast?*"

"*Na, na, zendeh,*" he answered me.

Bud stroked the matted coils of black hair. "Is it all right, really?"

"*Besyar khoob rasti?*"

"*Bali, bali,*" said the shepherd, smiling. His cape was of quarter-inch thick brown wool, two peaks about two inches high on the shoulders, like support points for a tent. Down the panels in front a riotous stream of flowers had been embroidered, probably by the shepherd himself during his endless hours of exile here. At night the voluminous cape could be drawn close about him, like a snail going into its shell for the evening. The lamb was now a stole around the youth's collar bone, its liver-colored muzzle against the boy's neck, the rest of the body hanging limply down the back. At night under the cape, curled on its master's chest, it would be warmed by the heat of the human body.

We saw Thompson striding along the ridge high above to the west; he moved with the fluid tread of an Indian scout, his rifle like a lance in front of him. The professional ease with which he covered the rough terrain was indicative that to him the style of one's pursuit of game was as important as the object of the hunt. Joining up with him, we set off in the direction advised by the Frenchman, with the idea that we were swinging toward camp, as well. Upon mounting the last barrier before the earth fell away to the sea, we looked below—toward the end of a canyon—but saw no ship in the bay. We were farther to the south, obviously; already it was quite dark.

On the sharp incline of the mountain, we heard a rustle. A small herd of mouflon stood above us, seventy-five yards away;

dim in the gloaming, they looked bigger than I had expected. Standing close together, frozen by their sight of us, they were buff-reddish in color, perhaps a yard high at the withers; their heads lifted, the coils of horn gave them a wild dignity. The moment of confrontation lasted but a few seconds, only the fading light was a factor of uncertainty. The mouflon knew we were enemies but counted on their disguising color and the way they blended into the dusk on the mountainside; with a blink of the eye they were almost lost to sight, or replaced by the rocks they stood next to. There were perhaps a dozen animals. Bud, without a bullet in his rifle chamber, hastily snapped one in; the ratchet sound sent the mouflon bounding away, over the sandy terrain, rocks clattering. Thompson fired immediately—quickly followed by a shot from Bud; both missed.

Thompson reprimanded Bud for not having been ready. Though he was only a boy, considering his extensive hunting experience his negligence was indeed surprising. Rather than vent the full force of his anger, Thompson scurried up the mountain slope in pursuit of the animals. Since it was nearly dark, the evening hour alone might quiet the mouflon quickly; perhaps on the other side of the ridge they were already calmly grouped. Bud and I decided to turn for home. A thin moon in the east helped somewhat, and we began to pick our way along by the faint luminescence of objects in twilight.

With the fire on shore as a beacon we descended slowly down a cliff, our only real danger being rampaging sheep dogs, trained to rip apart any strange living creature prowling in the brush at night. We were the last to arrive at camp. The tents, cots and camping equipment made the beachhead seem a civilized refuge. Thompson and McCaffrey were preparing hobo stew over a brisk bonfire, and whiskey was passed around while we waited for supper to warm. "No, no, thank you," said the doctor when the bottle came to him.

"It'll warm you up," said Thompson.

"Unfortunately, that is not true. One may feel warmed at first, but when the effect of alcohol wears off, you are colder." The Frenchman agreed, but he would take the whiskey anyhow, since he enjoyed the taste of Scotch; on special occasions such as this, must one always be sensible? He produced a bottle of wine, which he suggested we drink with our meal; after we had enjoyed such a repast, surely we would all crawl into our sleeping bags and snore blissfully, despite the wilderness in which we found ourselves.

We sat on our hunkers close to the fire; it seemed to give off less and less heat. Hawley and his buddies, hooting and shouting in their tent, were black silhouette monsters on the canvas walls.

The meal seemed over too quickly, devoured out of tin cups, the gravy sopped up with bread. Our fire was now scarlet charcoal and disappearing fast; we all made forays for bits of driftwood, weeds and roots, but only the German managed to find authentic wood, greyed and salted by the waters. It sparked blue when thrown on our blaze. The chill beyond our illuminated circle was surprisingly vicious. We repeatedly searched the area with flashlights, ranging wider and wider, but there was no fuel; when what we had gathered burned away, we'd have to go to bed. I got so close to the paltry flames, part of my wool glove went up in smoke. Finally it seemed best to stand in a huddle, taking the heat emanations on our faces, enclosing the column of warmth with our bodies.

We talked of mouflon. The name was French, *n'est ce pas?*

Yes, Monsieur M. replied, the creatures were in the mountains of Corsica and Sardinia; a smaller animal, he thought, with a marking on its back. Personally he had not hunted them on Corsica, nor in North Africa, where he'd been stationed previously. The Berbers hunted an animal called *aoudad,* or ruffed mouflon; the wool was used by the natives for their garments.

"But how did mouflon get way out here?"

"Wild sheep are sheep after all," said the doctor, "and where man grazes his tame animals, there you will often find the wild ones, of a similar species. In this region the sheep are the Armenian version, but toward the south, near Pakistan, there is still another kind of mouflon, called by the Punjab name, *urial.* I have read accounts of hunting there, in the earlier times. Wild sheep are said to trust more to their vision for protection against enemies than to their noses, unlike the wild goats. I think ibex, too, have great powers of sight. The mouflon—call them what you will—are famous for their sentries. They are standing on hill-tops all through the country; you can see them when you drive along. It is this cleverness which has intrigued hunters for many years."

The drunken strains of "Roll Me Over" came from the tent of revelry; none of us were much amused. Their whiskey brawl seemed such a curiously pedestrian way of spending the evening. "They'll never get up at dawn tomorrow," said Thompson, shaking his head.

We were all under the illusion that the real hunt would begin the next day, that our misadventures of the afternoon meant nothing. In the dim glow of my flashlight, I sat on the cot, removed my boots, and climbed into the Arctic bag. Thompson, who was undressing in his bag, urged me to part with everything, otherwise I'd be too warm. His advice was sound, but for the wrong reason. I didn't heed him. Had I stripped, the duck down would have had a chance to hold the body heat. Dressed in a thick Scottish sweater and long underwear, I lay very still and shivered. The Khoi stocking cap was a noose over my head, down to my chest; a wide slit over my nose allowed for breathing; with its faint, lanolin smell it was rather like being encased in the shank of a sheep.

I should have dreamt of mouflon but didn't. Sometime after midnight I awoke, having drunk too much wine; a trip to the weeds was necessary. The wind had come up and heavy breakers dashed upon the shore; it was so cold that the water we had used for making instant coffee was frozen solid. With the moon going down, a scimitar above the black mountain to the west, and the incessant boom of the heavy salt waves, the scene was utterly desolate, beyond a mere quality of stark remoteness; the hour partook of the primitive so completely that the presence of human life seemed an anachronism not to be believed. I hurried back to my sack, crawled in, and drew the darkness over my head.

A short while later it was dawn. The lake greyed into being; the mountain rimming the camp emerged in its implacable barren contours of yellow rock and tawny sand. The Frenchman and the German were stirring about, but I did not move for fear the sleeve of warmth I lay in would unravel. Face turned to the east, I saw striations of rose and pink behind the remote, refrigerated dome of Sahand. Red began to smear across the entire unclouded sky, caught in the desert dust particles of the atmosphere; then the lake was molten and a stroke of gold touched the top of the fore-mountains of Eshek. The iridescent surface of the sea turned from red to purple to blue. The sun flashed on my brow, needling my eyes, and it was time to arise.

On the ashes of our last night's fire, the Europeans had built a crackling little blaze. I tried to get into my boots, but they were frozen stiff, unyielding. Thompson laughed at my efforts until he tried to pull on his own. The Frenchman squatted near the fire and roasted a wiener on a stick. "Would you care for it?" he asked me.

"Thanks, but I think we've got some breakfast." I thought his meal very queer for this hour. Leaning intently over the fire, in his heavy military overcoat and helmet, he looked like a sad trench soldier.

Dressed at last, I found that our fresh fruit was frozen solid. The plates from last night's supper were waiting to be done, and while Thompson heated water for coffee, I went down to the lake. Food was frozen as well as stuck on. With sand and water I tried scouring the metal bowls in which we'd had our stew, but my fingers became so stiff from the cold, they were like using chopsticks. At last, giving up, I went back to the campsite, only to find the fire going out from lack of fuel. Even in daylight there was no wood to be found, though we might have burned the flash-fire tumbleweeds, one every ten seconds. Thompson admitted that it would be impossible to cook C ration sausages, as he had planned. Our oranges, apples and pears were like decorative glass fruit for a centerpiece. Disconsolately, we munched frozen pieces of bread, left over from last night. I asked the Frenchman for a hot dog, which he gave me, and set about trying to roast it before the fire died entirely. Unable to feel heat at all, I burned the whole finger of one glove before I smelled charred wool. Thompson succeeded in finding a can of fruit cocktail in such heavy syrup it hadn't frozen. We shared it with

Monsieur M. "Where's the doctor, wouldn't he like some?" asked Thompson.

"I think not. *Le docteur n'est pas ici.*"

"Already?" said Thompson.

"You can't tell me he's not digging for Hulago Khan's tomb," I said.

"I just want to know when he comes upon those twelve virgins."

"Not that they'll do any of us much good."

"Lord no, they must be frozen solid."

"He said he wished to collect scientific specimens," said the Frenchman.

"Well, that's a new word for it," said McCaffrey, who had come up while we talked.

"Are you all set to go?" asked Thompson. Father and son, snug in turtle-neck sweaters and wool-lined windbreakers, had their guns in hand.

"Sure, why not?"

"Is it not time for reveille?" asked the Frenchman, gesturing toward the army tent.

"I'm not going to try to work with those guys today. We'll be better off on our own."

After a bottle of whiskey was passed around, our libation for luck, we shouldered arms and set off, climbing the mountain by the north trail; the McCaffreys struck out in a southerly direction. Our strategy was to spread to all parts of the island, preventing the mouflon from hiding in one spot; we hoped to get a crossruff going.

Upon gaining the crest of the ridge, we came upon a shepherd who told us that the mouflon were now in the southern region of the island. More important: he said his fellow shepherds were grazing their flocks on the sloping, lower land in the western part of the island. Mouflon could not seek refuge there, and a pincer movement now seemed feasible. The Frenchman subsequently turned west, while Thompson and I skirted the shoreline cliffs on the north. Raw rocks of a grey, porous texture overlooked a steep drop-off to a jagged beach below. I looked in vain for signs of lamb skeletons down on the birdless shore; nor were there any eagles hovering in the sky. Several thick-leaved cactuses, deep green against the sand, were thriving along the edge of the cliff, as well as mottled orange and green lichen and bits of moss.

Suddenly, leaping up from nowhere like a couple of jack rabbits on the prairie, a ram and an ewe sped away ahead of us. Thompson had long since turned over his rifle to me; but in the few seconds while I raised the weapon, trying to find the speeding creatures in the telescopic lens, they were already two or three hundred yards away.

We circled the backbone of Eshek, traveling down the top of the central chain, which afforded a spectacular view of the entire island, including the western pastures, where the cooperative shepherds were on the alert, ready to scare off any mouflon. All along, we passed nascent canyons which dropped away on both sides, becoming deep valleys farther on. Cautiously, we peered down each ravine, hoping to come upon game.

I caught myself, just on the brink of falling into a shallow trench. "What in God's name . . . ?" I began, but didn't have to wait for Thompson's reply. Here were some excavations for Hulago's grave. The trough had been partially filled in with rocks and stones and was only six feet long, three feet deep. But, looking around, I noticed incisions elsewhere on the slope, some half-hearted, some in earnest—none were fresh diggings. They might have been a year or two old; sprouts of weed, frozen dry, tufted the sandy lumps. "Come on," whispered Thompson. "If there'd been any gold here, he'd have found it. Let's hunt mouflon."

The shallow ravine in which we were traveling ended, forcing us over the top into a small valley on the other side. A mouflon straggler—a large, handsome ram—wandered over the hill opposite and descended toward us, very soon dipping out of sight below a ridge of a branch canyon. "There's your trophy," Thompson murmured. "Go after him. If you keep descending here, you should reach the bottom and be able to see up the little ravine where he is. He'll be in easy range. If he wanders back over the hill—that's the direction I'm going in now—he'll run back, right past you. Either way you've got a sure shot coming. Be careful with it, it might be your only chance left." I nodded and he left me, soundlessly picking his way out of the gulley, until he was safely over the edge and gone.

Then I started my descent. The hillside was steep and bulging with rocks, many of them loose. I dug my heels in securely with each step and anxiously searched the opposite slope, fearing that the ram might come out of the coulee before I was ready for him. The trip down took nearly twenty minutes; I was on my knees the latter part of it, creeping behind rocks. There was no sound of wind, nothing at all to intrude upon the stillness; when a hawk flew over, its wings creaking, I jumped in surprise. Finally I rounded the nose of the hill between me and the ram; by now I was an experienced enough hunter of mouflon to realize that I might look up an empty cleft, the creature having simply disappeared.

But he hadn't. He stood with nose lifted seventy-five yards away, the horns making great curls over his head, each about thirty inches long. I branded him with the cross-hairs of my sights; he filled the lens, and I saw his shoulder muscles tense. His head jerked slightly with an awareness of unease or danger, but he had not yet discovered what it was. All of this happened in a matter of seconds. My arms were trembling with such excitement I could not stop the bouncing circle of vision in the telescope; it roamed over the target at random. I tried with absolute concentration to stop the tremble of my hand, but it was no use; the crosshairs continued to wander over the mouflon, above, behind, beside him. I realized I would have to squat, making a tripod of my elbow on a boulder, before I could take proper aim. In doing so, a tiny pebble hit another. That was enough. Immediately the ram tensed for flight. I took aim and fired. He leapt away as if my shot had given him energy; I still hoped dimly that his bound was the last surge of life before he tumbled, but knew, as he ran, that nothing at all daunted him. I fired again, and missed. Then he was over the hill and away.

Thompson scrambled down to my side. "What happened anyhow?"

I began to describe my stalk, but faltered; such talk is useless and depressing; neither of us said much.

A shepherd—the same fellow we had encountered earlier—came up grinning. Yes, he had seen the ram going off, and he knew where more of them could be found. He begged to be our guide. We needed one, and we loped along behind him, heading south. His pace was so fast even Thompson had difficulty keeping up. "These guys are a cross between a mountain goat and a mouflon," he said.

We walked several miles in the direction of the distant winter sun, then paused to rest. We sat down on some table rocks that made good benches, and for warmth, set fire to a small dead cactus bush. Though the sun was out and felt warm where its rays struck, everything not touched by the sun was bitterly cold. I had a few frozen hard-boiled eggs in my pocket and Thompson had two hard oranges. Since we'd been exerting ourselves and were comfortably heated, we imagined the fruit and eggs would be thawed out by this time, too; they weren't, but we ate them, giving some to the shepherd. He said he'd been on Eshek six months, and he and his companions were out of sugar and bread. We commiserated with him and promised to give him some of our provisions when we left. "Why do you put up with this kind of life?" Thompson asked him, in Turki. "Isn't there some other work you would rather do?" The boy replied that he had never done anything else. "How old are you?" Nineteen. He would like to go school, to learn to read and write. "Well, why don't you?"

"Pedaram be-man farman dad," he said in Pharsi; his father had ordered him to do what he was doing. Thompson interpreted his switch to Pharsi as meaning that he was bilingual. "If you want to leave, come on the boat with us," he said. Then, getting no response, repeated his suggestion in Turki. The reply came slowly, in the tongue of the peasants:

"No, I'd be afraid to."

We heard shots to the south, a regular volley of them, and Thompson said, "Those are Springfield army rifles; the sergeants must be in the field. Come on, we'd better be on the lookout; they may have stumbled on the main herd."

"Anja, anja," said the shepherd, pointing. Indeed, far down the valley, pouring out of a gorge, were hundreds of stampeding mouflon. They seemed to be fanning out toward the east, in the direction of our camp.

A short while later we saw two black human figures, bug-sized, scrambling on a mountain slope; then two more. "Where'd those people come from?" I asked.

"The sergeants must have a couple of native guides with 'em. Look at that one shepherd run! He must be nearly as fast as a mouflon."

Shouting voices echoed up and down the canyon walls; then there were more shots. McCaffrey and Bud, attracted by the shots, came up as we deliberated what to do next. "This is like beating yourself over the head with a hammer," said the road engineer. "It feels so good when you stop."

No, they'd seen nothing, hadn't even had a shot. Bud now decided to team up with Thompson, who was confident of running into a fragment of the flock we had just seen. His father announced he was frankly tired of it and wanted to get back to the ship. The two of us headed north; it was, however, six or seven miles to the northern cliffs and a couple more from there, back to camp. About half way, we decided to go cross-country after all, but for our descent to the valley floor foolishly chose a point which was almost perpendicular, requiring extreme care. We clutched the roots of bushes, clung to rocks until they came apart in our hands, and slid on our backs when necessary. Now and then I noticed the ground trampled in front of grottos of soft, knobular yellow rocks with hollowed places where the mouflon obviously curled up at night. The recesses were so smoothly worn, the cupped rocks so cozy, they seemed almost to have been constructed by the mouflon, rather than discovered by them. We also came upon another shallow trench, at the base of a prominent outcropping of rock. "That damn German has been everywhere," said McCaffrey. "I almost broke my leg on one of his holes."

"But I didn't see him digging anywhere, did you?"

"No, he kept out of our way."

The ship gave a long, mournful blast on its whistle. "It's one o'clock—that's when we were supposed to leave."

"Well, we're not going to. I doubt if I'll make it over this mountain."

The more we rested, the wearier we got; we decided to push on and not stop until we reached camp. But on the ridge we paused in triumph. With the ship in full view and the camp clearly visible below us, the trip down was hastily accomplished. But as we were nearing the beach, a gun blasted. McCaffrey turned to me, astonished—both of us feeling the irony of the moment; while we had been stumbling all over the island in desperate pursuit, the mouflon were occupying our camp. Rifles cocked, we stealthily crept through the brush and down the slope to the beach. Then we encountered the Frenchman, his blunderbuss still smoking. He looked up, giving us a melon-mouthed smile, and exhibited a large black and white magpie, which he had just brought down. He held it up proudly by the tip of the wing. "I had to shoot some-sing, no?"

The ship in the bay hooted.

We found that none of the other hunters were yet back. I made it to my camp cot with a conscious sense of forcing my bones to keep up their jointed workings, and flopped. I felt I could sleep that instant, but was too exhausted. Turning, I saw the German neatly tying a bowstring around his collapsed tent; his sleeping bag was a snug little pillow; his gear was stashed together in a civilized way, as if he were waiting for the next train out. He saw me looking. "Don't you think you had better pack up?"

"Yeah—in a bit."

"Did you shoot anything?"

"No. Did you find any treasure?"

"I collected some fine specimens and an unusual mollusk."

The Frenchman came over with a bottle of Vichy and two cups; we mixed a couple of Scotch and sodas and waited for the others to arrive. Thompson showed up ten minutes later with Bud, turning him over to his father, saying he would never hunt with a teenager again. He had had a beautiful shot set up, but the boy had fired too soon, from half a mile away.

The Iranian shepherd guide, standing next to Thompson, looked with interest at our gear; then he shared lunch with us, eating with his fingers out of the tins of C rations. Thompson gave him a number of cans we had left over.

The two sergeants straggled into camp empty-handed, with a long, bitter tale of how their Iranian guides had kept shouting and dancing about, scaring off every mouflon in sight. Finally they'd gotten so angry at the shepherds they had chased them away, firing over their heads to scare hell out of them. "You should have seen those Varsees run! God, you should've seen 'em go!"

"We *did*," said Thompson. "But where's Hawley?"

Neither of them knew. They had last seen him following several mouflon up a canyon. To reassure the ship captain that we were actually breaking up camp and getting ready to depart, Thompson decided to send out a boatload of supplies and one passenger—Bud. The *Pahlavi* was due to reach the port of Sherifkhane to the north by nightfall, but at this rate, would never make it.

At last Hawley arrived, bellowing from the foothills and dragging a mouflon through the brush behind him. He shouted for help with the critter. We all went to his aid, eager to witness at least one trophy of our hunting expedition. "You guys didn't get nothing? Nothing at all? Well, what the hell was the matter with you? Can't none of you shoot? Do I got to do all the work around here?" He let out a laugh and took a slug of whiskey from the bottle proffered by one of the sergeants.

"But you've got a ewe!" said Thompson.

"I've got a what?"

"It's a female. You know you weren't supposed to shoot them!"

"Hell, you think I was gonna get skunked? I seen it had no horns—thought maybe it was a young one. Anyhow, I figured one was better than nothing. I couldn't show up here in camp, the only guy without a mouflon, now could I?"

The small female was the color of undyed kid gloves, its coat burred and scrofulous, some of the hide showing. It had been shot through the head and now lay sprawled in the weeds, crumpled over on itself, a sickly pile of fleece-covered bones. Obviously, she had been one of the diseased mouflon.

"Hurry up now, the ship's waiting on us," said Thompson.

"I got to clean her, first. Lemme get my knife. You just tell those Varsees out there to wait up on me, hear?"

The sergeants walked to the tent with Hawley and began pulling out the stakes; they assembled their gear and took down the canvas while he bent over the carcass in the weeds, talking aloud to himself, while he worked. Since there was no place to string up the mouflon, he had to cut her where she lay. "No meat on *these* ribs. Whew! There ain't much to 'er, is there? All that work for a little bastard like this." In a few minutes three buzzards circled overhead, ophidian necks lowered. "Lice and ticks—God, I've never seen the like!"

By the time the equipment and most of the hunters had been transported to the ship, Hawley was ready to depart, the beast on his shoulder as he stepped into the lifeboat. The Iranian shepherd left on shore called *"Khoda-hafez"* as we set off for the *Pahlavi*. The ship's anchor was already up, the motor throbbing. As soon as we had scrambled aboard, it chugged out of the bay, past the strange rocks. I glanced back and waved at the shepherd on the beach, and in doing so, noticed two figures silhouetted on the horizon, standing on the rampart overlooking half-moon bay in almost exactly the spot I had been an hour ago. "Hand me your binoculars," I said to Thompson.

He knew immediately why I wanted them. "I'll be damned. They're looking at us go, just the way they watched us coming in. Probably the same two mouflon, at that."

In the lenses I easily made out the buff-colored rams, mounted serenely on the topmost rocks, horned heads high, as if they were gazing over our ship and far out to sea.

13 AMONG REVOLUTIONARIES

THE day of my departure for Hakhapur, Mahmoud arrived at my door before seven in the morning, and we proceeded down empty streets to the bus station, where he purchased two tickets, refusing to allow me to reimburse him. As the motor roared to life, a man in the rear was our muezzin, begging Allah for a safe journey, and all the passengers save Mahmoud bowed their heads. He looked straight ahead, watching the driver's skill in maneuvering past the sharp corner of the depot.

We crossed the Bitter River, a wide, aimless, rock-filled salt stream which ran through the middle of Tabriz, and headed for the red and purple mountains rimming the valley. Chickens in the aisle, their legs tied together, squawked in protest at the vehicle's speed. There were frequent stops to pick up anyone who flagged the bus; dust poured in the windows from passing traffic; we bounced over potholes and forded small streams. Mahmoud conversed with me on a wide range of subjects, struggling to uncover an English vocabulary acquired largely from reading, forcing himself to speak sentences and demanding that I correct him when he committed errors. "Did you know, in some villages the teachers tell the pupils to go out and hunt for food?"

"What sort of food?"

"Before winter, before the cold comes and kills everything, the children go out and hunt for grass. This they will eat when winter comes. They have nothing else."

"You mean, during a famine they do this? The year when there has been no crops?"

"*Na, na,* all the time in some places, this is what the children do. I have seen it. They gather the grasses; they do not go to school. They are too hungry."

"In Hakhapur does this happen?"

"Not recently, while I have been there. But maybe this year it will be famine, who knows? The government would do nothing."

There were rest stops now and then at *chai-khanes;* the passengers being too many for the toilets, they squatted behind low mud walls or scrambled into ditches. For refreshment, Mahmoud carried raw potatoes in his pocket. He peeled and sliced a few wedges, and we crunched these happily. Less starchy than raw Idaho potatoes, they had the clean crispness of water chestnuts.

"Iran, I do not believe, is a civilized country," said Mahmoud, shaking his head. "It is not civilized, is it?"

"No, in many ways it isn't."

"But Russia and the United States—they are civilized."

"And England and France and . . ."

"No, no, not France!"

If he thus excluded France, I couldn't imagine what he meant by the word "civilization." I queried him, and he explained that he did not like de Gaulle. "That man is very, very bad man." Over Radio Moscow he had heard de Gaulle described as a fascist, "a wicked man." But he had little notion of the exact charges, nor was he curious to explore the accusations. Genially firm in his repeated statement about de Gaulle, *that* ended the conversation on civilization.

We arrived in Hakhapur at noon and walked a few blocks down dun-colored walled lanes to the *khane* where Mahmoud lived. "I am a poor man, as you know. I have nothing here, but you are welcome." We entered a bare, enclosed courtyard and walked to a small open hallway, which gave on to a medium-sized room: he shared this chamber with two other young men. Cooking facilities and a little loft where Mahmoud slept were located in the hall. A bed had been fitted into the niche, which was reached by climbing a ladder; here, Mahmoud said, he studied at night while his roommates joked around in the room below, frittering away their lives.

Removing our shoes, we walked into the heatless living room; the floor was covered by a cheap, brilliant red carpet. Instead of the tinted portraits of Mohammed which adorned walls of most homes, there were large décolleté photographs of Elizabeth Taylor, Sophia Loren, and Gina Lollobrigida. "My roommates put those up."

He urged me to sit down and be comfortable on one of the two camp cots, but he made no move to start the iron pot-stove. My feet were numb, and I rubbed my gloved hands briskly. He wore only a suit, with a scarf around his neck, and no gloves; it did not occur to him I might be cold. He showed me his German-made radio; next to card-playing, listening to the wireless was the chief source of entertainment. There was no electricity at this hour, however; we would have to wait until six o'clock, at which time we could listen for five hours. The current stopped at 11:00 p.m. Mahmoud clearly wondered what to do with me, now that I was here. He dashed out to the hall several times; once he was gone for fifteen minutes, but insisted that I remain where I was. I concluded that he was preparing lunch.

"You have your pajamas with you?" he asked. "Good! Would you care to change now?"

I shook my head, puzzled; I understood his invitation more clearly when one of Mahmoud's roommates, a bank clerk, came home for his meal. He quickly took off his pressed trousers, white shirt and tie, and carefully laid them out on the bed, then got into pajama bottoms and a denim housecoat, for relaxing and working around the place.

Mahmoud brought out his photograph albums. "Would you care to see some pictures?" I looked at snapshots of his family, some of whom had been killed or imprisoned following the collapse of the abortive People's Republic of Azerbaijan in 1946. These men were his heroes, and he spoke of their deeds in a reverent, slow voice. There were photographs of Iranian wrestlers and weight-lifting champions. One athlete—Mahmoud pointed his blunt finger at him—had been invited "by your government to visit America and teach wrestling. But he went to Moscow, instead."

"Why?"

"I do not know—you tell me why?"

In another photograph I saw an emaciated Teheran man who lived by selling his blood for five tomans a liter. Mahmoud said he had sold too much and nearly died. "For such things to happen! *That* is the kind of government we have here."

He closed the volume. "I have other books for you to see, books of great wisdom which I study. Do you have knowledge of the science of magnetism?"

"I don't think so."

We are all born with a certain amount of natural magnetism, he explained, which gives us influence over other people. Some men, like the Shah—and all great leaders—have an immense amount of this capacity. One time the Shah was in his garden when two lions escaped from their cages and came bounding toward him. Whereas the gardeners fled over the walls, the Shah simply stared at the beasts without fear, and he stopped them in their tracks. This sort of natural magnetism comes through one's mother's milk. The second kind of magnetism is acquired through great study and concentration; it gives you the power to make people do as you wish.

I shook my head. "You study how to take unfair advantage of people?"

"Unfair? No. Never unfair, only what is right. But I must have strength and power to do that; otherwise people are led by bad men with trashy ideas. I have also learned hypnotism. A Russian doctor in Teheran taught me this science. I learned it very quickly."

The other roommate arrived, a pharmacist who spoke some French, and my hosts set up a small dining table. Mahmoud handed me a pair of heavy rayon pajama trousers, urging me to change clothes, and I did. The stove was now going, and the heat of our bodies had somewhat warmed the room. Wooden chairs were brought in from the hall, though I noticed there were not enough; the table, I concluded, was a concession to me, their Western guest, for normally we would all sit on the carpet in our pajamas and dip with scoops of *nun* into community bowls set between us. The restaurant catered the meal, which consisted of *chelo kebab*: a mound of long-grained steamed rice with lumps of water buffalo butter, two uncooked eggs (which we mixed in), strips of broiled mutton dusted with red shavings of sumac, and raw onion slices. Mahmoud opened a bottle of Pepsi-Cola for each of us, then noticed he had provided only three chairs. "I'm a poor man," he said, picking up his plate and moving over to the window sill, where he sat. Despite my protests, he would have it no other way.

The bank clerk, who knew nothing but Turki, smiled agreeably but did not venture to speak with me; the pharmacist and I exchanged a few remarks in French. I noticed on the index finger of his left hand a large gold ring: a skull beautifully executed, red stones in the eye-sockets; the little tabs of teeth were meticulously etched into a grimace. He was called "doctor" and served as physician for the town; how macabre, I thought, if one were sick, to have this ringed hand upon one's feeble pulse!

After lunch the two roommates left and Mahmoud and I explored the town. Our aim was to look over the school, where I would speak the following morning; it was a handsome brick structure, fairly new and well equipped. The lanky principal, who was pale, soft-spoken, and black-haired, said he had one request of me, but, simpering shyly, declined to say just what. Mahmoud strode about his boss's office as if it were his own. I begged to know what the limp official had in mind and urged Mahmoud to extract an answer from him; they spoke rapidly in Turki. The principal blushed deeply and lowered his long-lashed eyes.

"He says: do you know any American girls who would marry him? He, too, is tired of conditions in this country and he wishes to live abroad."

We all laughed, as if the proposal were a joke, but each of us knew the request had not been made lightly. No, I told him in Turki, I knew no American girls who might be willing.

Do you think I am handsome enough?

Yes, I assured him, he was good-looking. (But I felt him to be such a spineless creature no girl in her right mind would have him.)

Going into the classrooms, the children I saw were as alert as wild animals; visitors seldom came here, said Mahmoud; this was a day they would never forget. They ranged in age from eight or nine to sixteen and wore the poor schoolboy's uniform: bluish grey cotton coat and trousers, thick shoes, but no socks. Their heads were shaved to the skull to prevent scalp diseases, and their skins had been burnt a deep brown. Mahmoud strutted about in front of the classes, the impresario responsible for this show. He suggested I ask his English-speaking students some questions. I found it best to stick to queries phrased in *Brighter English*: How old are you? Where are you from? How many brothers and sisters do you have? And so on.

I happened to ask one child what work his father did, and his reply was: "My father is dead."

"I am sorry."

Mahmoud sadly put his arm around the boy and hugged him. "This lad's father was a brave man. He was an officer in the army. A few years ago the Shah discovered a plot against him and murdered all the officers involved, including the colonel who was this boy's father. Perhaps you read about that in America?"

"When did it happen?"

Mahmoud frowned, concentrating: I knew he must be trying to transpose the Mohammedan calendar into the Gregorian—but he gave up. "Some years ago. Three, four years ago."

"I'm sorry," I said to the boy again. He looked at me with an unblinking, distant, implacable expression in his eyes, as if the familiar tale of his father's history had now absolutely no meaning for him—or, more likely, that he could not comprehend that it would have any meaning for me.

"You may sit down," said Mahmoud, and the pupil obeyed. Next we visited a manual training room; he wished me to see how clever these students were with their hands. While we were there, classes were dismissed, and he and I played Ping-pong in the central gallery, with most of the student body as audience.

He was a tricky, skillful player, the champion of the town; since the children idolized him and expected him to excel in everything, some of his prestige was involved in our match. The first game was a smashing triumph for him; he had a spin-stroke that sent the celluloid ball over the net a few inches—then it arched back over the net, and I lost the point because my paddle hadn't touched the ball in the interim. He was fussy about the rules and gleeful over my confusion. There were ohs and ahs and shouts each time he won a point; but a few students were rooting for me, the stranger in their midst, in a perverse withdrawal of loyalty. These anonymous cheers when I scored a point greatly distressed him, and each time he heard the applause he wheeled around, trying to identify the betrayer. For any player with a short reach, his trick shot would have been impossible to combat, but my arms are long, and I mastered a quick slam return that effectively handled his spin. We were tied at twenty-all; in the play-off, I won. The defeat was so disturbing to him that he laid down the paddles and suggested we go out to the volleyball field. There, for nearly an hour, he worked off his humiliation, leaping in the air, spiking the ball, demonstrating his skill for the few students still hanging about. The sun had set behind the dazzling snowcapped mountains of the Elburz, and the students began to leave for home.

Walking back through the dimming streets, what I first thought an evening star turned out to be a small lantern atop a minaret of a mosque. We visited the Hakhapur sport club, Mahmoud showing me the dark enclosure, padded with mats, where he had tested out his championship and thrown every challenger in the region. All citizens of the town met along the way bowed to Mahmoud with an unusual display of respect, considering that he was merely a teacher, without wealth or social standing. When we reached home, the pharmacist was busy preparing our supper: a stew of potatoes, onions, carrots, and mutton, which Mahmoud assured me would be "very delicious" far better than that food from the restaurant we'd eaten at noon, which was "bad, not good, not clean."

"I thought it delicious."

"It'll make you sick."

"I hope not."

The supper now was being *properly* made, Mahmoud assured me, "very hygienic." The "doctor" understood how to cook "without making disease." When I offered to help peel potatoes, the pharmacist said no, I was their guest; I must allow them to serve me.

Mahmoud took out a pack of cards from a drawer and began to entertain me with numerous card tricks, all deftly executed—disappearing aces and flying Jokers. We sat down at the table, in order for him to perform a clever disappearing-lumps-of-sugar game. I was a good audience, properly dumbfounded when the pieces of rock-sugar were never under the cups I chose. At the start of each new trick he would caution: "Don't get mad! Now, careful, don't become angry!" Laughing, he would waggle a finger at me. "I confuse you? Do I? Now, don't get mad." He thought I would be annoyed if I were outwitted; he assumed that my laughter was from embarrassment, not delight. Each time I was the dupe and chose the wrong card or indicated the empty cup, he would laugh in triumph. His parlor games were merely another facet of his determination to show that he was a better man than I, a mere representative of a capitalistic society.

"Where did you learn these tricks?" I asked.

"From my father."

"I'd like to know how you make that sugar disappear."

"You would? Ha, ha! Do I ask you how Americans make atom bombs?"

"I wouldn't tell you if I knew."

"Why not?"

"You'd learn how to make them and drop one on me, just for the fun of it."

"Oh, no, sir, I am your friend."

"Are you?"

He rose, laughing, and turned on the radio. It was six o'clock, and the lights sprang on. The news broadcast from Radio Moscow had just begun, and he hung his head over the speaker, taking it in. A short while later the bank clerk arrived, changed to pajamas, and with his help in the kitchen, it was soon announced that the food was ready to be served. We had a hearty meal of garlic-flavored stew and *pilhav,* and we showed our appreciation of the cook's efforts by eating with rapt attention, wordlessly.

Mahmoud, wiping his lips with the back of his right hand, interrupted the silence to say that he knew an interesting proverb, a Persian proverb. By the mischievous look in his blue eyes, I knew that he intended it for me. "Khrushchev and some Americans—important people—were sitting down together for dinner. There were toasts of vodka to America, to Russia, to peace, to friendship, to health, and many other things. They all drank much vodka, and the Americans got bad drunk, so they behaved foolish. They were out of their wits. But Khrushchev, he remained a thinking man, clear in the head. He knew what he was saying. He knew what he was doing." Mahmoud stopped; that was the end of the anecdote. He saw my puzzled expression. "It's an Iranian proverb." He dropped his chin and continued to eat.

"Is that another story you heard on the radio?"

"*Na.*"

The "doctor" began looking at me intently, then asked in French what I thought of the situation in Iran, the condition of the country. "Yes, let us have a pol-it-ical discussion," said Mahmoud.

"Be truthful," said the pharmacist. "Say what you truly think. What is your opinion of the welfare of Iran?"

Although the bank clerk understood no French, only Turki, Mahmoud rapidly translated for his benefit. All three of them scrutinized me closely, waiting for my reply. "From what I have seen, I am saddened by the poverty, the sickness." In my mind flashed the thought: yes, Iran is those ragged, diseased people suffering the cruelty of deprivations—not the picturesque *chaikhanes,* quaint bazaars, exciting hunting trips, and skiing expeditions. I told them I had seen terrible living conditions, but improvements were starting. The economy was gaining each year.

"The rich are getting richer," said Mahmoud with a sneer.

I pointed out that a large percentage of the oil revenues were going into the Shah's Plan Organization to better Iran. My government was spending additional millions each year on aid programs in agriculture, medicine, engineering, "and even teaching. That is how I happen to be here." They looked at me with the distant scrutiny of strangers, as if they were thinking: so that is why you happen to be here—it is odd, isn't it?

"What is the good of these things?" asked Mahmoud. "There are rodents who eat the grain, and when the people come to eat, nothing but shells remain."

I tried again to cite the accomplishments. Patience, patience, I urged; the country was so backward it could not be changed in a day. The Shah was pushing reforms and curbing corruption; living standards were rising. The average worker earned more now than he did a few years ago.

"But the cost of living has gone up so much," said Mahmoud, "he is actually earning less. America has caused inflation."

The pharmacist shook his head. A catalogue of accomplishments was not what they wished to hear from me, only whether I thought there was hope.

What the future might bring, no one could know; but what did *he* think should be done?

"*Az an mard bepurs,*" he said, pointing to Mahmoud. (Ask that man.)

"Revolution," said Mahmoud in English. "There must be a revolution."

The word jolted me. I had never heard its sanguine sound uttered among conspirators in a darkened room. And even while I argued that the bloodshed of rebellion could never accomplish what peaceful reforms might bring about, I knew that Mahmoud had the word "revolution" between his teeth, and that he shook it out with the irrevocable directness of a call-to-action, the magnetic appeal of the stroke of the knife, the blast of the gun.

Mahmoud translated my arguments for the doctor's benefit, and he replied: "*Kudam behtar ast?*" ("Which is better?")

"We must kill the rich! Kill the rich and give to the poor, as Karl Marx has said."

"You would turn your country over to Russia, if you did that."

Mahmoud kissed the air, defiantly. The bank clerk squirmed unhappily and began saying he did not like this talk. "*Bi-sedah!*" ("Be quiet!"), said Mahmoud. "*In khaili mohem ast.*" ("This is very important.")

The present government was obviously corrupt, argued the pharmacist, in French, and life would continue much the same as it was now, as long as this government remained in control. He asked me to consider his own plight, for instance: he worked night and day, always on call to administer to the sick, but these people were so poor they could pay *rien*. The medical board had assigned him here to Hakhapur, a backward, forgotten village, whereas he was a city man, even an aristocrat, and not used to these primitive ways. He was engaged to marry, but his sweetheart lived in Tabriz. He had not enough money to marry her, anyhow. His days were spent uselessly, with no advance, no sign of progress.

The discussion was no longer political, said Mahmoud in disgust; it had become personal. Would that every man lived as *he* did and had no personal life at all. "Love is the opium of the people, not only religion, as Karl Marx has said." He began clearing away the dishes. On the radio, the Voice of Cairo was now broadcasting; although I frequently heard the word "Amerikai," neither Mahmoud nor the pharmacist would translate the Arabic for me. The latter was not listening to the radio; he wanted to know how much money I made, per month.

"Nine thousand five hundred rials," I told him, which was my living allowance, "and a salary in dollars paid to my bank in the United States."

"The professor is a rich man," said Mahmoud.

The pharmacist told me he earned five thousand rials a month and could barely manage a bachelor existence. We were at this point interrupted by visitors in the hall. *"Salaam. Salaam,"* we called. Mahmoud urged the four young men to enter; they were teachers from the school, who wished to make my acquaintance.

"Esme man Harnack ast," I said, shaking their hands.

"Befarmeid beneshinid," said Mahmoud, and at last they sat down on the three chairs—one occupied the window ledge—while the rest of us stood. He offered to make tea, but they insisted they could only stay a moment. They inquired after my health and I asked them the state of theirs. Soon they got up, bowed, shook hands again, and backed out of the room.

The four of us began playing cards to see who would buy Pepsi-Cola and vodka. Realizing that this was a chance for me to help contribute to the expenses of my stay, I tried desperately to lose. It was a game somewhat resembling rummy, and although I threw away every promising card that came my way, I could not lose. The pharmacist ended up paying the bill for refreshments. Twice in the course of the evening he was called to his office to dispense medicines; he returned cheerfully each time and resumed the game. "These people are always sick, and I must forever be ready to help them. *Quel dommage!*"

Eleven o'clock arrived, and the room was plunged into darkness and silence. Ancient Persia seemed to take over; lanterns were lit and preparations for the night began. Mahmoud crossed the hall and climbed the ladder to his loft. Were we both to sleep up there, I wondered? There seemed scarcely room anywhere for a fourth person in these quarters. I slipped into my shoes and made a last trip to the outhouse, the "unclean" lunch beginning to have its effects. The air was bitterly cold, astonishingly quiet, and countless brilliant stars were awash in the deep blue sky. "Where are you going?" called Mahmoud, alarmed. I believe he feared I was off to try to find a room at an inn.

"Where do you suppose?" I replied with a smile, picking up the can of water and gesturing with it. Toilet humor being much appreciated, everyone laughed.

While I was gone, Mahmoud dismembered his bed in order to get it out of his tiny chamber; then all of them set about putting it back together again in the main room. I felt embarrassed by the trouble I was causing and I saw that I was depriving Mahmoud of his bed. Was he to sleep on the floor? Of course, he responded cheerfully. "I shall enjoy sleeping on the carpet."

The other two young men insisted that I seat myself on one of the cots until the bed could be made up. Mahmoud unwrapped a small bolt of white cotton cloth, which he had probably purchased in the bazaar. I wondered for a moment if he really knew what a sheet was, though he had undoubtedly seen them in the movies. Iranians normally slept without bed linen, under quilted comforters. Mahmoud snatched a couple of wool blankets from the cots and dumped them on the guest bed. Someone would be cold tonight, I said; but they would not listen to my protests. Carefully, Mahmoud stretched the yard-wide stream of cloth across the pile of blankets and draped the end over the headboard. Deciding this wouldn't do, he asked the bank clerk for a knife. I knew they were embarrassed to have me watch, and so I looked away, just as a great ripping noise filled the air. When I glanced up, the sheet was the proper length, and there were two of them, with the blankets assembled on top. Two bulky pillows were placed at the head, and the pharmacist took a bottle from his closet and liberally anointed them. He noticed me looking and said: *"Eau de cologne."*

I nodded. *"Merci."*

The fire glowed through chinks in the stove, and Mahmoud made up his pallet nearby. I got out of my underwear and put on sleeping pajamas, which caused them to stare, since they wore pajamas in the house while lounging about, but underwear to bed. I realized later, however, that they were probably not as interested in my sleeping garments as in glimpsing my "unclean" body, for they were all as hairless as sheared sheep, having been depilated at the baths, and had never seen the likes of me before.

I lay down and said good-night. The pharmacist was still up, and before extinguishing the lantern, he threw an object on the floor, then began bouncing up and down. I turned over to watch, not knowing what was up. On the carpet was an amulet about the shape of a fifty cent piece, covered with a flowered *chedur* material. The pharmacist began his evening devotions very vigorously: jumping up and down, first on his knees, then head to the floor, murmuring prayers all the while. Mahmoud began snickering and finally outright laughing. His roommate ignored the derision, quickly doused the light, and suddenly we were immersed in the thick silence of the village. I guessed that Mahmoud's mockery had been because of my presence: he thought *I* would think Moslems a queer people, and he wanted me to know that he at least was modern and scientific in his views and did not honor such beliefs.

Just as we had gotten to sleep, there was a knock on the door. Another sick man! The pharmacist lit the lamp, got dressed, and Mahmoud, wrapped in blankets, for a joke followed him to his office. They came back after dispensing medicine and we settled down for the night.

I was awakened by my stomach in violent turmoil and dashed to the outhouse. The sun was just coming up. When I returned, the other men were stirring. "The Russians are a poor people, but a brave people," said Mahmoud, lying in his bedroll on the floor—as if this were the tag-line of a long Russian dream which had occupied him most of the night.

How did I sleep, asked the pharmacist? Well enough? We exchanged a few pleasantries, and Mahmoud, seeing he was ignored, began wrestling with the bank clerk, throwing him to the floor and pinning him there, then lifting him to the ceiling, despite the young man's shouts of protest. Soon the radio came on: male vocalists with whining, nasal songs, especially disagreeable at this hour of the day. We all went out to the pump to wash up—an icy gush of water—then settled down to a breakfast of tea and *nun*. Mahmoud proudly offered me water buffalo butter, which was as white as lard, and a comb of black honey. I took some of each and rolled the paste in the thin, farinous *nun;* it was absolutely delicious. We had cigarettes afterwards, the one thing I could freely provide, and Mahmoud's roommates puffed away with pleasure, though Mahmoud eschewed tobacco. Again he said he did not smoke, drink, or fornicate. He would not marry until he was forty-two or forty-four; his father, however, had had thirteen wives. I scoffed, incredulous. He repeated the statement and his roommates confirmed him. "But what happened to them all?"

"He still has four. The others were sent away."

I remembered that to be divorced in Islam, the man had merely to say in the presence of a mullah, "I divorce thee," to his wife, and it was done.

Some time later the subject of military service came up. They asked if I had ever been in the army, and I replied that I had enlisted in the U. S. Navy toward the end of World War II. I questioned Mahmoud on when he planned to do his tour of compulsory service in the Iranian military forces. "I'm not—not for this government." After he had obtained his university degree, saved some money, and acquired a full knowledge of political science, he would "go to another country."

"Where?"

"Iraq, perhaps. Or the Arab countries. Things are happening there."

"How could you get permission to leave?"

He kissed the air. "I would go over the border. They would not catch me."

214

The two roommates hurried off to their jobs, and I inquired what time classes began at school, when he was due, and when I was expected for my talk. "Ah, there is time. Do not worry," he said with the ease of a man who makes his own rules.

We cleaned up and leisurely walked through the sun-filled town to the school. Student patrols on the look-out observed our approach, sounded the news, and when we arrived in the compound, the entire school was lined up on cement steps which led to the front door. The principal and the teachers flanked the company of school children, who were standing at attention for our arrival. The extraordinary marshalling of the entire school population had undoubtedly been planned beforehand by Mahmoud. A number of pictures were taken of me in the center, the schoolboys fanned out beside me; then in an orderly fashion, the pupils were marched off and re-formed in the courtyard. I was to stand on the top step for my address.

The speech I gave concerned the importance of education and the nature of schooling for boys their age in America. Mahmoud served as translator into Turki, but I suspected he was a very bad one, from what I understood. I had been surprised the day before to hear no Pharsi in the classrooms, the official tongue used in schools. When I asked Mahmoud about this he had scoffed at the government regulation and said that laws or decrees could not change the speech of a people; Turki was the native language and Turki he always used, though of course he himself was fluent in Pharsi.

During the question period following my address, Mahmoud's translated remarks became very long, whereas in the course of the speech he had scarcely done my words justice. I could not follow Turki at the swift rate he was going, but I caught enough to realize that he was expatiating on my remarks, at *my* expense. His puzzling purpose in having me here in Hakhapur was suddenly revealed in its true propagandistic light. I had been wondering why he would allow me the opportunity of making a favorable impression on his students, thus ameliorating some of his venomous charges against capitalism and the decadent West. Now I saw his game. He openly exhorted his audience to ask "pol-it-ical" questions, and when they came, they were trenchantly phrased, as if he himself had molded them beforehand.

"What about the black men in America? Why do you treat them so bad?" asked one boy.

I tried to explain the history of slavery, the evil that had been started long ago and still lived on in persecutions and injustices toward the Negro. But I also spoke of Abraham Lincoln (the one American all Iranians revered) and the Supreme Court decision, which promised a future of equality.

Mahmoud made a good deal of my response, saying that in America we had slavery. I argued with him in English, but he jauntily passed on to the next question: a student asked what caused the vapor trails behind our jet airplanes. "Ah! A scientific question!" said Mahmoud. I gave a simple, layman's answer; and this was rendered in Turki with dispatch. Another boy wanted to know what I thought of their school; others asked how old I was; what my father did; where I lived—familiar queries from *Brighter English*. Mahmoud was impatient with these students; he picked out a favorite pupil standing on the end, a tall, gawky youth of twelve, and insisted *he* ask a question. Through the interpreter, Mahmoud, he responded by asking if in America the situation was the same as it was in Iran: what was the use of getting an education, when there were no jobs to be found? Was it not true, Mahmoud amended, that in capitalistic countries there was always unemployment?

Even as I replied to this charge, I realized the futility of my efforts, for he smilingly waited to translate into Turki a loose and highly annotated account of my words. I thought I heard him say that I had affirmed that in America there was much unemployment and people were starving. When I interrupted Mahmoud and asked if this was what he had said, he denied it. I insisted he tell me what he had said, and then, slowly, he tried to repeat verbatim my original response, which was no guarantee that he would not go ahead, just the same, and tell the students what he pleased in Turki. The teachers standing off to the side seemed only half-aware of what was going on. Now Mahmoud called openly for "revolutionary questions." The students asked what I thought of the Soviet Union? Why did America want to start a war? Why did not America believe in peace, as the communists did? Why did we make trouble in Berlin?

I decided to end the performance. I said in Pharsi to my audience that I had been pleased to have seen them and I wished them well. *"Omidvar am baz ham shomah rah bebinam."* They applauded: they, too, would like me to come again. I walked over to the principal and shook his taffy hand. The teachers began herding the students into the school building. "I did not make you mad?" asked Mahmoud, grinning. "Are you angry with me? Did I upset you?"

"What do you think?"

"Ah ha! sir, you are angry! I am very, very sorry to have displeased you." But he could not keep a smile from his lips.

"When does my bus leave?"

"You have time."

"Time for what?"

Again he laughed. "Ah, sir, do not be so upset. Come, let us look at things in the town. It is market day in the bazaar. Very colorful. I think you will be interested, as a tourist."

I walked down the street with him, fully aware that I was no longer a tourist, though I missed that comforting, carefree, old-fashioned cognomen. But I went through the motions of the traveler in the remaining hour before the Tabriz bus arrived, feeling odd in the role, despite the fact that I saw many interesting, picturesque sights: in the animal bazaar on the edge of town was the traditional carved stone sheep, a talisman for stockyards; dozens of peasants with their animals were in the throes of business, arguing and shouting as if their lives depended upon it (and in most cases it did), feeling the limbs of sheep and goats and poking fingers into their mouths.

Later, in the small covered section of the bazaar a jeweler implored me to pause at his shop; I admired a heavy gold ring with turquoise stones, one of which was missing. The shopkeeper asked one hundred and fifty tomans for it; I offered seventy-five, by way of conversation, though I had no real desire to purchase it. "Let us go," muttered Mahmoud irritably. He said the ring was worth the price the merchant had stated; if I wished it, that is what I should pay, since I was a rich American whereas the jeweler was a poor man.

I replied that I would get my bag from his house at once and have nothing further to do with him, since our acquaintance was becoming mutually annoying. I would find the bus myself.

Immediately he apologized, but the rift was not that easily repaired, for I was too angry; we walked on in silence. And yet I was not sorry I had come. I had learned so much. While waiting in the cafe which also served as bus depot, I hastily ate a lunch of *chelo kebab,* Mahmoud sitting opposite, watching me eat. "We shall see each other in the city, sir?" He was afraid he had gone too far and that this distance between us could not be closed. "I shall come to see you, when I am next in Tabriz."

I broke off a piece of *nun.* "No doubt I'll see you in class next week."

"I wish, sir, that you would not take roll call so frequently. I fear you have marked me absent too often, and I shall not be able to take the examination. Why did you do that to me? Why could you not overlook my name?" A Persian whine had crept into his voice, his manner was wheedling.

"I'm sorry, but you know the rules."

"Ah yes, I do. But we are friends."

"That is what you keep saying, but I find it difficult to believe."

"I promise I shall be a devoted friend to you, honored sir."

"Anyhow, I couldn't make an exception about class attendance. If I did there would be a dozen students with similar requests."

"I swear I would tell no one! I swear!"

"I'm sorry, Mahmoud, but it cannot be."

He shrugged his shoulders. "Your bus," he said pointing toward the window, "it is here—no, no, do not hurry. It will not leave for some time yet. I will tell the driver to wait."

When finished, I got up, shook hands with him, and said goodbye. "You have honored me by your visit. I am a poor man, but your presence has made me rich. Here—your bus ticket."

I tried to reimburse him, but he would have none of it; somehow, when I'd not been looking, he had even paid for my lunch. The proprietor bowed, smiled, but would not take my money. Again I shook hands with Mahmoud at the door of the bus. "You have, sir, my card?" He handed one to me. Many students had given me their name-cards as a token of friendship; Karim had even printed up a box of cards for me, with my name in Pharsi and English. I read out Mahmoud's full name, and he beamed. "Do you know what my surname means?" I shook my head. "It says, 'seat of government' or 'place of government.'" He noticed my meditative look, and his eyes glinted merrily. "It is my destiny, even in my name I find my future."

14 TRIP TO THE
CASPIAN SEA

Nau-Rooz, the Persian New Year in March, delivered me back to
the happy guise of traveler, since at holiday time the university
was closed and all Persians who could afford it became tourists
themselves, journeying south to meet the spring in their favorite
cities, Shiraz or Isfahan. I booked passage out of Iran, flying to
Greece and later stopping in Turkey; upon my return in the
middle of April I was told by students and professors alike that
the memorization of texts was now beginning, hence attendance
in class was not mandatory and absences would not be recorded
by the clerk of the Faculty. I found my audience dwindling each
day, and more and more students were feverishly pacing in court-
yards and parks, book in hand, committing to memory everything read. At last the university closed down, releasing all pupils
to their agony of preparation for the final examinations.

Now that the highest mountain passes were open, I decided to
visit the only region of Azerbaijan I had not yet seen: the subtropical lowlands along the Caspian Sea. Student friends helped
me chart a route through Ardebil, Astara, Resht, and Qazvin,
though most of them had never been east of the mountains and
could not understand my interest in traveling there. The first city
I would stay in would be Ardebil, an historic metropolis of the
Safavid period; the shrine built in the early seventeenth century
by Shah Abbas, who was responsible for the splendor of Isfahan,
was still standing, though infrequently seen by tourists, since
Ardebil was inconveniently situated. My students told me that

Ardebil was known as a city of pederasts, and when a traveler crossed the river and entered the town, if he saw fish in the river he would become a boy-lover, too. Thus, when anyone was going to Ardebil, the immediate remark was: "Oh, and will you see the river full of fish?"

I left at six o'clock in the morning in a bus crowded with livestock and people; a couple of chickens sat on my teal blue Iranian suitcase, which loomed in the aisle. After stopping for tea in Sarab, we proceeded higher and higher toward Mount Savalan, the highest peak in northeastern Azerbaijan. My seat-mate, a young army officer from Ardebil who spoke some English, advised me to stay at the Tabriz-Nau hotel, though he was sure I would find it poor and urged me to stay "with friends." Green valleys, cultivated fields, and flowers along the roadside were increasingly in evidence, the higher we rose. I was troubled because the lieutenant had never heard of the Safavid mosque I planned to visit; he assured me that there was no such thing in Ardebil. There was nothing at all in his home-city for a foreign gentleman, such as myself, to view, and it would be better if I passed on to the Caspian Sea and stayed at the bathing resorts to the south. I suspected that the dome of the mosque would be much smaller than that of the Imperial Mosque in Isfahan, but surely, I felt, a resident of Ardebil would be aware of its presence, brilliantly set against the sky in tiles of aqua, gold, and green.

At close to noon the bus crossed the famous "river full of fish," which was completely dry, and we entered the mud-walled, dun city of Ardebil. The streets swarmed with black-garbed people, all exceedingly poor and dirty. As we disembarked, the lieutenant offered to find a droshky for me (he assured me that there were no taxis in Ardebil) to transport me to the Tabriz-Nau. I accepted but said I planned to go directly to the office of education. In my pocket was a letter of introduction to a Mr. Mohseni, head of education in Ardebil, from the U.S.I.A. office in Tabriz, asking his friendship and help and saying that I would like to give a lecture to school children, sometime during my stay in the city.

My army friend quickly found a droshky, and I set off, lurching through the cobbled streets in the frail, antiquated buggy, my feet propped on my suitcase; the driver had been instructed by the officer to take me to the office of education. Squalid little shops along the way—and the curious, sometimes hostile, gazes from the people—seemed unpropitious for a pleasant sojourn here, but I was highly pleased with myself for having arrived. Although the beginning of anything is charged with possibilities, in travel the thrill is direct, visceral, and unspeakably pleasant.

Suddenly, before my eyes was the glistening pale blue dome with yellow faience which I recognized to be the mosque; the gaudy, columnar minaret nearby was equally dazzling. The education offices were located in the same compound; I got out of the droshky, paid the driver, and hauled my suitcase up the steep dark stairs, telling the servant that I wished to see Mr. Mohseni. I was ushered into his office at once. Rather disheveled after the journey, I no doubt appeared somewhat wild-eyed; I wore a zipper jacket rather than a suitcoat and tie; sponge-soled sport shoes rather than oxfords. Perhaps I interrupted a conference of some sort among the eight men there. In any case, I threw them into utter and complete confusion.

Mohseni refused to talk French with me, although I had been assured back in Tabriz that he could; and when a fat, fortyish French teacher arrived to interpret my remarks, I found myself flustered and unable to put a decent sentence together. They had the letter spread out on the desk before them. They had each read it several times—looking up at me between paragraphs. *Could* I really be a professor? Or was I an impostor? And why did I wish to give a lecture? And to whom? And when? They were much put out, as if I were asking an extraordinary favor when I announced my availability as a speech-maker. Where would I stay, inquired Mohseni in Turki? And I replied, "Tabriz-Nau" before the French teacher had a chance to interpret. This evidence that I knew some Turki further darkened the suspicions of everyone, and they turned to the letter again, examining closely the seal of the United States of America. In rapid Turki, Mohseni addressed me, protesting that a telegram should have been sent announcing my arrival. Then they would have been ready. I realized that the U.S.I.A. office in Tabriz must have assumed that provincial, out-of-the-way Ardebil would quickly and enthusiastically take me in.

The student who had helped me purchase the proper bus ticket to Ardebil had sent his card with me, on which a note had been penned to his friend in Ardebil, a teacher of English in one of the schools. I produced the card, asking to see this man at once. Mr. Mohseni darkly undertook to meet this sally, announcing that it would be impossible; the day was only half over; this teacher would still be with his classes. But at four o'clock I might expect to see him at my room in the Tabriz-Nau hotel. I *did* have a room there, did I not? Then I confessed that I *hoped* to have a room, *"Enshallah,"* in good time—whenever it could be arranged. Mr. Mohseni set the time for my address at ten o'clock the following morning; this was the earliest possible hour I could be accommodated. Of course, a full week's preparation would have been more suitable. I nodded and begged my apologies. The alarm in Mohseni's dark, square, rather Arabic face did not subside much; I saw that it was compounded mostly of worry and fear that he would not do well in this emergency. I realized fully that no one ever "dropped in" at Ardebil.

I left the office with Mohseni and the French teacher and hoped they were taking me to lunch, since I was rather hungry. But we walked across the inner courtyard toward the mosque. I remembered my suitcase, left in the public hall outside the director's office, and I expressed concern for its safety. Mohseni sent a servant to fetch it, and he lugged it along, twenty paces or so behind us; each time I turned around he grinned, nodded, and bowed, as if to say, "See? It's safe. I'm here!'"

The French teacher, a curator of the mosque, which was no longer used for religious services, pointed to the façade and to the glazed, brilliant dome, which was an early example of baked tiles, executed in the technique called *haft ranghe* (seven colors). The splendor of the colorings I found too overwhelming to be really satisfying; perhaps the spectacle seemed to demand too great a response from the viewer—the enormous Easter egg against the sky was so astonishing! Or perhaps I found it vaguely disturbing that there was no predetermined distance from which one viewed the edifice to its best advantage.

Removing our shoes, we entered the dank, musty shrine; so bad was the ventilation that, as in dim old Italian churches, the painted murals and wall decorations had turned dark and were flaking away; it was difficult to make them out at all. The grilled portals to the various sections of the mosque were of solid silver; entire doors were silver—lintels, knobs and hinges. Under the crystal chandelier, which contained no candles, the famous Ardebil carpet (now in the Victoria and Albert museum) used to lie. The pattern of the carpet had been extended to the walls and ceiling in paint, now nearly faded away, as if in palimpsest.

We stepped forward to visit the carved sarcophagus of a Safavid king; bit of turquoise, ivory, semiprecious jewels and wood were fashioned into a gem box the size of a coffin. After pausing in another chamber, so dim I could scarcely make out the tombs and effigies, we entered a large chamber in which the traditional series of joined arches reached high overhead. The surface above was honeycombed; there were niches and pedestals for thousands of Chinese vases, but of course, my guide told me, Turkish invaders ages ago had destroyed all but a few of them. Shah Abbas had installed here a great collection of blue and white Chinese porcelain, and many potters of the Safavid period had learned their art from the several hundred Chinese artisans employed by the Shah to decorate this mosque. What a shooting-gallery time the conquerors must have had, throwing stones at all those vases!

Thanking my guides, I took leave of them at two o'clock and hailed a droshky to transport me to the Tabriz-Nau. The hotel looked extremely unpromising from the street, with a flight of grimy stairs leading up from the filthy roadway—a mire of mud and offal. The proprietor hurried up the steps at my heels, and I got him to understand that I wanted the best room in the house, entirely to myself; and so, for eight tomans (about one dollar), I bought bed space for four and had one fourth of the hotel. Geraniums blooming in the window seemed a homey note, but the place was suspiciously vermin-ridden. The bed linens were the familiar blanket-type coverings and had not been laundered for some time; the pillow was soiled from the heads of many customers. The smiling proprietor saw that I was pleased with my room. Was there anything further I wished?

I asked where the toilet was located, but used the word *hammam,* which means bath. I wasn't aware of my error until I was marching off with the friendly innkeeper, down the street several blocks to the bathhouse. Realizing my mistake, I could think of no way of reversing direction without causing him consternation. We passed a landscaped *golistan* (city park), and the view of Mount Savalan was splendid, but rain clouds were gathering near its dome.

Leaving me at the *hammam* door, the hotelman departed, and I immediately asked the bath attendants for a *restoran*. Helpfully, one of the men came with me, down the street; he would take me to the best cafe in Ardebil. Soon we arrived at the *Tabriz-Nau; inja,* said my guide: behold, the finest eating place in town. The proprietor was astonished to see me so quickly and asked if the *hammam* did not please me. No, I told him, it did not, and now if he would kindly lead me to the toilet (this time I used the right word) I should like, thereafter, to sit down to *chai* and *chelo kebab*.

Later, mounting the stairs to my room, I scared off a couple of pigeons roosting on the hall banister. They flew up and down the aisle and finally out a window. I had time for a nap before the English teacher arrived, and after sprinkling a little DDT powder on the casters of the bed, to prevent bugs from walking up, I lay down uneasily. The door could be locked from the outside but only propped shut from the inside. After a few minutes I had visitors. The proprietor came in without knocking, along with a younger man who spoke a little French, and a fagged-out young woman who appeared to be drugged, and whom I guessed was the house prostitute. She smiled toothily at me, but as if from afar. The hotelman wished my passport and Savak card (special permission from the secret police to travel in this restricted district of Iran). I gave the credentials to the man and lay down when they left, using a towel for a head-rest, rather than trusting the pillow.

Rain began splashing on the white and pink geraniums; I slept a little. Close to four o'clock I awoke, read an airmail edition of the New York *Times,* my touch with reality, and awaited my caller. I opened the door, so that he would have no difficulty finding me, and a pigeon flew in, circled the room, and flew out the window. The strange, bedraggled woman was sitting on a chair directly in front of my door; she did not seem to notice I was standing behind her. I squeezed past her in order to make my way to the toilet at the end of the hall; upon my return she was dream-walking about my room. *"Befarmeid,"* I said. The zombie did not look at me, she merely moved out of the room as if drawn away by a rope around her neck.

Promptly at four, Ali the English teacher bounded up the stairs and into my room; his English was fairly good, and he was over-joyed to see me. He inquired news of his friends in Tabriz, which I was happy to supply; he was constantly grinning. At first his gaiety was exhilarating, then something of a strain, for I saw that he was displaying his company manners: in front of me he wished to appear light-hearted, carefree, and enormously pleased with life. Close to 5:30, just as we were making plans for the evening, the chief of the secret police arrived, wearing a soiled brown snap-brim hat, a four days' growth of whiskers, and, hav-ing probably seen detective movies, a manner that was arrogant, authoritative, and at the same time rather stupid. He fixed me with a searching look and through his interpreter announced that he intended to ask me questions. What was I doing in Ardebil? How long would I be here? Where was I going? What did I teach? What was I up to, anyhow? He wished me to understand that he was in charge of security in the entire area of the Russian border near Ardebil.

Ali said nothing through these rather sinister proceedings, then suddenly with a shout and a smile, he embraced the ugly fellow and after a torrent of Turki, told me in English that here before his very eyes was his former grade-school teacher, the very man who had taught him to read and write back in Tabriz when he was a tiny lad. The police chief cracked under this sentimental gambit, heartily shook hands with his former pupil, and they chatted about the old days. Towards me, now, he was most genial; he noticed on the bed one of the pamphlets I had of the Howard Baskerville commemoration ceremony, and we dis-cussed the noble sacrifice of the American, Baskerville, for the cause of Iranian freedom fifty years ago.

When he left, Ali and I set off for a walk around the city. I met a number of his students and teacher friends. As the evening strolling hour wore on, the streets were jammed with people; they overflowed the sidewalks and filled the thoroughfares. Despite the genial looks on individual faces, there was something ominous about the milling crowd—perhaps because of their dark clothing, the emaciated looks in their faces, the critical poverty that was everywhere and the sheer numbers of them.

Ali told me he had been assigned to teach in Ardebil, though Tabriz was his home, and his mother, alone there, missed him greatly. Perhaps someday he would pass the examination to become a Fulbright scholar to America. This was his dream. But I knew by his speech, and by a specimen of his writing I saw later, that he was not good enough to qualify and never would be. We inspected the school where I would address a crowd of children the next morning; on the auditorium stage a group of Iranian soldiers were dancing a kind of gavotte. Ali told me they were rehearsing for an Army "Show" the next day. Dancing to the flute, drums, and a couple of stringed instruments, the men were going through a rather courtly series of steps, arms about each others' waists.

We turned down a *koutche* to Ali's apartment, which he rented with two Army officers and their orderly. They all slept in one room and had cooking facilities in a hall. The officers turned out to be extremely young, naive country boys, wild-eyed and full of fun. There was a simple, ingenuous quality about them that was quite winning, but it was difficult to imagine them in positions of responsible leadership. They immediately began "cutting up" like a couple of dormitory freshmen, with obscene gestures, practical jokes, funny noises, and the like. The quiet, brown-faced orderly, Hassan, who was from Mazandaran, made tea for us. Ali offered me his pajamas, which I put on, and he donned a pair of old trousers; carefully, we put aside our street clothes, then sat on the carpeted floor, for there were no chairs. On the wall were magazine clippings of movie stars, plus a few pictures from the U.S. Information Agency, a view of Mt. Vernon and another of the Washington monument.

The soldiers left, and Ali and I listened to the radio; conversation became rather heavy-going; I had to start a topic and keep it afloat, though he seemed pleased enough to have the talk. A cloud of boredom lurked over his life, and to protect himself from it he adopted a determined gaiety; occasionally he would burst into song, mime, or show extravagant zest in performing little tasks, homiletically saying that it was necessary to be full of joy. This was his way of keeping from sinking into that morass of deep sadness which afflicted so many Iranians. He wanted me to tell him about teaching in America, how much money I made, and what my sex life was like; he hoped to absorb from me all I could tell him of the outside world—and immediately—for he felt his time with me was short; he had only this one chance, for when I left, there would be no one interesting coming his way again. Now and then our discussion lagged as we listened to a song from the radio station in Baku, Soviet Azerbaijan. At last he set out a simple supper of *nun,* goat cheese, and tea. I was soon ready to go back to the hotel, but the Army boys came home, ready for a session of rough-housing before bed, and they didn't want me to leave. They danced about the room, sang, and then insisted that I sing an American song for them. I obliged, although they remarked, truthfully, that I wasn't much of a singer. When I finally left they told me it had been the most wonderful evening they'd had in years. I walked back to the hotel through the silent town and climbed the stairs to my room. Chair propped against the door, I fell asleep.

In the morning before Ali arrived, I shaved, using a tea glass of hot water, dressed sprucely in a suit, white shirt, and tie (seemingly highly inappropriate garb for Ardebil, and, therefore, such a necessary costume). The hotelman served tea, *nun,* and marmalade in my room, and while eating I noticed a packet of official-looking papers on my table, all in Pharsi (which I couldn't read). When Ali came at 8:30 I showed him what I had found; he shook his head thoughtfully, concluding that they had accidentally been left here by the chief of the secret police, Mr. Agdam. "We will take these to him, and he will be most grateful," said Ali.

A careless official, after all, I thought; or just a rattled one.

We ambled over toward the school, but I had difficulty fathoming from Ali's remarks just what sort of arrangements were being made for my talk. Very likely nobody was doing anything about it, but to press or inquire would be inexcusably rude. Persians were very oriental in this respect; one waited to see what would evolve, all in good time. I guessed that there was some trouble about having chairs in the auditorium, and also confusion regarding the procedure for rounding up students from the various schools in Ardebil. For a while I was sequestered in the principal's office, while hurried conferences were taking place in the hall among various officials, including some of the assistants I had seen in Mohseni's office. I learned later that the Iranian army colonel, whose men were giving the "Show," heard of my scheduled speech and ordered chairs set up in the auditorium early in the morning. The chairs would be used again at night for the performance; and so the military neatly solved what had been a muddle in the educational world.

One by one, for my diversion, Ali called in bright students for me to interrogate. I was to ask them the memorized questions from *Direct Method # 1* their English manual; the pupils responded mechanically, having little notion what these vowels and consonants signified, and were invariably astonished that I seemed to attach something meaningful to their rote utterances. The most pathetic scholar was a tiny boy no taller than a four-year-old child. Daneshvar was thirteen, but undeveloped in every way except mentally; his mind, Ali told me, was brilliant; he remembered everything but alas, it would come to nothing. The boy's family was destitute because his father, an army officer, had been implicated in a plot against the Shah and had been put to death. It seemed to me odd that I should encounter two such political orphans—Mahmoud's student and Daneshvar. Perhaps it was a coincidence; perhaps there were more purges in Iran than the world knew about; or it might have been a current myth, sprung from the oppressed classes. Ali said friends in Ardebil had given the dead man's family money, but the situation was nearly hopeless for them. It would be impossible for this midget to attend school next year (since he obviously could not work, it had seemed best to have him attend classes), for there would be no money for tuition. But due to Daneshvar's physical condition, which was increasingly poor, there did not seem much likelihood that the boy would be alive next year. And perhaps it

229

was best that way. Ali put his arms around the tiny creature and tears fell from his eyes. Daneshvar, who sensed the gist of our words, also seemed about to weep. I felt like crying over both of them; then the principal walked in, cheerfully announcing that students were filing into the auditorium.

When we entered, the audience of six hundred students rose to their feet. I went to the front, and with Ali standing beside me translating as I went along, spoke for an hour, then answered questions. At the conclusion we left the hall to a shouting, tumultous ovation. The students beat upon the chairs with their hands and stamped their feet; I could not imagine why, unless they were exuberant at having been pulled out of their usual routine. There was a peculiar fervor in the air, a dynamic intention, as if every one of them was fully aware that he lived on the edge of portentous events; somehow my presence sharply brought the matter into focus.

Following tea, compliments, and courtesies, Ali and I made our way to the office of the chief of the secret police. Mr. Agdam was overjoyed to get back his papers. He had a spent a miserable morning, looking everywhere, but it had not occurred to him that he had lost them the evening before. Any favor he could do for either of us—we were just to say the word (and it was understood, we would tell no one of this error). I kept saying his name, to engrave it in my mind, in case I needed it later on my travels. Ali was thoroughly delighted with this turn of events. "One never knows when such a friendship could make a lot of difference."

It was a storm-threatening, windy day, and my bus for Astara on the Caspian Sea was due to depart in forty-five minutes. I had been told the road was hazardous or impassable if wet, and should a downpour develop, I might find myself spending a day in a mountain teahouse. My time was too limited to wait for fair weather; I decided to push on. After a hasty lunch of *chelo kebab* in an upstairs, secluded dining room, the only light filtering down through a dusty skylight, in a restaurant characterized by private dining nooks, balconies, and murmured, clandestine talk, we hurried back to the Tabriz-Nau. I changed into my informal travel clothes, gave Ali a pair of cuff links, and with bag in hand, descended to the street to hail a droshky. We found one at last; the driver, learning from Ali that we must catch a bus, shouted at his scrawny team of horses and flailed their bony hides with a wicked-looking whip. The cruel, sadistic pleasure showing in the driver's face was disgusting, and I shouted in Turki for him to slow down. But having been given an excuse to abuse his animals, nothing would stop him, and the whip cracked over the mangy horses' heads all the way to the bus station, which was located some distance away in an exceedingly poor section of town.

Ali dashed into the office and made arrangements for my passage; I paid for the ticket, and we learned that the bus would perhaps not leave just yet—it would depart, *Enshallah,* in good time. A porter dressed in rags, who had the manner of a fool (but I gathered a wise one, whose words people listened to), begged me to send him a postcard from America. He was cross-eyed, with a withered hand he carried just over his stomach; lifting the dead fingers with his active right hand, he forced his dead left to participate in his gestures. The station agent examined my papers, morosely shaking his head; the porter, too, and the other passengers waiting on the wooden bench in the cubby-hole bus station, all seriously doubted that I would manage traveling alone along the frontier. Surely I would be arrested and questioned somewhere on the way.

At last a yellow Chevrolet town-and-country station wagon (or it had originally been this), rebuilt and extended at the rear, arrived, and I saw my suitcase hoisted to the top and strapped into place. There would be only eight passengers to Astara. Ali took out his card and wrote on the back the name of his friend who taught English in Astara; I put it carefully away in my wallet, after noting that Ali's first name was signified merely by the initial "A." I had heard one or two of his friends refer to him as "Azam," and I asked him, now, what his full name was.

"Unfortunately, seven years ago I lost my birth papers. We could not find them anywhere."

"Was there no record in the city offices?"

"Perhaps at the mullah's, but we could not find it. Someone had made a mistake. Then about that time my brother died, and so I took over his papers. Therefore, I am officially Ali, but my friends still call me Azam because that's who I really am."

I had a Kafka-esque feeling when I heard this. "Well, are you really twenty-eight, as you said, or the age of your brother?"

"My brother's age would be thirty-two, and *officially* I am that old. But actually I am only twenty-eight."

No wonder, I thought, the friendship of police chief Agdam might someday be important.

Ali spoke to a young man, requesting him to look after me on the trip, and then we all filed out to the station wagon. I was to sit in front between the driver and Ali's appointed guardian. At the bus door Ali and I said farewell, shook hands and then embraced; the motor started up. A man in the back begged Allah for a safe journey, and we set off, driving northeast out of the city across a wide valley toward dark mountains. *"Russe! Russe!"* said the driver, gesturing ahead at the mountain range of the Caucasus.

"Bali, bali," I replied.

In the exceedingly high altitude the desert landscape was being transformed by outcroppings of greenery, brilliant poppies, daisies and small yellow flowers that looked like buttercups. We came to a dingy outpost, a small mud village, where sentries stopped us. The driver and Ali's designated companion for me took my passport, visa, and Savak papers and went inside the military headquarters. I sat wondering if my arrest were imminent and kept repeating to myself "Agdam, *telephon* Agdam."

Smiling, they returned and handed over my credentials; we proceeded to wind up into a very high, beautiful mountain pass, where rivulets splashed over rocks and scrub oak thrived in side ravines. The air began to feel decidedly different, it was lighter but also quite moist. The sky was heavily overcast and we traveled just under the cloud layers. The road became a much eroded raw track clinging to the side of the mountain. We crested the pass and began a winding descent which would take several hours, bringing us from an altitude of close to nine thousand feet to the below-sea-level of the Caspian shores. The roadside was immediately green with thick weeds, trees and grass. The occasional houses were not the familiar flat mud adobe edifices, which would melt in the rain climate of the Caspian, but built of wood, with heavily thatched roofs rising to peaks like the "Pahlavi hats" still seen in this region. The present Shah's father had ordered his subjects to wear Western-type high crowned felt hats, instead of tribal headgear, when he came to power in the 1920's. An enormous mosquito buzzed on the inside of the windshield, and the driver squashed it; I remembered that this lush, subtropical region was also malaria-ridden.

The side of the mountain we were descending was really a gorge; at the bottom one could see a fast, glistening stream, and across the narrow valley, just on the other side of the water, was Soviet Azerbaijan. I began to notice the watchtowers, high wooden structures resembling forest ranger lookout stations, and back away from the stream there appeared to be a mud wall. As the road descended closer to the river, I realized that what I had taken to be a wall was actually a strip of plowed earth covered with coils of barbed wire. From watchtower to watchtower the entire barricaded frontier was under constant surveillance. The driver told me in Turki that there were lights all along here at night. About every mile I observed white-painted wooden barracks set under the trees. We passed an Iranian encampment located within shouting distance of a Russian barracks, but sadly amateurish in contrast. In order to preserve some privacy, the Iranians had erected a high thatched fence festooned with dried limbs of trees, making a kind of large duck hunter's blind which shielded them somewhat from the gaze of the Russians. Again we were stopped by troops and my papers were inspected by the authorities; my mute friend bought me a Pepsi-Cola while we waited for the outcome.

On our way once more, the air became increasingly moist, now and then the sun breaking through overhead. We passed a small collective farm, sprucely painted—even the cows looked curried— and many people were milling about the barns. An hour later we had descended to the level of the rice fields, gleaming and flooded, the dark bullocks wallowing in the muck; the farmers in wide coolie straw hats, cotton trousers rolled to the hips, were laboriously moving in slow motion. I saw tiny, intensely green patches of rice seedlings; these would be set out into the large, irrigated fields, one seedling at a time. All vegetation was increasingly lush, magnolia trees flowering brightly and huge, many-trunked banyan trees; the roofs of whitewashed cottages were in bright red tile. I was clearly in a different country.

The people, too, had changed in physiognomy: they were short, rather squat, with very dark, greyish-brown square faces—it was as if we had arrived in India. Almost no women wore *chedurs;* instead, they were swathed in a series of gay petticoats, many-colored cotton prints, and stately headdresses; a number of women were carrying baskets on their heads. With the sun shining brightly, the air perfumed with a mixture of burning charcoal and the scent of flowers, I was reminded of the odor of Florence. That familiar lower-intestinal smell of the Middle East was not here. The streets of Astara were wide, though not paved, and great, improbable roofs arched high into the air, with handsome wooden balconies underneath, carved railings and balustrades; the flying roofs, I realized, were necessary for the heavy rains and some straw roofs had supplementary roofs lower down, like a series of umbrellas. The world here was clean, and children played innocently along the grassy roadsides.

When the bus stopped in front of the Hotel Javan-Nauma, I went inside with the other passengers; a small crowd began gathering around us in the lobby, which was also a restaurant. Gossip was exchanged, some of it concerning me, the *Amerikai.* I had given my "protector" Ali's calling card with his friend's name written on it and inquiries were now made about the room as to where this English teacher might be found. I sat down to tea knowing that in good time he would show up. But nearly an hour passed, and though I had exchanged a few words in Turki with a young school-aged boy who sat across from me, I was surprised to hear him suddenly say in slow English, "Would you care for more tea?" I nodded and asked him who he was and where he had learned English. His name was Nersy, and he was a pupil of the Mr. Cyrus I wished to see. And where was his teacher, I asked?

"It is the hour for volleyball. He is playing with the other teachers. He will come, I think, after a while."

"Enshallah," I said.

"*Bali, enshallah,*" he agreed, and we sipped our tea leisurely.

Another half-hour passed; he wished to order more *chai,* but I was getting restless. Once Nersy was certain I wished no more refreshment, we got up and walked down the street toward the school. When we arrived at the side lines, Cyrus came over and introduced himself; he was a stocky, black-haired, dark complexioned young man with large, somber, brown eyes; he was sweating profusely. Cyrus invited me to take his place in the game, but I declined, and leaving Nersy, went back to the hotel to engage a room and get a change of clothes from my suitcase. The proprietor, once he understood my singular request to have a room entirely to myself, obligingly began moving beds out to the veranda. I put on a fresh shirt and went downstairs, finding Nersy hanging about the lobby again. He was about sixteen, lanky and languid; he was quite successfully sporting a curved, toothbrush mustache. We strolled along the river bank of the frontier and watched two Russian soldiers pumping water from the stream for use in their gardens. Across the bridge lay a modern-looking town with paved streets, painted houses, and prosperous-looking citizens. Exactly in the center of the bridge was a barricade with the soldiers of the two countries on either side, in small toll houses. A tower of latticed steel loomed in the near distance; from the top of it, loudspeakers broadcast propaganda into Iranian Azerbaijan. At times a woman was ranting, but usually the announcer was a man, his voice high-pitched, hortatory. Nersy said nobody paid any attention, but at night the Russians sometimes shot off flares from the tower, and then everyone looked, in fear of what might happen next. The blue sea lay beyond us about a quarter of a mile away. I picked up a stone and threw it into Russia, just for the hell of it, and then we strolled back to the hotel.

In the lobby we found Cyrus, dressed in a black and white checked sports shirt, open at the throat, and a light tawny sport jacket. I noted the informality of his dress in surprise, for none of my student friends or teachers in Tabriz would dare appear in public without a tie. Cyrus was very nervous about his English and exceedingly reserved. I knew he would take some bringing out. He and I went up to my room, which was now ready, and for which I had agreed to pay ten tomans (about $1.20; Cyrus felt it was shockingly exorbitant). My chamber was on the second floor in a building separate from the main one, and it could be reached only by climbing an outdoor staircase. On the back veranda cots had been placed close together, to be rented out as the night wore on. My room contained only one table, two chairs, and the bed; there were no shades on the windows, which adjoined a balcony above the main street of Astara. I later discovered that strollers made free use of both the front balcony and back veranda and would pause, nodding and smiling, to look in at me. The room was rank with body odor, and I propped open the window and door to get a cross-draft. "Very pleasant," said Cyrus, sitting down on a chair.

"Yes, isn't it?" I sat on the saggy, mesh-spring bed, over which a small cotton pallet had been placed.

The evening was here (it was six o'clock), and he wondered if I would care to attend a "concert." Yes, indeed, I thought that sounded interesting. The performers would certainly be very good, said Cyrus, since they had come up from Bander-Pahlavi, the resort city to the south, where the Shah had a summer palace and kept his yacht. Since the concert was soon to begin, we went downstairs and were joined by Nersy and a Mr. Khayyam, who taught geography and who turned out to be more fluent in English than Cyrus. In a touching attempt to save face, Cyrus told me that Khayyam had learned English from him, though I later discovered that the man was a relative of an English professor at the Faculty of Letters.

Astara was astir, for tonight was equivalent to a Western Saturday night; tomorrow was Friday, the holiday, and the auditorium of the town hall was crowded with entertainment seekers. School would not be in session next day, and Cyrus would be free to show me the sights in the vicinity; he talked with the others about renting a "machine." Nersy suggested I come for lunch at one of his father's villages back in the mountains. Delighted, I accepted, and there was much further discussion of renting a "machine" for transportation. I immediately insisted upon paying, knowing how little money teachers made. I earned in one month what Cyrus earned in a year. Also, I was carrying eighty dollars of Iranian money, for I had not known exactly how long I'd be gone, nor what situations might arise where a bribe would be necessary. After my repeated offer to rent the "machine," Nersy said, "I feel sorry for you."

"Why?"

Cyrus smiled. "He means, he feels sorry for you if you are always thinking about money."

That put me in my place, and I realized that further protests would be ungracious, would deny them the pleasure of being my hosts. I let them buy the concert tickets, which were probably quite expensive. Although the affair was to start at seven, it was postponed for an hour because all the tickets had not yet been sold. We walked out toward the sea and sat in a pleasant park filled with orderly beds of flowers and dominated by a large oiled-bronze statue of the Shah, gazing toward the Caspian, cement waves washing at his feet. The Russians were blasting away over their loudspeakers, and the noise was becoming irritating. I could catch none of the Turki and kept trying to find someone who would enlighten me but no one would. They preferred not to think of it and begged me to ignore the sound. The mosquitoes were plentiful, but the waning light in the *golistan,* the auroreal blush over the sea, and the deep blue dusk arriving from farther out, put us in a contemplative mood. The air was soft, wet, and caressing, and I welcomed the familiar feeling of wet-country climate and realized my preference for it.

We continued our tour of the village, and I noticed that every house had a summer cottage called a *lam* in the backyard; charming little huts built of wood, usually rather high and open to catch the evening breezes, with a thatched roof conically shaped overhead. Often the railings were elaborately carved and painted white. They were something like the bandstands one sees in city parks of small towns in the Middle West. Many of the homes were of brick, or stucco painted a brick color, and trimmed with white paint around the windows and doors; eaves and porches were decorated with wooden gingerbread, and grass and flower beds surrounded the buildings. A bluish haze had crept into the air; the distant mountains, set against one another, had the look of a misty Chinese print. Going through the bazaar on our way back to the concert hall, Cyrus handed me a small green fruit called *aloocha,* about the size of a plum and very hard; it tasted of citron, something on the order of a lime. "Very high in vitamin C," said Mr. Khayyam.

I nodded and had another; delicious.

At the concert we had the choice seats, four rows back, front and center. However, too many tickets had been sold, and a fight for available places began developing in the back. Things looked rather ugly, before the police arrived and hauled outdoors the rowdiest patrons. The curtains parted, and an ensemble played a few wailing Persian tunes. Then came a play—the familiar master-servant routine, with the servant being the comic character, a buffoon who was actually clever, and who wisely instructed the master in how to mend his wicked ways. The scene took place in a foreign country, where the young man had traveled to undertake studies; but he had succumbed to foreign temptations, profligate living, and he had forgotten his family and his duties to his native land. Finally, after a series of mishaps, he concluded that it would be best for him to return and resume life under the Shah (as soon as the king's name was mentioned, applause burst forth), and the play ended.

There were a few vocal numbers, one of which the audience didn't like, and they hissed the sultry wench off the stage. Then a small girl, scarcely eight years old, came on and performed a sexy, nymphet dance; she wiggled her hips, lifted her dress suggestively, winking slyly, and began to do the bumps and grinds in a thoroughly professional way. Her lips were rouged, her hair henna-dyed and curled. Everyone thought the number very cute and gave her a roaring ovation. Next we were treated to another play, this one set in a madhouse; but who was to say which of the people were insane, the inmates or their caretakers? This was the point, and there was a good deal of cheap humor over several loony characterizations. The variety show lasted three hours, until eleven o'clock, and I was weak with hunger. Back at the hotel I dined on *chelo kebab,* though rather tired of the dish, and after bidding my friends farewell, went up to bed.

The town awoke at 5:30 A.M. with radios turned on loudly, gathering of friends in teahouses, and much movement in the street—a custom, I assumed, which was a carry-over from the

Moslem sunrise worship, though I was told by Cyrus later that most residents of Astara were not devout Moslems. I rose and shaved in cold water at the sink on the veranda, the outdoor sleepers still rolled in their chintz quilts. Downstairs at breakfast I saw another European: a German engineer employed by the city to rebuild the power plant. We nodded and exchanged a few words; he was having eggs, and I requested the same, *abpaz* (hard-boiled), but I knew the result would be the runniest eggs this side of the hen herself. The grey day was growing brighter. I took a walk along the frontier and gazed at some bay colts gamboling in a field behind the Russian barns.

My friends due to arrive at 8:00 A.M. were on time; Nersy was already on his way to the village, Cyrus said, to make preparations for our arrival. We strolled down to the sea, and I assumed we were waiting for the car to become available, and I mistakenly mentioned this; the remark was met with puzzled glances between Khayyam and Cyrus. I learned later that our amble along the waterfront was merely a diversion while Cyrus and Khayyam tried to think of what to do about transportation. Had I known their problem, I might have done something to make things easier; as it was, I sensed that I must show the good manners of enjoying myself. This I did sincerely, for the beach was beautiful—black sand sprinkled with pink and white seashells; the mountains to the west were shrouded in a grey-green haze. The surf washed almost to our feet. I talked about swimming but saw that it was much too cold. Fishermen's nets marched out to sea; poles marking the mesh fences swayed in the rolling waves. There was one swimmer, a student of Cyrus'; we held a brief conversation in French, as he stood in the cool breeze, his limbs blue, his flesh clammy to touch when we shook hands. He wore a faded purple bathhouse *longhe,* tucked and folded around his loins; he said he would go out to the nets and try to find a fish for me. I was relieved when his repeated divings were to no avail. He kept swimming farther out, lifting up the nets, though Cyrus called to him that we were leaving, that he should not trouble himself.

The sun was hot on our backs, and I removed jacket and tie, resolving to change to a sports shirt before setting off for the hills. I happened to mention droshkies, as we were walking back, and

Cyrus immediately said that perhaps we could go to the country in a rented droshky. Would that be suitable? I understood then that plans were still unformulated. At this point Khayyam had the courage to mention bicycles, but he quickly added that of course the distance would be too far, fifteen kilometers each way, at least. Unfortunately, Cyrus said, a droshky probably could not travel the roads we would have to take. Also, it would not be so pleasant having to deal always with the carriage-driver—some of them were very stubborn and ill-tempered. I realized that a bicycle was the only "machine" they could afford. Immediately, we went to hire good English Phillips bikes; I raised the seat into proper position. Not having ridden for ten years, I was a bit wobbly at first. We stopped at Cyrus' and Khayyam's home, where they shed their jackets; I decided to keep mine with me, in case we returned after sundown. They lived in a house built high on piles, perhaps as a guard against termites. Although there was a false ceiling to their rooms, the actual roof soared up. It was a simple flat with native carpets on the floors, a couple of beds and two chests of drawers, a few books and a dog named Jimmy.

"Take advantage of this," said Cyrus, offering me a bottle of cologne. I didn't know quite where to dab myself and saw that they were watching. I guessed it was intended for the face, like shaving lotion; I also rubbed my arms, saying that the perfume was wonderful, smelled marvelous. I handed it back.

"You took little of it. Please, you must have more." He pressed the bottle into my hand again.

I had on a clean shirt. I really didn't think I smelled so bad, having washed up rather thoroughly in the sink on the veranda only a few hours earlier. I put a little more on my face and vigorously handed it back to him, thanking him for his kindness. Then I watched where *he* put it.

"Freshens one," he said sententiously, rapidly dousing himself under the arms; he opened his shirt and rubbed cologne on his chest, then poured some on his feet. "Very refreshing."

We walked out of the house, pausing on the high wooden steps to survey the view; they were located almost on the river bank. "We live dangerously," said Cyrus with a smile.

"That is Russia there," said Khayyam.

"I know."

We mounted our bikes and rode through the town. Cyrus, who was beginning to confide in me, kept close. He told me he was from Teheran, which he missed. He looked back nostalgically to his time of service in the Iranian navy, when, as an officer, he had been assigned to a ship in the Persian gulf. He had loved his life at that time, for he received a good salary, had an orderly in constant attendance, wore a handsome white uniform with gold braid, and had known the company of women. Now he had none of these pleasant things in his life, nor could he expect them, ever again; what a boon it was, therefore, to have the unexpected pleasure of my visit, which he would remember for many years to come, though I, of course, would soon forget. I assured him to the contrary, and then he changed the subject. "What do you call this road in English?"

I wasn't sure what he meant; we were traveling down a gravel thoroughfare beyond the outskirts of the town.

"Is it 'asphalt'? The same as in French?"

"Yes, here and there I see asphalt, though it's been pretty badly worn away."

Little troubled by automobile traffic, we briskly rolled along the flat road through seacoast, sandy country, covered with gorse and scrub brush. Bird life abounded—finches and warblers, flocks of ducks, and many bright blue birds with yellow throats and rust wings. Now and then we left the main road to take a short cut through the thicket along a footpath. We were on our way to Lavandervil, which Cyrus said was "not far from here." The near-sea terrain made pumping difficult on our bicycles, and I was always relieved when we returned to the highway. Cyrus announced that just ahead of us was a graveyard containing the tomb of a famous dervish. It was a holy spot.

"Shall we stop?" I asked, eager for a rest.

"If you like."

Many Persian families were picnicking on the grounds, samovars steaming; since we were not serious pilgrims, Cyrus thought it inappropriate to actually visit the shrine in a small pavilion on the grounds. I happily sprawled on the grass. "Shall we flag the bus when it passes?" asked Cyrus. "Are you too tired to continue?"

"Oh, no, I'll be rested in a minute."

"This is ordinary for us. We are used to riding bicycles."

Five minutes later we pushed on, traveling through a vast rice-field country: a patchwork of dikes holding the water at various levels; black bullocks and tan water buffaloes harnessed to plows, peasants behind, all in somnolent slowness, moving in mud. We came to a village but speeded on through. "No, this is not Lavandervil," said Cyrus. "But it is not far from here."

Each kilometer gained, I knew, would have to be retraced on our return. Our way was suddenly impeded by a washed-out bridge; we would have to ford the stream (which Cyrus thought was too deep to traverse) or cross on an extremely crude footbridge fashioned out of a couple of tree trunks. Carrying my bicycle in one hand, I inched along the narrow beam high over the swift stream, thinking: what in the world am I doing here? I began to laugh and almost fell off.

On the other bank was the village of Sibleh, where Nersy met us, quietly glowing with pleasure. The hamlet Lavandervil, he told me, was located back from the sea, far inland, where there were no roads. Nersy sat on Cyrus' handlebars as we journeyed toward the interior. Soon we came upon a large crowd of people gathered in a circle. In the center was a dervish with a snake in a sack at his feet; now and then he poked the snake with a stick; it wriggled angrily, causing the audience to Oh! and Ah! apprehensively, clacking their tongues against their teeth. They were also induced by the dervish to offer prayers to Allah, because the power of their faith and their belief in him as a representative of God would charm the snake, working miraculous things before their very eyes—*enshallah*. Cyrus begged us to continue our journey; the dervish would tantalize the people for hours before letting the snake out of the burlap bag. The holy man, turban-wrapped, his brown, soiled kaftan dragging in the dust, began flashing large cards at his ring of onlookers, cards that bore certain magic symbols and cabalistic imprints. "Now it is he collects money," said Cyrus. "Unless the people pay, they will see no miracles." Friday morning was the usual time for the dervish performances, since they had usurped the religious prerogatives of the mullahs and sometimes claimed that they were the true manifestation of spiritual powers. They successfully lured Moslems away from the routine of mosque worship because they were invariably more of a show.

The road out toward the mountains was a rutted cowpath and cycling was increasingly difficult; worse was yet to come. In addition to dodging ruts, one had to watch out for livestock, especially the humpbacked white Brahma cows. Most of the travelers were on foot or horseback. The land became a wooded, brush-filled pasture with moss dripping from the trees: a scene resembling the cattle country of interior Florida. We turned right, down a small path, occasionally traversing open spaces under high trees, where herds of grey-white cattle grazed. "Here is Lavandervil," said Nersy at last.

It consisted of a few white-washed adobe huts on stilts, high thatched crowns for roofs. Most of the houses were windowless, the living and sleeping transpiring on the wide verandas in fair weather. We passed a mud hut I took to be the mosque; hand-prints in brilliant henna orange were splotched on the white-washed walls. Nersy informed me we were to lunch at his father's overseer's house, on the edge of the village, a larger dwelling than the others. We parked our bikes against the *lam* and sauntered over to the porch. It was quiet and peaceful in this spot, with many trees overhead, stretches of lawn, and some garden enclosures fenced in by the weaving together of branches. A chickenhouse was in the rear, connected to the main building.

The overseer welcomed us with dignity and a mixture of pleasure and anxiety, understandably attendant upon a visit from the master's son, with his guests. His wife hid in the kitchen, but three children played on the porch with kittens, and two fierce short-haired dogs were vigilant in the yard. We climbed a short ladder to the "good" room, and I saw that a table had been laboriously hauled into the low-ceilinged space, obviously in consideration of my Western habits; there were also a couple of strange-looking crude wooden chairs. Having left our shoes below, we lounged on the thick carpet, ignoring the chairs. The open windows were four inches above the floor, and one could look out on a charming pastoral vista. The servant brought us tea, and we each had six glasses. Then we sat at the table and were served a large platter of saffron-flavored rice, *kookoo* (potatoes, vegetables and eggs baked together, with a pastry crust), a couple of chickens apiece (the size of robins), Pepsi-Cola, smoked sturgeon, and onions. While we dined, two hawks swooped down and very nearly got a couple of small chickens in the yard below, but the dogs were alert, and the poultry raced for cover. "Look at that!" I cried. It was all over in an instant.

"Here it is always a question of life and death," said Cyrus, smiling.

Nersy turned on the radio, but the reception was so poor he soon turned it off. "I have a gift for you," he said, reaching into his coat pocket. I immediately regretted having nothing along for him; I should have anticipated this moment of the courteous exchange of presents. He handed me a model of a rocket, carved in a greenish colored wood, the spike on the end whittled to a sharp point. I placed the five-inch-high model on the table, complimenting Nersy on his artistic skill; it sat by my plate as if on a miniature launching pad. We both fell silent.

The overseer brought us *corsi* bedrolls and removed the table and chairs. We unrolled the quilts and bolsters and stretched out, facing the windows, breezes wafting over us. My companions slept, but I didn't, even though I was exhausted; flies kept crawling over my face, and the hinges on the window shutters were extremely squeaky. After about forty-five minutes we rose and took our leave, down the path to the rutted road, and back to the village of Sibleh, which by this time the dervish had left. Nersy borrowed a bicycle for himself, and now, Cyrus proclaimed, we would *really* begin our journey and see some of the sights. They discussed the whereabouts of a lake, in which we might go swimming; it was still a fine day but becoming increasingly hazy. The three of them sang a good deal as we rode along.

Coming to an obscure path adjacent to the road, we turned left and found ourselves among picnickers on a green sward under trees; it was the Mayor of Astara and his family. I was introduced—yes, he knew all about me and my arrival yesterday. Would I not pause and have tea with his people? Cyrus indicated that we had far to journey this day and must immediately press on. A short while later we came to a stagnant, eerie tarn, with many dead trees around the shore and hundreds of ducks wheeling in the skies. A number of buzzards or vultures sat brooding in the trees; some of them seemed caught in a trance with their wings stretched wide. A very unhealthy place, and I, sweaty, began to feel a chill; the sun was now behind mist and burning dimly. There were croaking frogs, blue herons, white egrets, and an abundance of mosquitoes. One end of the shallow lake was held by a crude earth-and-rock dam, where wild orchids grew profusely. We struggled along the boggy, rocky way, carrying our bicycles most of the time. The mountains began just ahead, rather steeply. It was now four o'clock, and we seemed far from Astara. I saw tiny villages perched like swallows' nests on the hills; we struggled along half-lost paths, branches scraping us, raspberry canes slashing across our arms and legs, we forded small streams, lost our way, asked peasants for directions, and then stumbled on. Thoroughly warmed again, I couldn't imagine where we were going for our swim, but I was thankful we hadn't stopped at the stagnant lake. Toting bicycles in our arms, we staggered up the side of a mountain, and upon gaining a brief plateau, found an apple orchard, where a cuckoo sang. Ahead I noticed brick buildings, orchards, and fields. "Here is the tea plantation," said Cyrus.

"Is *this* our destination?"

"You will find it interesting, I believe."

Passing between the brick gateposts of the estate, we parked our bikes and picked several roses for sniffing, some pink, others red. The custom was to hold out the rose, offering sniffs to your friends. We walked around the grounds a little, inspecting a few banana plants and palm trees. Lodged on the side of the mountain, the plantation overlooked the flatlands and the sea in a magnificent way. We went inside to the place where the tea was processed; green leaves were spread out on racks of white cheesecloth to dry. In another room the moist, fresh tea leaves, smelling like damp hay, were being cured over charcoal in hamper-sized straw baskets, open on the bottom save for a wide-meshed cloth filter. Cyrus led the way to the veranda facing the sea, and we flopped down on straw mats. The plantation manager brought out a chair for me, urging me to sit on it, but I insisted on staying comfortably where I was, Persian fashion.

While waiting for glasses of tea to be served, Cyrus told me that the other teachers of Astara always held picnics on Fridays; today the site of the picnic was here, at the tea plantation. Now I understood why we had come: he wanted to show me off to his friends. Soon through the gates below us, four teachers in suits and ties came into view, were hailed, and hiked up to the veranda to join us. Only one man knew English, and the others refused to go far in Turki with me; they were friendly but shy, and had exceedingly smelly feet. We drank several glasses of the too-fresh tea (it tasted like grass steeped in hot water) and started off. I assumed we were returning to Astara, but no, we turned in still another direction, which seemed to take us farther from the town. I began to doubt I could make the return trip. Perhaps we might stay overnight at Nersy's father's village, where I would happily sleep with the squeaky hinges and flies.

On our bicycles—now we made quite a troupe—we traveled down a potholed road, through another village, and up a mountain side. Carrying our vehicles most of the way, we arrived at last in a sort of farmyard. The whitewashed mud house was decorated with murals in henna dye: some primitive artist had etched rice plants on the white walls, the frond tips almost coming as high as the two windows. An old woman on the porch cast us a baleful look. Under trees behind the house, on a grassy knoll, were several more teachers with their blankets, samovar, and card games. They were playing bingo, I discovered. It was a fine cool spot, and when I sat down they offered me vodka and Pepsi-Cola, which I was to drink bottoms up, Russian style. We drank to friendship, America, Iran, and peace; soon there wasn't much vodka left. From out of the woods two soldiers came strolling toward us. They made directly for me and asked to see my identification papers. I was amazed; fortunately, I had my passport and Savak card, but I surely did not expect to encounter troops in his remote spot. Cyrus told me that soldiers were constantly tracking through the hills along the border, usually in twos.

"That is so that one of the men doesn't run away," said a teacher, smiling.

There were twelve of us now, many of the men in lounging pajamas. Someone spied a girl herding a cow across the ravine, and there was a great deal of ogling; some ran down the hill to see her better. "A hard-breasted girl," said Cyrus. "Pretty, very pretty." Although they lived in monastic good fellowship, with volleyball every night after school and picnics Friday afternoons, it took a mere country cowherd to set them gawking and tittering in adolescent excitement, and to remind them of a world they were missing.

Now the hour had come to journey home; the men took off their pajamas and got into suits and ties, folded the blankets, and put their eating utensils into baskets. We took a different road, much to my relief at first, but it turned out to be terrible, too. We cycled through rice paddies, and the road itself was often flooded. Then we traversed a heath on a path with stunted trees very thick and close to the road. We made it to Astara by eight o'clock. On the outskirts I saw the same dervish we had encountered earlier, back in the hills. Now, in addition to the snake in the bag, the holy man had a rather large rodent with a string around its neck. The rat was about the size of a prairie dog. I wanted to stay and watch, but my presence annoyed the dervish, and he told Cyrus I must leave. My friend informed me that the climax of the act was near; the dervish feared his magic might not work, with a foreigner, an unbeliever present. The snake, I was told, would be released from the sack, and the rodent would confront it, but the dervish would control them both and they would not kill each other.

After leaving our bicycles at the rental shop, Cyrus and I wandered past a *hammam*. The night before he had told me that the chief thing wrong with living in Astara was that there were no baths. I thought at the time, indeed that *would* be a drawback, and wondered if the people were forced to bathe in the sea the year round. Now he told me that there were two *hammams* in Astara, but they were not modern: that is, they were not equipped with shower-stalls, but merely had a common pool, the water changed once a month. The thought of a steam bath appealed to me, and I'd even have enjoyed lying on the stone slab and having a masseur work up and down my back with a gritty bag; but I was leery of the common pool. A British physician friend in Tabriz had just returned from a stay in a village in which hundreds of people were suffering from what appeared to be arsenic poisoning. The inhabitants' tongues were blue and their skins splotchy. After exploring the sewerage systems and writing Scotland Yard for further information about the effects of arsenic poisoning, he had concluded that the bathwater had been contaminating the wells. The salve used as a depilatory thoughout Iran was largely composed of arsenic. Reminded of this story, I declined Cyrus' invitation to join him at the baths as an end to our day.

Before the bus for Bander-Pahlavi left next morning, Cyrus stopped at the hotel on his way to school; I gave him some books, and we clasped hands in farewell. My suitcase was loaded on top; he observed that I would have glamorous traveling companions: the actors from the show last night. I found a seat near the front, and the bus started up. Every few blocks the driver stopped to pick up passengers, bargaining over the price of the fare. On the edge of Astara we paused for a long time, and suddenly Nersy came dashing up. He had overslept and wished to bid me goodbye. I got out of the bus, regretting that the book I had for him was in my suitcase and inaccessible. He was so excited he had forgotten all his English. I found a U.S. penny in my pocket, which he was pleased to receive, especially since he saw it was stamped with the head of Abraham Lincoln, about whom he had "heard many good things." He gave me his picture, with his name and address on the back; then we parted.

Our progress was slow because the driver stopped for people wishing to post a letter; he hauled aboard crates of fish, sacks of grain, and clumps of chickens tied together. On the odometer I noted that the distance to Sibleh was twenty kilometers; by rough calculation I figured I must have cycled from forty to fifty kilometers the previous day, or about thirty-five miles.

We forded streams and took detours; although I had expected to reach Pahlavi by noon, at 1:30 we were still far short of our goal and stopped at a *chai-khane* near the seashore for lunch. The dunes of clear sand were tufted with grass, and empty beaches were washed by a gentle surf. The driver of the bus offered to treat me to a *chelo kebab* lunch, but having had a hearty breakfast, I wished only *mast* and *chai,* which disappointed him.

At four o'clock we pulled into the resort city of Pahlavi, with its modern, new buildings, paved streets, and well-tended parks— a city of about 40,000, perhaps more, depending on the season. I took a taxi to the Grand Hotel, which Nersy had recommended, and on the way passed the Shah's palatial summer residence, done in late Stanford White style. I was looking forward to a comfortable room with a bath; it was off-season, and there would be no difficulty about reservations. I disembarked at a shabby wooden structure, asking the driver incredulously if *this* were the Grand Hotel. He, nodding and smiling, assured me it was. The hotel appeared to be empty, but I found the front door open, and a woman came out to the desk, greeting me in French. I engaged a room, *avec bain.* Just as the porter left me at my door, an old man with a goatee, standing in the hall, said in crisp English: "So, we are neighbors. Come and see me later. I believe we are the only guests in the hotel."

We agreed to have dinner at the same hour. I took a nap and then walked all over the town, inspecting the summer homes of the foreign embassies, the beaches, the parks, and concluding that attractive as it was, I wouldn't be interested in spending much time at such an imitation Mediterranean watering place. Returning to the hotel, I found the old gentleman in the dining room reading *War and Peace.* He was a seventy-eight-year-old Russian, who had fled St. Petersburg (leaving behind a priceless collection of antique furniture) at the time of the revolution, because, he said, he was a member of the aristocracy. Upon receiving his Ph.D. in law from the University of Berlin, he had earned his living as an entrepreneur of various sorts. At present he was inspector of the Iranian government's grain monopoly, and he was being consulted about the purchase of a large crop in the grain exchange at Resht, where he planned to motor tomorrow morning. He assured me that his wealth was considerable, and although he could have "retired" long ago, he preferred keeping busy: alas, he could do nothing but make more money. Such a boring thing to do and so easy, once you have made money in great quantities.

He boasted of his friendships with Russian princes and princesses in exile; we had something in common on that score, since I had known a sample of the breed myself, having served as a butler for a Russian prince one summer during my college years. *My* prince, he assured me, was of a mere common Georgian variety, whereas *his* acquaintances were real Romanoffs. We talked of books, business, and women, the latter subject clearly his favorite topic, and only a thin line of humorous self-awareness kept him from being a rather dirty-minded old man. We had an excellent *ragout* for dinner, preceded by caviar. Then we made arrangements for the morrow: if I cared to leave as early as 7:30 would I go to Resht with him? We agreed to meet for breakfast, and I paid the woman behind the desk before going up to bed. As I was doing so, a third guest arrived, whom the old man later informed me was the grandson of a sheik who had ruled southern Persia at the time of the present Shah's father's rise to power. Reza Pahlavi had bought off the sheik, because he didn't think he could successfully fight him, and now this Arabic-looking grandson lived a luxurious life traveling from resort to resort, the year round, amusing himself with his blonde, pretty wife. "A former French actress," said the old man. "But there are other delectable women that young rake has! How I envy him! The worst thing about old age is that the desire is still there—but what can I do about it?"

After an early breakfast of strawberry jam, hot rolls, eggs and tea, the old man and I got into the long black limousine waiting under the porte-cochere of the Grand Hotel; his chauffeur hastily took my bag (which smelled of chicken manure). It is not a cliché, I thought, Persia is a land of contrasts. There were Kashan carpets on the rear floor of the Rolls Royce; we rode through the streets in splendid smoothness, then raced down the straightaway to Resht, twenty miles in the distance, through shimmering rice fields. As we entered the city, my host said: "This is a typical Russian provincial town of fifty years ago. You could find it anywhere in the Ukraine. I know, I saw them." Ahead of us was the massive city hall, with its grey, metallic onion dome. Nearby was the Iran Hotel, which was old, battered, and had high narrow windows and an onion-topped tower. The Savoy across the street sported no Russian dome, but there he advised me to stay. "This town was built by the Russians, you know. Occupied by Peter the Great early in the eighteenth century—long under Russian influence." He had a luncheon engagement; we said farewell. He urged me to look him up in Teheran, where he had a magnificent apartment, "properly uniformed servants," and "an excellent Continental cook." He said he himself was on a diet and could eat nothing interesting, but he enjoyed feeding his guests sumptuously.

I explored Resht, finding the streets so clean I walked for a block, orange peel in hand, hunting a receptacle. The tree-lined boulevards were characterized by homes with continuous second-story verandas, the red-tiled roofs overhanging them. What wasn't of wood was stone, neatly whitewashed. I sat in the sun in a manicured park before a geyser fountain, amid beds of pansies, irises, profusely flowering rose bushes and mock-orange. Later I wandered through the bazaar, buying a box of delicious apricots; it was largely a culinary shopping district, with displays of many fowl in feathered opulence, like a Victorian hatshop. For lunch at the hotel the head steward asked if I would like roast pheasant; I thought he must surely mean duck, perhaps wild marsh duck. I said yes. But pheasant it was, in savory gravy neatly spiced. It was a rainy day, later on, and I went to bed early, since the bus for Qasvin was leaving at 5:30 A.M. As the boy from the bus station toted off my suitcase in the dusk (for it had to be loaded during the night) I wondered, as I gazed down from the balcony and saw him crossing the square, if I were seeing it for the last time. The only thing in the bag I'd really regret losing would be the donkey saddlecloth I'd purchased in Ardebil.

All the next day we climbed out of the seacoast country, up to the high desert plateau, which is most of Iran; I planned to board the Teheran-Tabriz train around 4:30 in the afternoon, in Qasvin. Although the mud-walled city of Qasvin contained some unusual Safavid landmarks, I had little time to explore, and the rains came heavily. In the Qasvin depot an old man with a

bucket of iced *mast*-and-water (called *doh*), which is the refreshment drunk with *chelo kebab,* came over and offered me a glass
for two rials. I saw the buffalo hairs on the ice; the mixture
looked revolting; I shook my head. But I had struck up a des-
ultory conversation with a student and an older man—now they
bought glasses of the stuff and insisted I be their guest. I could
see that neither would guess I might refuse on the grounds of
cleanliness; I was affronting their offer of friendship, and I saw it
in their faces. Finally I took the *doh,* drank it hastily (the taste
was something like buttermilk) and returned the glass to the
peddler.

The stocky older man, now satisfied that I agreed to be
friendly, began talking to me in a mixture of French and Turki;
he had sharp-bargaining eyes, but a direct, somewhat affable
manner. He lived in Mianeh, a town near Tabriz on the railroad,
and he had come from Resht and Pahlavi, where he'd been vaca-
tioning. Bathing, at this time of the year, I asked? The waters of
the Caspian were cold, and few people went to the seashore so
early in spring. He scoffed—bathing, no. He'd gone to visit the
whores. In Azerbaijan it was rather difficult to find clean and
attractive women. Therefore, all who could afford it went to Pahlavi and Resht, where the prostitutes *had* to be good, since much
of the trade came from wealthy Teheran vacationers. Off-season,
as it was now, a man could have a fine time for very little money.

When the train arrived, he went with me to inquire about
space; no tickets could be sold until it was ascertained just what
accommodations had not been taken in Teheran. I hoped for first-
class, which would give me an upholstered seat upon which I
could stretch out. But my friend from Mianeh reported that only
third-class was left; this meant spending all night sitting up on a
hard wooden bench, four people in a row. We found a compartment which was fairly empty; then, hour after hour, the student,
the Mianeh man, and I taught each other our languages. We
played a Russian card game, rather like Hearts; they were surprised I caught on so quickly. Soon all speech was in Pharsi, and
I found myself "inside" their language. Later we had some
vodka, although the train police interrupted us in our drinking,
as it was forbidden to drink in the coaches. At last the gentleman

from Mianeh reached up to the luggage racks overhead and brought down his supper wrapped in a blue and white bandana: cold chicken, *nun,* hard-boiled eggs, radishes, cucumbers, and *mast* in a small pot. I bought tea from the porter.

As night came on I slept a little, head against the laminated wall. A game of blackjack was in progress when I awoke, fitfully, now and then; the stakes were surprisingly high, five tomans a card; I saw sweat forming on the student's brow and guessed he was getting in too deep. At last I sat up and found myself alone, except for the student; he noticed my surprise and told me that we had been to Mianeh and gone. The next stop was Tabriz. We had tea together, watching the dawn; and then we arrived in the station.

He declined to share a taxi with me. Our exchange was in Pharsi, while the driver stood there, waiting for us to make up our minds. Then I got in and instructed him in Turki; I sat back and commented on the weather. He chattered away as we drove into *koutche* Ark, and I replied fluently, with mounting confidence and a peculiar exhilaration. After he had deposited me at my garden door, I realized what was giving me such a flush of triumph: the cab driver had taken me for a native. I had journeyed forth, an American tourist with D.D.T. powder, Pharsi phrase book, and a note-sheet of names and places, but I had come back a Persian. I had achieved that unspoken, insistent longing of any tourist: I had become, for a moment, one of *them.*

15 "AZERBAIJAN IS OUR COUNTRY"

It struck me as portentous when Hassan, later that same day, ushered Mahmoud to my veranda door. "Where have you been, sir? What did you see? May I come in, please?" He was already in the foyer, removing his shoes. "Were you in Russia? No? Ah, too bad for you!"

Having been asleep, I was still somewhat dazed; but the mere sight of his florid face and sandy hair and the sound of his sharp, overly loud voice had already awakened me from the dream of travel I'd been living the past few days. "I'll put on the tea kettle. *Befarmeid beneshinid.*"

"Do not use Persian to me, let us speak English!"

What he really wanted was a chance to practice English and at the same time air his political views. We settled down to tea and argument; he was not interested in hearing of my travels, once he learned my itinerary.

Did I realize, he began, that there were three million Communists in Iran? Most of them lived in Azerbaijan. Many of the men who led the Peoples' Government, the Pishevari regime of 1941-1946, were incarcerated in Teheran jails. They'd have been shot long ago, had not the Shah feared an uprising of the people of Azerbaijan, in the wake of the assassinations. "Two of my cousins were killed, trying to escape." His blue eyes darkened, his expression was lowering. "The students of your classes—they are educated—and they are all Communists."

"No, I believe they're not from what I've learned. Mostly they're in favor of the National Front."

"Ah, they would tell you nothing. But they have read and they know that there is nothing in the way things are now. Our government is trash."

"The religious students hate the Communists because they're atheists."

"Only the old people are religious, not the younger ones. Not me, not my brother, not my friends. Not most of your students. We know religion is only to puzzle the minds of the people. We know that with the Moslem religion we carry along the old ways. There is nothing in it."

"But your own roommate," I began, "the pharmacist, he prayed! I saw him."

"Yes, but he is an aristocrat."

"So?"

"The aristocrats pray and keep on with religion, but even they do not believe it, in actual fact. Otherwise, when you borrow money, they would not ask for ten, twenty tomans extra for . . . for?"

"Interest?"

"Okay, *interest*. They want the old way to continue. Of course the people of Iran think the people of America are good and kind, but your government is trash."

"What makes you say that?"

"Oh, *I* don't believe this. I think American government—democracy—is good, because you have freedom. In Russia it is all discipline, and that is not good because you are not free. Right?" He smiled, confident I would be reassured by his statements, having forgotten that back in Hakhapur he had extolled the necessity of discipline in the management of state affairs and the usurpation of freedom. Leaders having great personal power and magnetism were needed, he had said, for the proper regimentation of a society. What he most admired about Abraham Lincoln, for example, was not his humanitarianism but the extraordinary force he displayed in his relationships with other men.

"The American government contains people we hate, the heads of departments. If America didn't have this—these wicked men—

255

Russia would not be so mad because Iran is friendly. Especially here in Azerbaijan, we are afraid. If the Americans left Iran, in a moment the Kurds and the Azerbaijanis would revolt."

"And what kind of government would they set up?"

"Communist."

"Isn't that just what you want?"

He pretended not to have heard me. He went on to tell me of the Shah's brother, an evil man hiding his cowardice under the cloak of royal immunity. He had used his pistol to shoot one of the revolutionaries—"that is the kind of man he is!" He also informed me that a mathematician from Tabriz named Khasrow Roozbeh, who had written many books and was revered as a kind of scholar-saint ("a very good man, a very brave man"), had been killed by the government. And there was also Dr. Radmanish, who escaped to Russia at the time of the collapse of the Pishevari regime, and who was now in Iraq serving as a court theoretician. "It is too bad that America continues to support the Shah of Iran, for his government is corrupt." He shook his head. "But when the time comes, he will not be able to escape to America, anymore than Faisel or his uncle got out of Baghdad. Do you understand me?" At that moment his glance rested on a book I was reading, *The King Must Die,* and his face brightened. "What's this? What is this you are reading?"

"It's a novel—historical—about Crete."

"Oh, it is fiction?" he said sadly.

"You think the Shah must be killed?"

He sighed. "I do not want to be a revolutionary."

"But you are one."

"I must help the poor people. We have nothing. The rich men have everything, and they are the ones supporting the government. It is very bad. Very bad." For a moment he was silent, brooding. "Do you remember Azerbaijan Day? Were you here?"

I nodded. On December twelfth, the anniversary of the liberation of Azerbaijan from Russian domination in 1946, Tabriz had been festooned with flags, ropes of colored electric lightbulbs and patriotic posters. Carpets hung like tapestries from the windows and balconies, and through the streets rumbled scores of tanks, motor trucks with troops, companies of foot soldiers bristling with guns and flag-decorated armored cars.

"Do you know why there were so many tanks and soldiers? Because a revolution was to start in Kurdistan. Do you know, sir, what all these tanks and guns are for? These military things from America? They are to keep Iran strong, says the Shah, to prevent outsiders from invading us. But can you compare Iran's military force with Russia's? No, no, it would be ridiculous. The guns are to protect *this* government—and the Shah—and they would shoot the people if necessary, as was the case in 1946 and again in 1952. Citizens were shot down in the streets! This is what we have to thank America for. Are you surprised that we are not grateful? You are prolonging the tyranny we suffer under."

Loud knocking at the door startled me. I went out to the foyer and found Hassan, returning with my groceries from the morning shopping. Now having supplies for my larder, I urged Mahmoud to stay for lunch. He reluctantly agreed, provided I would prepare something simple, nothing more than soup and *nun*.

While waiting for the bouillon to heat, he chided me for not providing him with radio music, which would have been so suitable on the present occasion. "You shall have to make your own music," I said.

He obliged without a moment's hesitation, his voice clear and melodious; he sang a tremulous love song; then, laughing, began to accompany his next song with a hip swinging, wriggling, Iranian dance. Around and around the room he whirled, beautifully coordinated. "Now I shall do rock-and-roll," he said, and his parody was painfully on the mark, his gyrations tellingly weak and decadent. "Rock-and-roll is trash, but here now is a Russian song." Immediately he snapped out of the limp gestures; his body was vigorous, his movements linear, legs kicking, arms akimbo.

Finally tired, he sat down to eat his soup and bread. If I knew of any Americans or other foreigners with money who would like to hire him as an entertainer at parties, he would be willing. "I would go very cheap." He reminded me that he knew many card tricks and magic jokes; there was no end to his talents. He

257

could draw, too. Did I have a sketch pad and pencil? When I supplied him, he began doing some caricatures with a ballpoint pen. His hand was sure, his creations rapidly executed. He signed his name in Pharsi with elaborate, sweeping decorations, of the sort found in illuminated manuscripts.

"Is *that* the way you always sign your name?"

He grinned. "Of course. See?" He pulled out, from an inner pocket, an American Express travelers' check. In the upper left corner was his name; the denomination was one hundred dollars.

I was astonished. "Let me see it more closely."

He laughed and handed it over. As I studied it, I began to see that it was an exceedingly skillful forgery, all the lines artfully, painstakingly inked, the lettering, everything, carefully reproduced. "You did this?"

He chuckled. "I can do anything. Let me see your signature."

I scrawled my name on a piece of paper. With a flourish he copied my name so remarkably well that I knew my bank in America would honor it without question. A bit unnerved, I changed the subject, and when he wasn't looking, casually pulled the sheet away from him.

He slapped his hand down, holding on. "I want it," he said, smiling.

Hastily, I tore it away and crumpled it up. He roared with laughter. "You're afraid of me."

"I just don't trust you."

"But we are friends."

"Are we?"

"You have been to my house, I have been to yours."

"But that doesn't mean we are friends."

"Now you are angry with me. I am sorry. Let me sing you some more songs, to make you happy."

"Do you know any native songs?"

"Of course. There are many beautiful songs from Azerbaijan. Here is one." He cleared his throat. The song was in Turki, and when he finished, he translated—though I had understood it fairly well.

> Azerbaijan is our countreee-eee
> We want no government from outside

258

<blockquote>
May God help us exterminate our enemies
Azerbaijan is our countreee-eee
</blockquote>

"That is an old folk song, I suppose?"

"No, it is not so old. It was written by a man named Beria."

"Oh, come now," I shook my head, "not *the* Beria of the Soviet Union?"

"Not that man. I know who you mean. This Beria was number two man in the Pishevari government, the People's Republic of Azerbaijan. He was married to a girl in your second-year class, did you know that?" He told me her maiden name, which was how she was listed on my roll, and went on to say that after the collapse of the Communist government, Beria fled into Russia; his wife had heard nothing from him since. "But she cannot marry again—and I believe she has a little boy—for she does not know when he might come back again." He cocked his head and smiled wisely. "Perhaps quite soon!"

The next number Mahmoud sang was "a very old song," about love, and when he had finished, translated it for me as follows:

<blockquote>
My dove, my sparrow, you belong to Azerbaijan
You belong here with me.
Why do you want to go away?
Do not leave Azerbaijan
You belong here, you belong to Azerbaijan.
</blockquote>

"It is a patriotic love song," said Mahmoud, "because Azerbaijan *is* a country. Do you know the five Marxist points on what makes a nation? They are as follows: number one, common language. Turki we speak, not Pharsi; it is the same language they speak in Soviet Azerbaijan, therefore, Azerbaijan is one country no matter what the borderline divides. Two: land mass. That is obviously a true fact, and I need not tell about it. Three: living together as comrades. As illustration, if peasants are fighting landlords, it is no nation. All must work for the common good. This is what the people of Azerbaijan would like to do, if we are not oppressed by the Teheran government. Four: common characteristics or habits. For example, Americans are industrious and kind, that shows they are a country. Germans are disciplined, they are a hard people; Persians are good businessmen. You understand? Each people has a characteristic. Azerbaijanis are not like Persians, they are Azerbaijanis, they are, according to Marx, a separate country. Fifth point is . . . ah, too bad. I have forgotten. But you must look it up. Now it is growing late, and I have to go. Will you come to my house here in Tabriz? I have books there to show you, books from Russia."

"Will I see you in class this afternoon?"

"Of course."

"And do you speak your thoughts this freely, among your friends at the Faculty of Letters?"

"Why not?"

"You must know that government spies are in each classroom."

He kissed the air contemptuously. "I do not care. I have friends in important positions."

"It is a criminal offense to belong to the Tudeh party. You could be arrested."

"They could not hold me. No jail can hold me. And besides, I am not a Communist. I do not belong to the Tudeh party. I am just a simple lad, learning what I can about *all* forms of government. I am interested in political science. Did you know that there will be a seminar in political science in Teheran this summer? And I shall be there. We are going to study SEATO and NATO. I have been invited to attend."

"Indeed, you must have friends in high places."

"There are not many from Azerbaijan going. But I am one of them."

We went out to the door, and as he slipped on his shoes, said: "The other thing I wanted to tell you is this: I have just won a crossword puzzle, a puzzle for the whole of Iran."

"Did you win money? Was it a radio contest?"

"No, no, it was put out by the Iran-America Society, in Teheran—you know . . ."

"Yes, the Iran-America Society promotes friendship and understanding between our two countries."

"Of course. And I answered the contest by correctly explaining seven English language idioms and doing the crossword puzzle.

'In a scramble'—that means, 'all mixed up.' 'He lit out'—that means, he got away. Am I right?"

I nodded. "You have learned your lessons well."

"No, sir. What I know, I have learned by myself. There has been no one to teach me, and so I taught myself. 'See you later'—ha!"

After final examinations soon to take place, I was scheduled to embark on a speaking tour of Isfahan, Shiraz, and other cities of Iran. There were farewell parties given by Americans in the community; among them, the Roger Thompsons. My hunting companion, over cocktails, chided me for quitting the country so soon. After ten months, which was a mere beginning in any foreign land, how could I know anything about Iran? I should write to Washington at once, requesting a renewal of my grant, and he would see to it that I got around Azerbaijan a little more than I had—attend some Kurdish festivals, hunt wild boar and tiger, and continue our just-begun archeological diggings in some ancient mounds near Tabriz. We would do all the things we had spoken of. Since his tone was somewhat patronizing, I heatedly assured him I had not been idle, that I had gotten to know some lives so intimately I would never forget them.

"But what, for instance, do you know about village life? Have you ever stayed in one?"

I told him I had, and something of the circumstances of my visit to Hakhapur. He was immediately interested in Mahmoud and reminded me that I had promised to arrange a student bull session for his benefit. Although he had frequently attended the teas for Iranian teachers of English, he claimed to have lost his close association with the Faculty of Letters, where in previous years he had lectured. Months ago, when he had made his request, I had been reluctant to arrange a student discussion hour in my home for his enlightenment, since I had gone to some difficulty establishing the fact that I had no political capacity and therefore all students might speak freely with me. Should Thompson be present, they would be on guard and distrust my guileless role in their midst; hence I had done nothing about furthering such a meeting.

Despite our frequent talks on a wide range of subjects, the whole official side of Thompson's activities were never discussed—nor would I have queried. I merely enjoyed stepping inside the Thompson home: the "Billy the Kid Suite" on the hi-fi and a ham and sweet potato dinner on the table seemed to remove me, by magic carpet in reverse, to America. His bland, genial manner was so impenetrable that I never had much clue as to what he was actually thinking, had experienced, or was considering. But I had the feeling that despite his lack of accoutrements of intrigue (he wore neither slouch hat nor trenchcoat), he liked to promote an aura of secrecy and importance about his life something in the manner of a boy playing a dangerous fantasy war on the barricades of the backyard fence.

Whenever he and I discussed international politics, I became uneasy over the familiar sprinkling of anti-communist phrases in his discourse, as if he had learned his lesson well and that was that. In college on the G.I. Bill after the war, he had studied political science, government, and history. The drama of the fluid, unformulated moment here in Azerbaijan—he knew that later all of these events in which he took an active part would be in history books, studied by future scholars—greatly enhanced his sense of importance. And, I felt, lamentably caused him to overestimate his astuteness in diplomacy. There was nothing in his talk about communism which I felt was really inaccurate, nor anything with which I disagreed, except perhaps in the sweeping nature of his generalizations and the easy way familiar arguments were served up again. His dialectic was prefabricated—much as Mahmoud's on the other side.

For all his pride in rational discourse, his response to communism was as emotional as was Mahmoud's. Thompson hated their system because it advocated a mechanistic view of life, which in its Stalinist form had denied the spiritual virtues of natural affections. It placed a cold hand upon the feeling heart. The communist faith perverted a man's capacities for decent family feelings and hindered the proper burgeoning of love and love's responsibilities. It threatened the "home," therefore, as well as the freedom of the individual to develop his own peculiar interests, ideas and talents. The calculated use of human beings, an insistence on making an individual's own wishes subservient to the best interests of the state, disgusted him.

But as Thompson talked, passionately, on this subject, I was frequently surprised to realize that we might have been conversing in some remote, hinterland region of America not within sight of the mountains of the Soviet Union. I felt that in actual experience with communists (of course he had seen them through his binoculars across the border), he was as strangely lacking as I. We were two insular Americans, and his need for education seemed more imperative than mine, considering his job, which, though never clearly defined, had something to do with intelligence. In fact, thanks to my spirited discussions with Mahmoud, I had actually sensed the workings of the communist mind, albeit found here in a literal and often ignorant display.

I wanted to share my Communist with Thompson, and after one of the last classes at the university, Mahmoud having invited me to his home to see his library, as we walked along the *jube* I asked if he would consider going to Mr. Thompson's house and discussing politics with him. "Who is this man?" Mahmoud asked.

"I think you've probably already met him. He's been in Tabriz quite a while. He often comes to those teas for English teachers —didn't you ever meet him?"

"Is he the dark-eyed man? Tall, thin? Why does Mr. Thompson wish to see me?"

"He is a political science expert, too. He shall probably argue with you about capitalism and communism, as I have done."

"You are my friend. I talk to you privately."

"He works for the American government. Politics is his business, and I know he would enjoy the discussion."

"That should be very interesting. Is he a good man?"

"I think so."

We walked along the Bitter River, past shops with kerosene lamps, and he said nothing for a while. Then he smiled and smacked his lips over a girl in a blue flowered *chedur*. "Oh, oh, a pretty girl!"

"How can you tell? She's all covered up."

"I know by the look in her eye. I would need nothing else."

"You told me you were giving up girls for the sake of your freedom, until you were forty-two or forty-four years old."

"I said that?" He looked surprised. "Now, here we are." We walked through a narrow walled garden and up a flight of stairs to the single room he rented. I saw a carved Russian wooden casque on a table; two glittering Nicolai lamps standing four feet high by the windows; an ormolu clock with a painted portrait of a daughter of the last Czar; a huge, handsome pierglass in one corner and the *corsi* bolster where he slept.

"Where did you get all these things?"

"Ah, sir, is that a polite question?"

There was a small pot-stove for heat, a table in another corner with left-over food in bowls, swarming with flies; noise of children next door; the entrance was draped with damask to keep out the sound. "Here is my radio, you should have a radio, too."

He told me he sent responses to radio puzzles and contests. For example: Napoleon's hat and five others were in a completely dark room. "How did Napoleon know which hat was his?"

"I think even I could answer that one; there's something about Napoleon's hat that seems familiar to us all."

"Here's another: of the following birds, which are native to Iran? Magpie, jackdaw, raven, grasshopper, eagle. Do you know the answer? Do you? It is easy. The grasshopper is not a bird!"

I saw that he had letters of reply ready to be mailed. In one contest he expected to win a tape recorder, in another, an electric razor. Also, he had composed a stern letter to the head of the Iran-America society contest, asking why the books he had won as first prize had not yet been sent. "See, I have all these books from Russia; they make good books in Moscow. I should like a few more like these." From America he had paperback editions of *The God That Failed,* the writings of Alexander Hamilton, and Tocqueville's *Democracy in America;* he had not read them, for the language was too difficult. He valued them little because they were not hard-cover volumes.

"My favorite is Gorky. He was praised by Lenin, too." He began reading the preface to Gorky's *Stories*: " 'Gorky paved the way for that new and free type of literature to which, as Lenin said: ". . . more and more writers will be drawn because of their sympathy with the working people and the ideas of socialism, and not because of considerations of gain or personal ambition. It will be a literature of freedom, for instead of serving a few spoiled ladies or the fat and bored "upper ten thousand," it will be written for the millions of working people who represent a country's pride, its strength and its future.' "

"That sounds fine. It sounds like Walt Whitman."

"It's good? It's true?"

"It's good and perhaps it *should* be true."

"Here is the book I got for being the number one boy in my graduating class. Notice, it is signed by the former Governor-General of Azerbaijan. A book, it is, of Persian poetry. I read it sometimes; it is very beautiful, but not political." He took out another volume with a colored illustration of the prophet Mohammed on the endpaper. "This was given to me by the Shah himself—again, because I was the best scholar. *The Life of Mohammed,* that is a safe book for students to read," he laughed. "That is why the Shah gives it away." He stroked the spines of his books affectionately. "The others here are Stalin prize novels. My father would not allow me to have these in his house. That is why I cannot live at home anymore. My father's ideas are trash. He told me if I kept thinking as I do, he would turn me over to the police and I would be thrown in jail."

"Did he say it when quarreling, or did he really mean it?"

"He would—he is afraid he will lose his job, if I get into trouble with the police. He does not understand that nothing can hurt me."

A plastic, multiple-photograph stand on his bookcase contained pictures of his friends, family, and idols. He pointed to snapshots of his cousin and his brother-in-law's brother—both had been killed in the abortive uprising against the Shah in 1952. "Brave man, my cousin—a wrestler, too. Both good men."

Later, walking along the Bitter River until we came to an intersection, where I found an empty droshky, he told me that this was his last year of teaching out in Hakhapur. "Next year, what shall I do?"

I did not quite understand what he was driving at. I suggested he apply for a post in Tabriz, where he could easily attend university night classes and thus finish his program for the degree.

"But what shall I do?" he said again, and his voice had a familiar whine. He was asking me to use influence in order to get him a post in Tabriz, or perhaps a fellowship abroad. And yet he did not come out openly and suggest it. We parted, agreeing to meet again in a few days, when he would come to my house and I would escort him to the Thompson's.

At the appointed hour he arrived at my door. "This man, Mr. Thompson—why does he wish to see *me?*"

I explained that he was interested in learning what ideas the people of Iran were holding. "He is a political observer, but I do not think he knows much about what the students are thinking. I mentioned you to him, since you are the most outspoken of any I know."

" 'Outspoken'—yes, very good," he chuckled. "I am not afraid. There is a Turkish proverb, 'If a man has been scalded by milk, even when served yogurt he blows on it three times.' I have been injured many times, but it has not made me cautious. Only brave men will change the world, do you not agree?"

When we arrived at Thompson's, I sensed that the rendezvous was taking on some of the aspects of a trap for Mahmoud, and I was beginning to feel culpable, for having instigated the thing. Thompson's house was in luxurious good order; it was almost on display, as if in the hope that once Mahmoud saw how Americans lived, he would be persuaded to adopt Western democratic beliefs so that he, too, might acquire "nice things." I saw Mahmoud hesitate on the threshold; he wanted to kick off his shoes rather than walk on the exquisite Kashans in the hallway.

"Come on, come on, never mind about your shoes," said Thompson.

Mahmoud walked into the vestibule gingerly, stepping in the spaces between the carpets, but in the living room he found himself confronted with a wall-to-wall beige Wilton rug. He gazed at it, astonished. "Very beautiful home. You must be a rich man, Mr. Thompson."

"This is an ordinary American home. We all live this way in the States—don't we?" he glanced at me. Walking over to the Stromberg-Carlson, he put on a record, offered to mix highballs for us, and then went into the kitchen to instruct the servants when to serve lunch. For a moment I was a man without a country. Seeing this home through a Persian's eyes, I felt alien to it; but Mahmoud because of his communism was a stranger to me, too.

"You have gone to much trouble," said Mahmoud, when Thompson came back. "I feel unworthy."

"No trouble at all. Just an ordinary lunch. I would have to eat anyhow."

"You have a family?"

"Yes, but they are out at the moment. I understand you don't believe in marriage—that you don't intend having a family."

"Why do you say that?" he looked at Thompson, then at me, puzzled.

"I told him what you said to me—that's all," I replied, embarrassed; then, turning to Thompson: "he didn't mean anything by it."

"Oh, yes he did."

Discussion between the two of them did not really begin until we were seated at the lunch table in front of the French windows which gave out on a pleasant garden. The theories of Karl Marx were aired, then the practices of Lenin, which Mahmoud viewed with approval and Thompson with horror. What transpired was rather like a debate: volleys of argument were fired from bastions of opinion. It was a fruitless display since there was no audience save me present, and neither one could convince the other. I had not expected Thompson to behave this way: I thought he would draw out Mahmoud in the manner of a journalist, until the boy stood revealed. Now and then Thompson slipped in a leading question about what men in Azerbaijan Mahmoud knew—he mentioned a few prominent Kurds who were Communist sympathizers—but Mahmoud, perhaps quite sincerely, claimed to know none of them.

As the hour wore on, Mahmoud gained in self-confidence and enjoyed the raillery from his host. "Oh, what a capitalist you are!

What a capitalist!" he laughed. After dessert—lemon chiffon pie, which Mahmoud looked at with curiosity but would not touch—we listened to recordings of music from Port Said. Despite the pulsating, hypnotic rhythms, Mahmoud could not be induced to dance for us, fearing that we might secretly be making fun of him. Now he looked at me, across the room, as if I had become a stranger. How else could I have joined in with this man asking for a dance? He sat with a certain rigidity in the foam-rubber chair, suspicious of its softness.

Our session broke up rather early, and I felt that Thompson had been too insistent on promoting his own line of argument. In the face of such belligerence, Mahmoud's manner had become less revealing; here was a game with too many unknown factors to allow him to cavort with his old, rolling ease. Still, he had managed to scoff at the Shah, scold the American government, plead the dire cause of the poor of Iran, praise Russia, and assure his host that socialism would eventually dominate the world.

In the rush of final examinations, farewell parties, and packing, I did not see Mahmoud again. Having been absent from class too many times to qualify for the annual test, upon which grades were based and credit given, he did not come to the university at all. Nor did I see any students who might have talked about him. He was not very often in Tabriz, and I felt perhaps he actually had few close friends. In recent weeks, in class, when he had responded stridently to questions or read aloud from the mimeographed text, I had sensed a ripple of ridicule in the classroom that I could not account for. It was strangely inappropriate, considering the respect or fear of him they showed at the start of the course; had he become too cocky in his proselytizing? Or had he been boasting of his friendship with me, hence earning a kind of "teacher's pet" reputation, which they both envied and despised?

I was never to find out. In fact, though most of the students I'd known well came to my house with presents and well-wishes, Mahmoud did not appear. I was puzzled and uneasy, feeling guilty about the miscalculated luncheon with Thompson. When I saw Thompson for the first time after the session with Mahmoud, I was eager to learn his candid reaction.

"What did I think of him? He was a live-wire, all right."

"Not as lively as I've seen him. He felt inhibited by the luxury of your house."

"I'm waiting to see what the General at the police station has on him."

"What do you mean?"

"They've got every Communist on file—or should have."

"You turned in his name?" I said, dumfounded.

"I asked the General to check him out, that's all."

He could not understand why I was shocked; if the police didn't know about him now, it was high time they did, especially since he was a schoolteacher. There was nothing wrong in giving such information, since after all, Iran was our ally against communism. Mahmoud, in playing his dangerous game, Thompson argued, must have been aware of possible consequences. In this business, one could only lift one's attention from the personal level to that of the political and consider events in terms of the over-all struggle. That was easier for him to say, than for me, for my year had been spent mostly among the Persians, and I couldn't dismiss personal factors of friendship in my dealings with them. Thompson, however, was a professional; he always knew that soon he'd be moving to some other kingdom in the world, where the whole process of his role would be enacted again. He held on to his perspectives, as he knew he must, and kept his eye keenly on the present job to be done. As a visiting professor of anomalous status, I didn't have to. My acquaintanceship with Mahmoud could remain fluid and unresolved, though he was both friend and enemy. Howard Baskerville, a half-century ago, had made the mistake of merging his political and personal interests; but I had unwittingly avoided such an outcome by having brought Thompson into the picture.

Upon further reflection, I was not surprised Thompson had taken the move he had. He'd probably done similar things many times before, since our "advisory" capacity in underdeveloped countries was certainly not innocent of guile or political motives. I also better understood why Thompson's oversimplifications and easy arguments, his *certainties*—in our previous discussions—had bothered me. It was the old problem of whether or not a man of action could afford to let himself probe an issue until all the ambiguities were revealed, hence causing self-doubt and inaction. He wouldn't have been able to act so coolly as he had with Mahmoud, were it not for the fact that he saw issues in black and white—not a grey mass of the in-between. Or, as Joseph Conrad put it: "Action is consolatory. It is the enemy of thought and the friend of flattering illusions." For me it came down to a consideration of whether my country needed the Thompsons in far-flung places, who could do this sort of dirty work—if it were truly necessary for our national survival. Had not Darius, Xerxes, and other Achaemedian kings lost their satrapies despite gold, bribery, arms, intrigues, and puppet rulers? And how? Partially for these very reasons.

There was a further irony: though I never knew what happened to Mahmoud, I could see what had happened to Thompson from the incident. He was clearly convinced he'd accomplished one more tiny victory in the great world-wide struggle—and he was much too satisfied. I should have hoped he'd not taken such comfort from his collusion with the local strongmen. I should have thought it might have occurred to him that such arrangements, though sometimes convenient for keeping an unruly populace in check and a country in the camp of the West, were ultimately a poor way of holding our own in the world.

But even more interesting: he should have known that turning in Mahmoud's name was *not* an act likely to net one more conniving Communist, or to have any outcome at all. He was underestimating Mahmoud's guile and defenses. The pertinent question was, who in the police department had been protecting Mahmoud all along? He'd been swaggering around the university in front of Savak spies; he'd been outspokenly proselytizing for communism throughout the year; and in Hakhapur his political activities had been conducted in the open. Indeed, he must have had friends in high places.

And so the simplicity and directness of Thompson's action was also its very futility. How could he have lived in Tabriz as long as he had and not known that? Or perhaps, because *I* knew it, I'd already been too long in foreign parts.

16 *L*EAVE-TAKINGS

MY LAST days in Tabriz, with the summer heat coming on, were a welter of errands, farewells, and packing. I tried to get rid of everything I owned that could not go into two suitcases. I sold my phonograph and records, housewares, and even some of my clothes; I drank up all my liquor in parting toasts. I gave away all my books as prizes to the best-students. Darius wanted to buy my Burberry—I would have preferred giving it to him but knew the uproar it would cause among his friends—and finally packed it up, with the rest of my gear, since whatever price he might have offered would've been more than he could afford.

Student friends came to my door in groups and alone, exchanging addresses with me and indulging in their emotions—weeping and saying that we should never see each other again, but that *they* at least would never forget me. I found the gushing sentiment difficult to cope with, despite my year of experience with it, and cheerfully assured them all that we'd meet somewhere, sometime in the future. They reflected sadly that yes, obviously, I was happy to be going home to the United States, where I would find my friends and loved ones waiting.

The morning my plane left, a contingent was standing-by at the airport. Several bouquets were thrust in my arms, parting gifts were showered upon me, and then, with my samovar wrapped in the blue, Isfahan block-print tablecloth I'd become fond of, I embarked for Teheran. At that moment I felt I was leaving Persia, though for some weeks I would continue to remain in the country. Originally, when offered two or three choices of posts available in Iran, I had chosen to teach in Azerbaijan, because in childhood I had once lingered over a postage stamp picturing desert, camels, and mountains, and bearing the indescribably romantic name, *Azerbaijan*. And now I'd been there; it would pass into memory.

I'd think of things not remarked upon in the course of the year: of the smell—the odor of the Middle East—unmistakable and unforgettable. The air of Iran was never free from dust; you smelled the earth itself, barren, sandy, powdery, long bereft of vegetation; dust rose with the slightest breeze, and enveloped all living creatures moving upon the surface of the land. This was surely the central ingredient of the Persian smell—dust—but not the curly housedust of an American suburban home, or the soot balls of the city apartment, or the loam dust of the rural regions; this was more akin to what was meant by the phrase, "ashes to ashes and dust to dust." It was the ultimate end of dust, as Persia and its people, who went back to the fifth millennium B.C., comprehensively involved both the primitive beginnings of man and some of the decadence of the end.

In the following weeks I journeyed to other famous cities of Iran—Qum, Isfahan, Shiraz; I lived for a time in Teheran, in the course of which I began to move farther and farther from my life in Tabriz. Going from cocktail party to dinner-dance, from fashionable restaurant to evening party in the foreign colony, I discovered that few Americans had been to Iran's northernmost province, for, they told me, it was a long, inconvenient, and expensive trip ("and what is *there* to see?"). The Iranians I met were sleekly Europeanized, and when Tabriz was mentioned they sneered.

I bought carpets with my surplus rials and ransacked the bazaar for treasures. Then began the long process of trying to obtain an exit visa. This was complicated by the fact that I'd not gotten the proper Savak stamps-of-approval for some of my excursions, and whole weeks of my tour were unaccounted for. Officials in the U.S.I.A. office advised me to see the matter through in person, and supplied me with an Iranian aide; but they hoped I would not expedite matters by using *baksheesh*. It might establish a precedent, in Iranian-American dealings, and furthermore, we were a country that didn't believe in the use of bribes for getting what one wanted.

I couldn't seem to get my exit visa. I sat for hours in the waiting room of the police chief's office, looking through the barred windows at the blue-brown summer sky. I finally decided to stop this nonsensical struggle with a society that had *its* way of working. I handed out *baksheesh,* and was free of the place in ten minutes, visa in my pocket.

Then I returned to the U.S.I.A. office, where I'd been asked to fill out some sort of questionnaire, summarizing my year. The State Department was mostly interested in the effectiveness of the program, how it might be bettered, how I'd found the students, and what I suggested for improvements. The questionnaire blithely ignored what to me was still the overwhelming thing (or took it for granted): that the *idea* itself of sending visiting professors to foreign countries was a most extraordinary one. Who could imagine that the government of an enormously powerful country would initiate such an ingenious plan of furthering its interests abroad? And all of it done so casually, the recruitment so simple; the briefing, nil. By sending intellectuals overseas, straight from their college halls, it was inevitable that most of these professors would be more committed to their own values and beliefs than to some official policy set forth by the government in Washington. And yet they were sent. What was the result of such daring? *This* was what the State Department really wanted to know. For the most part, it would not be measurable.

But this one could say: the program itself demonstrated a faith in the individual American, and an admirable functioning of democracy. Perhaps in the early agrarian days of our republic, it was not unusual for a citizen to feel directly responsible for government, when called upon to run for office or asked to give up some time and self-interest for the sake of the commonweal. In these latter days, however, despite the slogans and the statements of our-democratic-way-of-life, most people didn't have a sense that their efforts might make any difference at all, nor did they feel connected to the organization called "government"—except as it inconvenienced them in taxes and conscripted service in the armed forces. But here was one program which allowed an individual to feel he was truly serving his society. No wonder my Persian students had difficulty understanding the nature of my mission, since its basic circumstances were essentially idealistic, its aims just about saintly.

But not quite. There remained a certain sore point: in all of these exchange programs in education, Peace Corps movements, and fellowships in "international living," the nature of the operations remained disturbingly ambiguous and the talk tended to be out of both sides of the mouth. On the one hand the United States was spending dollars to help bolster weak economies and persuade uncommitted nations that they should join the Western bloc (in short, our motive was political); on the other hand, we enlisted idealistic Americans and succeeded in placing them abroad because we liked to help those less fortunate than ourselves (in short, our motive was love). Both cannot be simultaneously true.

When my year was just about over, I realized that my students *had* been right when they'd kept insisting that I must be in Iran in some sort of official capacity. To say it wasn't so was merely to play the game we Americans were so fond of, self-righteousness, as we went about our business, whatever it might be. Therefore the official-ness of my role in Tabriz was not considered either by the State Department or by me and yet my students knew that I was supposed to be influencing their thinking and making them like the United States, as well as teaching them English. What was so wrong about *that,* they wondered? They accepted self-interest as natural in human behavior. *Of course,* the United States was seeking propagandistic profit by sending me to Iran. Why else would the U.S. government spend its money this way? As far as they were concerned, it was a rewarding bargain, all around.

I had happened to know, before going to Tabriz, that "public relations" would be part of my job. I'd even had some experience in that work (for a college) and knew how unctuous it could be, especially when involved with an area not "business," but somehow morally cleaner, such as a college, a foundation, a philanthropy, or the government. And I knew that any selling job involved compromising certain aspects of the truth—focusing on desirable aspects and not going into others—*mesmerizing* your customer, as Mahmoud might put it, whoever he might be. Hopefully, good sense, reason, and fairness would be uppermost, but inevitably some shady-side would be kept just a little more hidden than in all honesty it should be.

Years ago when desperate for money, I undertook to sell books door-to-door for Childcraft encyclopedias, and I received my instruction from a salesmanager who had himself been a former teacher. He hired me, he said, because he saw that I was the kind of fellow who *had* to be doing something worthwhile, who was not merely devoted to self-interest or only looking out for myself. Teachers were that kind of people. Now, luckily, I had landed a job I could believe in wholeheartedly, for Childcraft had been endorsed by *Parents* magazine and even had the seal of approval from *Good Housekeeping*. There was no better educational source-book produced anywhere, and every child would be enriched by having a set of these books on his shelf. By selling Childcraft (though it was expensive for most parents), by diverting money to educational purposes like this, instead of perhaps toward an unneeded new car or a dishwasher, I would be changing immeasurably the lives of countless children. Was it not wonderful? "Just believe that—know the good you're doing," he said, and he predicted I'd be a sales success. And with a Yankee wink he added, "It's wonderful indeed to be doing good and making money, all at the same time."

I supposed it was wonderful in diplomacy, too. At least I'd had a vigorous and successful year of it. I'd done my best to charm thousands upon thousands of young Iranians who'd never had a look at an American before. In one of those speeches, on Lincoln's birthday, I'd addressed an assemblage of townspeople, including the Governor-General of Azerbaijan. I described democracy and delineated the life of the one American universally revered in Iran—Abraham Lincoln. I told how he had freed the slaves. And then, in a neat shift that diverted attention away from the complex problems of Negro–white conflicts and civil rights agitation in America, I said: "There is, however, slavery of a different sort still common in the world. We no longer mean by

275

the term "slavery" the condition in which ignorant savages are chained together and forced to work for masters. The twentieth century has developed new and in some ways more vicious kinds of slavery. There is, for instance, the enslavement of one civilized people by another; there are restrictions of freedom and denials of basic rights. There is political tyranny of one faction over another within the confines of a country. We still find masters sapping the will and strength of victims. We have witnessed in our times, psychological as well as physical bondage. We still have a long way to go before the basic human rights of dignity and freedom are the heritage of every man in the world."

Of course, through the inept translator, it came out pretty diluted, but at least I'd been trying to make them think of the difference between a free society, such as the West believed in, and the constrictions of the communist countries. I was being a good propagandizer. I hadn't stopped to consider that the Governor-General might have been wondering if I meant the tyranny in Iran.

On that questionnaire, I should have reported my triumphs more clearly, assuring the officials in Washington that in the area of public relations it had been a bang-up year. I did put down frankly that the University of Tabriz was no great shakes as an institution of learning, but that I thought it worthwhile for the U.S. to send another man to take my place next year because of the fine spot it was for making friends and influencing people. No, the level of English achieved by all but the best was really inadequate to make sustained university work possible. The teaching of English as a foreign language took special skills and training that most college professors wouldn't have. I thought of Fanshawe, my British Council friend, and how we'd argued at first concerning the auspices of our respective programs, whether they should be under a "Foreign Office" or an "Information Agency." The British Council idea, really a series of academies set up throughout the world where people wished to study the culture of Great Britain, and pay for language lessons, seemed a good way of avoiding much of the duplicity I squirmed under, in my double role. A British Council job was a career in itself, however, and there was merit in the freshness brought into the U.S.

visiting professor program by having such a variety of people from all over America doing the job—usually only once in their lives.

Upon arrival back home, I sent a batch of cards to quite a few of my students, for old times' sake, showing a colored picture of the university where I was now teaching. One of them wrote as follows:

How can I thank from your fine post card. The faculty which you teach I think as good as heaven. This year I am studying in night school. Our American professor is a serious man, and never have a jok with students. He taches some stories of John Steinbeck, Sherwood Anderson, and Whashington Irving. He is very different from other Americans, he never wants to know his students name, and certainly I can tell, he never know am I his student?

Three days ago another American proffessor visited our faculty. He was a nice-looking gentleman with a white bird on his chin. He stayed in Tabriz 2 or 3 days and lectured about Walt Whitman in our faculty.

Will you send me some American or other countries stamps? I wish to have some Americian magazines too. Now I want to finish my letter please forward my greetings to your wife, and I am fond of to corresponding with girl or boy students. You can give my adress wich they want.

Your sincerly,

ABBAS

Another of my Persian students, whom I'd known a shorter time and less well, wrote:

It is nearly a month or so since you have left, but to me it seems even more than a year. You are now in another world which is quite different from the world I live in. You are in a large, busy world full of life and activity. You may have forgotten this small town in Persia together with the people who live in it. How can I forget the short, happy moments I was with you? Yesterday I went to Hafizieh in order to make fresh the fast memories you left there. Everywhere your kind, friendly face seemed to appear before me. Then this Persian poem came to my mind:

It is as if you are in my heart and eye,
For everywhere I look you seem to pass by.

I wish I could express in words my intense feelings, but unfortunately I have neither the talent for writing nor a knowledge of English language. I know that what I write down here is a confused heap of words without meaning and sense.

I am studying hard nowadays to improve my English. I read a few books by good authors.

I hope you will be kind enough to write to me and make me extremely happy by your letters and your advice and instructions.

I am,

Yours very sincerely,

SEYID

Several months later there came further news from him:

When I saw your letter this evening, I could not believe my eyes. As a matter of fact it was a long time since I had not heard from you, and I thought you had forgotten me. It is true that through my own neglect I lost the track of our correspondence, but the bad lucks which rushed to me from all sides last year had a great part in my carelessness.

Last year I graduated from the university and during that time I was carried to the operation hall several times because of the carelessness of a surgeon who had not taken my appendix out completely. Circumstances made it necessary that I begin to contribute to the family income as soon as possible. I got a job as interpreter and translator and my employers were very nice to me. Hardly had I got accustomed to my job than I was called to Tehran by the Ministry of Education. I had been first among my fellow students during my college years, and now I was going to be rewarded by having an audition with the king and going abroad afterwards. When I came to Tehran I got an application from one of London's Schools through the Ministry of Education. There were 129 others who were also top students from all over the country. After a little while 60 of us were sent to America and Europe, but the rest of us were kept in Tehran, because the Minister of Education was transferred and the new minister would not let us go. He said that the Ministry had no money to send us. We complained against this injustice to every man in authority without benefit.

You can imagine my unhappiness for all this, and my happiness at reading your kind letter at this time. My future now rests in your helping hands.

Your nation leads the world because it has such great and nice people as you. You are great because at the time of your happiness you think about unhappy people. This is greatness. Every corner of the world I may be, I will ever remain your humble lover and friend.

This was my story. I hope by your kindness and help I may fullfill my ambition in furthuring my education.

Looking forward to hearing from you,

your humble friend,

SEYID

This particular boy got his grant to England, finally, though I heard about it from another source. The letters from all of them have stopped, and some of their names are forgotten. But each one of them had his story—and this has been mine.